The Henry McBride Series in Modernism and Modernity

Le Corbusier

The Final Testament of Père Corbu

A Translation and
Interpretation of
Mise au point by
Ivan Žaknić

Yale University Press

New Haven and London

Mise au point first published 1966 by Editions Forces-Vives (Paris). New edition published 1987 by Editions Archigraphie, Geneva.

Original text of *Mise au point* copyright © 1966. Reprinted by permission.

Translation of *Mise au point* and all other English text copyright © 1997 by Yale University.

All works of Le Corbusier © 1995 Fondation Le Corbusier —Artists Rights Society (ARS), New York SPADEM.

Designed by James J. Johnson and set in Meridien and Syntax types by The Marathon Group, Inc., Durham, North Carolina. Printed in the United States of America by Vail-Ballou Press, Binghamton, New York.

Library of Congress Cataloging-in-Publication Information
Le Corbusier, 1887–1965.
   [Mise au point. English and French]
   The final testament of Père Corbu : a translation and interpretation of Mise au point by Ivan Žaknić / Ivan Žaknić.
     p.   cm. — (The Henry McBride series in modernism and modernity)
   Includes an English translation of Le Corbusier's last recorded interview as well as a critical commentary in English.
   Includes bibliographical references and index.
   ISBN 0-300-06353-9 (cl. : alk. paper)

   1. Le Corbusier, 1887–1965—Philosophy.
I. Žaknić, Ivan. II. Title. III. Series.
NA1053.J4A2   1997
720'.92—DC21   96-47812

A catalogue record for this book is available from the British Library.

The paper in this book meets the guidelines for permanence and durability of the Committee on Production Guidelines for Book Longevity of the Council on Library Resources.

10 9 8 7 6 5 4 3 2 1

To Vica, Jacqueline, and Elaine,
my three mothers, and
to the memory of my father

The Henry McBride Series in Modernism and Modernity

The artistic movement known as modernism, which includes the historical avant-garde, produced the most radical and comprehensive change in Western culture since Romanticism. Its effects reverberated through all the arts, permanently altering their formal repertories and their relations with society at large, and its products still surround us in our workplaces and homes. Although modernism produced a pervasive cultural upheaval, it can never be assessed as an artistic movement alone: its contours took shape against the background of social, political, and intellectual change, and it was always bound up with larger questions of modernity and modernization and with the intellectual challenge of sifting their meanings. The Henry McBride Series in Modernism and Modernity, dedicated to the memory of Henry McBride, focuses on modernism and the arts in all their many contexts.

LAWRENCE RAINEY, *General Editor*

Contents

Preface

Le Corbusier's *Mise au point* (Into Focus) is presented here as more than a simple translation. I hope this edition will appeal to an audience of architectural historians, architects, readers of biographies, students of modernism, and—in a special group—those interested in the final, triumphant and embittered years in the lives of great creative minds, in this case, one of the giants of twentieth-century architecture.

Mise au point dates largely from June and July 1965, the last summer of Le Corbusier's life. Intended as a sort of meditation, it has been interpreted by the few who have read it closely and who knew Le Corbusier intimately as his "spiritual testament." This edition supplements the text of *Mise au point* with an interview Le Corbusier granted in May of that same year and recorded on two 33-RPM discs. Finally, there is a short chronology to orient those not familiar with Le Corbusier's built oeuvre and artistic output over sixty years.

The task of a translator working with this sort of biographical and psychological material is complex. As the reader will observe, Le Corbusier often seems angry, but just as often he is chivalrous and inspired; he moves quickly from the public to the private regis-ter, making neutral references to well-known events and on occasion, as if the past suddenly struck him with fresh immediacy, indulging in moments of disappointment or bitterness. In translating, I have tried to make Le Corbusier's text as readable as possible in English, reflecting these abrupt changes in intonation within the demand for an accurate rendering of the original.

Minute liberties in translation can at times have striking consequences. In the history of Le Corbusier scholarship, perhaps the most daring license was the one Frederick Etchells took in 1927 when he translated *Vers une architecture* as "Towards a *New* Architecture"—inserting a single adjective and thus confusing the intended meaning and causing polemics that still rage among architectural scholars. As Hilaire Belloc wrote in 1931: "The art of translation is a subsidiary art, and derivative. On this account it has never been granted the dignity of original work, and has suffered too much in the general judgment of letters."

Yet a translator can bring dignity to the original text in many ways, without, ideally, using the original text as a pretext to recast a thesis or dazzle an audience. The mere matching up of words from source language to target language is only one way; another is the attempt to illuminate the possible concealed utterance and contexts, or, perhaps, to tell the story not only through words or additional commentary but also by means of supplementary images and photographs. Thus I felt that this edition should be both bilingual and illustrated, for those in a position to appreciate such texts. The French text, published several months after Le Corbusier's death, has not received full scholarly attention—beyond the occasional excerpting of fragments to suit specific purposes. To respect its integrity, the actual text of *Mise au point,* as Le Corbusier wrote it, has not been illustrated in its English version but only annotated. The appended French text appears as it does in the French original of 1966.

As I worked on this project, I realized that unraveling the many allusions and references would require a good deal of footnoting. This scholarly apparatus itself soon became insufficient, and I began to sense a more creative connection between Le Corbusier's recurring anxieties, literary passions, and enthusiastic outbursts. This led me to provide an introduction in which I explore some of these themes and link them with an occasional image. Although this speculative introduction is longer than *Mise au point,* I hope it will not drown out that original text but rather pay homage to it and make it more accessible.

What remains is a most pleasant task: to thank a number of people who have contributed to the completion of this book. First, my thanks to Evelyne Tréhin of the Fondation Le Corbusier in Paris for her cooperation and support, and to librarians Holly Reveloarisoa and Valerie Valentin, who helped with archival materials. In Switzerland I am grateful to Françoise Frey, librarian at the Bibliothèque de la Ville at La Chaux-de-Fonds, and Jean Petit, who published the first French edition of *Mise au point.* Among those who have been especially helpful in securing illustrations, I thank especially Angela Giral, director of Columbia University's Avery Library; the Honorable Tony P. Wrenn, archivist at the American Institute of Architects Library in Washington, D.C.; Susanne Mercier at UNESCO, Paris; and Joyce Rosenblum, photo librarian at the United Nations in New York. Special thanks also to several of Le Corbusier's associates and friends with whom I was able to correspond or to interview, including André Wogenscky, Jerzy Soltan, Roger Aujame, Charlotte Perriand, Jean-Jacques Duval, Jullian de la Fuente, Robert Rebutato, Dr. Jacques Hindermeyer, Lucien Hervé, and Henry Pessar. Many friends and colleagues were generous with their support at different times and in various capacities: Jacqueline Charon, Elaine Rogers, Kirstin Rääf, Isabelle Morillion-Roumagnac, Kenneth Frampton, John Gery, Harris Sobin, Jaime Coll, Jordi Oliveras, Hughes Bigo, Deidi von Schaewen, and Geysa Sarkany, Jr.

Special gratitude is due to the staff of Yale University Press, especially Cynthia Wells, my editor Laura Jones Dooley, and designer James J. Johnson. Their expertise brings to publishing the dignity of an art.

Through faculty research grants for travel to off-campus libraries for necessary archival research and interviews in Paris, Lehigh University greatly facilitated my work on this book. One special person played a crucial role at a critical time: Robert Geppert, artist, poet, ardent student of literature and the arts, and Maecenas in an era when such patronage is hard to come by. His generosity was indispensable in bringing this book to publication.

And then there are those who wish to remain unnamed but whose encouragement and support were at all times essential.

The Final Testament of Père Corbu

Introduction

Cet homme dérange, a toujours dérangé et mort,
il dérange encore. Les idées n'ont pas disparu avec lui.
Elles sont porteuses d'un message qui se moque du temps.
—EUGÈNE CLAUDIUS-PETIT

Le Corbusier's final piece of writing is a brief text of meditations known as *Mise au point*. It did not see the light of day during its author's lifetime; Le Corbusier annotated the manuscript in July 1965 and died several weeks later while swimming in the Mediterranean. By strange coincidence, this "omega"-narrative of his life shared a common fate with the "alpha" of his career, the travel journal he wrote in 1911, *Le Voyage d'Orient* (Journey to the East). Both texts were in his hands in July 1965; both were re-read and lightly annotated, and both were published by Editions Forces Vives posthumously, under the direction of Jean Petit the following year, 1966.

In *Mise au point* Le Corbusier declared: "The line of conduct of little Charles-Edouard Jeanneret at the time of "Le Voyage d'Orient" was the same as that of père Corbu. Everything is a question of perseverance, of work, of courage." The two texts, the master's first and last, do indeed make a puzzling juxtaposition. Whereas *Le Voyage d'Orient* has become a familiar text—translated into several languages and supplemented by the "Voyage d'Orient carnets" (the sketchbooks Jeanneret kept during his journey)—and is now an established part of the Le Corbusier corpus,[1] the status of *Mise au point* is much more tenuous. In

the final, posthumous volume 8 of the *Oeuvres complètes* (1970), a dozen pages from *Mise au point* were excerpted and reprinted under the title "Rien n'est transmissible que la pensée."[2] Few scholars refer to the parent text; now and then it is tapped for significant quotations, but as a primary source *Mise au point* is rarely acknowledged.[3] There are reasons for this neglect. As this critical edition of Le Corbusier's text shall demonstrate, the compositional history, genre, and thematic content of *Mise au point* has confused, and at times even appeared to embarrass, Corbusier scholars.

The present volume is an attempt to remedy this situation by providing a translation and an annotation of Le Corbusier's final work. For this short testament is both a meeting-point and a culmination of many events crucial to the final years of one of this century's most creative and influential architects and urban planners. Through its annotation *Mise au point* is placed in the context of creative themes that recur throughout Le Corbusier's life, especially the successes and disappointments of his last years. The text itself is beyond optimism and pessimism; although its predominant tone may be described as bitter, a verve and a gusto for life are also evident. Explosive and combative declarations and unfinished thoughts and actions abound. To round out the elusive portrait of Le Corbusier's final years, I have drawn on many resources: published and unpublished correspondence, archival material, and interviews with surviving members of Le Corbusier's inner circle and others who knew him. Finally, I provide a translation of a live recording session Le Corbusier granted during his final year, an interview that is in many ways more spontaneous and uninhibited than his "last will and testament" and provides a valuable context—and balance—for the often enigmatic written text.

Mise au point as it was originally published is not a polished work. Its literary merits can be disputed, and the text often reads more as a cubist collage than as an integrated narrative. But the historical and psychological value of *Mise au point* should not be overlooked. The work contains many layers, overlaps, and transparencies; drawing on a long life in which he had employed many writing styles, from the most vernacular and even pedestrian to the most subtle and philosophical, Le Corbusier appears to be pulling the strands awkwardly together in this final attempt to bring everything into focus—to explain himself. Some writers on Le Corbusier have translated the title *Mise au point* as "Explanations"—and that does capture the spirit of the text somewhat.[4] But "Explanations" does not sufficiently explain the phrase "Mise au point" itself—an activity of restating, shaping, and perfecting that is both visual and spatial, the bringing of an image "in-to-focus"—nor does it explain the intent of the texts its contains.

There is a symmetry in Le Corbusier's having conflated and raided previous writings to create *Mise au point,* choosing to include multiple points of view on events important to him. In the same way, *Mise au point* has been dismembered and used out of context by those who wrote about the architect after his

death, notably Jean Petit, who published *Mise au point* while he was preparing a major biography of Le Corbusier, *Le Corbusier lui-même* (which the architect read in manuscript in 1965 but which was published only in 1970), and Lucien Hervé, author of *Le Corbusier as Artist, as Writer* (1970). Since no single author's manuscript survives for *Mise au point,* it remains unclear how much of the version published in 1966 was "constructed" by Petit himself.[5] Petit's *Le Corbusier lui-même* contains embedded pieces of *Mise au point,* and given his constant editorial presence during Le Corbusier's final years, it might be difficult to confirm a primary author for *Mise au point.* Is the genre or voice of this final narrative in fact so *un*integrated that colleagues, friends, and students of Le Corbusier's work are free to pirate it, perhaps even invited to do so?

It is my contention that, except for the English-language publications *New World of Space* (1948) and *Creation Is a Patient Search* (an autobiography of 1960 that combines architecture, painting, and the printed word), *Mise au point* is the closest Le Corbusier ever came to writing an autobiography-memoir, or perhaps a final confession. But in these pages he is rarely repentant. His self-pity and stubbornness are mixed with an unexpected vulnerability, while a pessimistic gloom hangs over the whole. He is irritated with a world that has failed to recognize his genius; he travels backward and forward in time, revisiting his past in search of key intersections and interactions.

The work is constructed with a double focus. The first is Le Corbusier's utopian vision and the resistance it encountered: plans refused, commissions "stolen" or torpedoed, great plans unrealized. The second focus is more impersonal: Le Corbusier projects his idealism on the world at large, a world he often saw as unworthy not only of his visionary planning but in many other ways, too, hopelessly lost and at war with itself, on the brink of atomic disaster.[6] Here, as elsewhere, Le Corbusier has a good eye for the reductive and inspiring symbol. The single authorial sketch contained in *Mise au point* includes the words "derrière nous" ("behind us," where he seems to warn us that the world is going to collapse) separated by a vertical line from the words "devant nous" ("before us," where he offers the sunlit future of his three human establishments). As a young man on his first Journey to the East, Charles-Edouard Jeanneret saw himself as a Romantic or Byronic poet. By the time of this final, more metaphorical journey, Le Corbusier had become a prophet.

It is worth speculating on the implications of this role. There are many ways to "prophesize." Some prophets claim to have achieved a higher vision but then descend to the society of ordinary mortals and make it their task to adjust this vision lovingly to the world as they find it; these are patient and cooperative workers, the pastors and nurturers. Then there are those who, like Cassandra, are cursed with a knowledge of the future and share it mournfully, tragically, for it is fated that all who hear it will disbelieve her. And finally there are those who condemn the world as it is and are willing to live in stern isolation from it; many Old Testament prophets are of this thrilling sort, who thunder about the sinfulness of the world and refuse to partake of it. Often these reformers are passionate ascetics, indifferent to the world's pleasures for the sake of the world's salvation; they have ascended to a vision of the future light but are unwilling to adjust what they have seen to the reality of the present, which is to say, they do not "re-descend."

What sort of prophet was Le Corbusier? As we shall see, his final years were marked by a strong ascetic tendency in both his personal and his creative life. But Le Corbusier *did not let go of the world:* he continued to invest eagerly in it, to be bitterly disappointed

Le Corbusier's caricature of 16 May 1928 in defense of modern architecture and urbanism. From a student's book of impressions, program for lectures at Barcelona's Mozart Hall. The script reads: "Not so, Mr. Guitar, the young are not running after money, since they are busy trying to knock down old windmills!" Courtesy Jordi Oliveras, Barcelona.

by it, to expect that he would be integrated into it. In his final decade Le Corbusier began to take seriously and recall frequently—and, of course, always with his customary wonderful sense of humor—literary models for "misplaced creativity" and "half-lunatic imagination": Rabelais's giants Gargantua, Pantagruel, and Cervantes's Don Quixote.[7]

Here a comparison with *Journey to the East*—written half a century earlier but prepared for publication only in the last few months of its author's life—is fruitful. For in fact the prophetic and mystical strain in Le Corbusier's personality seems to have been present from an early age. Among the books that most influenced the young Jeanneret was Edouard Schuré's *Les Grands Initiés* (1889), a history of the lives of prophets and reformers, including Rama, Krishna, Hermes, Moses, Orpheus, Pythagoras, Plato, and Jesus.[8] In long letters to his parents in 1907–8, Jeanneret credits this book as formative for his choice of

Le Corbusier's postcard to his parents, 24 August 1931, with this message:

Hier Oran . . .	Yesterday, Oran . . .
Aujourd'hui Alger	Today, Algiers
Demain désert	Tomorrow, the desert
Ici j'ai tué mon premier taureau	Here I killed my first bull
C'était très agréable	It was a lot of fun
baisers à vous	hugs and kisses
Don	Don

Courtesy Bibliothèque de la Ville, La Chaux-de-Fonds / FLC, Paris.

career and temperament. What is interesting here is the continuity in style and tone between these letters of a young, impressionable Jeanneret, writing about Schuré's book of heroes and their ecstasies, and the old, irritated père Corbu observing and writing about his own life and its supreme crises. In both, Le Corbusier–Jeanneret seems to identify with the object of his description; he participates in it directly and passionately—even though his use of such French depersonalizing constructions as "on" (frequent in *Mise au point* and placing its genre between memoir and prophecy) blur the boundaries between his self-referential voice and an outside object. "One predicts an incredible authority which will be revealed one day, the authority which has made miracles of the prophets, of Egyptian priests, Hindus and Persians," Jeanneret writes again to his parents in 1908. "Schuré defines it as a terrible force, either highly dangerous or an almost divine influence, depending on the case. . . . As much as possible, never a word of doubt, I beg of you. The struggle is already passionate enough."[9] Perhaps the most revealing document of this year (1908) is Jeanneret's long letter from Paris to his schoolmaster Charles L'Eplattenier.[10] In it we find a young man ready to "struggle with truth itself," to undergo any abuse; almost every sentence contains words like "solitude," "strength," "battle," "force," "opposition," and "martyrdom." Images of a boundary reached and a Rubicon crossed permeate the letter: "Today it is all over with paltry childish dreams of success. . . . One day, shortly, perhaps reality will be cruel. . . . [To do battle with thought] one must go into solitude; Paris offers that solitude, to one who fervently seeks silence and arid seclusion." As Eduard Sekler and William Curtis (among others) have pointed out, "There is a strong messianic ingredient in Le Corbusier's career generally"; as illustration, they mention Le Corbusier's preaching of urbanism at Algiers and elsewhere, juxtaposing an image

La misère De vivre
          faite homme!
et le Dédain De la misère
De vivre
          Incarnée en
l'âme Du
GRAND CONDOR

Le Corbusier's Christmas card to his parents, 1909. The text reads: "The misery of life maketh the man! And a scorn of life's misery is embodied in the soul of the Great Condor." Courtesy Jean Petit.

In *Mise au point,* Le Corbusier's prophetic, abstract voice is responsible for many beautiful and intriguing passages. But time and again it is interrupted by disjointed commentary, jargon, and sudden harsh judgments, by a passing idea or emotion jotted down quickly in what is almost the verbal equivalent of that terse ideal he had long ago posited for his sketchbooks, "chose active en action." Contrary to the hopeful image projected in 1908, posthumously in 1966 the maze of Le Corbusier's mature life is revealed as full of doubts. The chief obstacle to his seeing his own past more objectively seems to have been his bitterness; a satisfying explanation for the world's indifference is what he wished to bring into focus. Le Corbusier's philosophical references and literary heroes are not casually chosen: Montaigne's "De L'expérience," Cervantes's Don Quixote and Sancho Panza, Friar John and Panurge in Rabelais.

And yet this pantheon of nostalgic, passive, failed, or ridiculous figures is really quite peculiar. Assessing the twentieth century, one would suppose that the accomplishments of Le Corbusier, world-famous architect and artist of acclaimed genius, scarcely require a defense. *Mise au point* must be read as a psychological document, as a series of experiences and reflections from one ultimate but limited perspective, coherent to the psyche of the one who wrote it but in its irritated details and utopian posturing often baffling to those who are outside reading it and trying to decode it. One possible source of additional insecurity in this text—which is, after all, a literary composition—might be Le Corbusier's Swiss origins and his anxiety over his mastery of the French language. It is possible that he felt this anxiety more keenly than his readers. Paul Valéry, for one, admired Le Corbusier's literary abilities: "I envy, sir, the effectiveness of your style. . . . You write like an angel," the famous poet informed the architect. It was a compliment that Le Corbusier loved to repeat.[12]

of Le Corbusier with images of "prophetic leaders of the past," including Christ.[11] Jeanneret identified himself with the image of a "Grand Condor" perched on a Swiss mountain, like a Nietzschean superman—graphically representable but unreachable.

Why was Le Corbusier so determined to write a book about himself, one that would liberate him from two contradictory (if not diametrically opposed) needs? On one hand, there was his need to justify his existence, to make manifest in himself that "terrible strength" that Schuré had allotted to the great "prophets" of world history; on the other hand, there was the need to justify his weariness, dissatisfaction, and ambivalence, his staunch belief "not to give a damn for honors" (*Mise,* 101). These two often abruptly shifting goals create problems in tone and thus challenges in translation, which I have tried not to smooth out in English. Wherever the original sounds dated, rhetorical, or overheated, every effort has been made to preserve Le Corbusier's voice and to remain true to his sentiment. This voice, it could be argued, brought Le Corbusier his first fame in France; his writing in *L'Esprit nouveau* was famous before any of these ideas were applied to plaster or concrete.[13]

It is also a fact of architectural history that until recently most Le Corbusier scholarship centered around his most polemical, theoretical, or systematically intellectual works: *Towards a New Architecture, The City of Tomorrow, The Radiant City, Modulor,* and his prodigious works published in the eight volumes of *Oeuvre complète,* covering the period 1910 through 1965. During the 1980s and especially with the advent of the centennial celebration of 1987, however, a more intimate, detailed, and vulnerable image of the man has begun to emerge. Crucial to this image were the first four volumes of the *Sketchbooks* (published by MIT Press and the Architectural History Foundation in 1981–82); H. Allen Brooks's edition of the *Le Corbusier Archive* (a thirty-two-volume set), and more than a dozen essays by the foremost Le Corbusier scholars. In addition, dozens of major catalogues, books, reprints, and translations of texts previously untranslated into English came out during the centennial or

soon thereafter (such as *Journey to the East,* 1987, and *Precisions,* 1991). The necessary materials were becoming available for scholars to investigate Le Corbusier's creative personality alongside his prodigious number of built works, planned projects, and more than fifty books. And often, having set out on this task, would-be biographers discovered that he had already covered the ground, but differently and, as it were, exclusively. As one early associate put it, "Look, my dear Corbu, I cannot do a book about you. Public opinion has placed you on a pedestal. You've kept yourself so far from that pedestal, so hostile to the pedestal, that in order to recover your life I would have to remove the pedestal altogether."[14]

Mise au point: *History of the Text*

Although the final manuscript of *Mise au point* was not assembled until 1965, some of its parts (notes, texts, letters, and essays) date from 1945, and some material echoes works whose origins are even further back. Most of these parts were in constant revision; Le Corbusier would write, rewrite, or edit a passage, send it to friends and publishers, and set it aside. Jean Petit correctly notes in his Introduction to the 1966 edition that Le Corbusier would have changed the text further had he been given the chance. But July 1965 was the last time Le Corbusier worked over the "definitive manuscript"; in August, toward the end of his vacation, he took his final swim. The manuscript, typed or handwritten, from which Petit produced the printed French text has not yet surfaced, despite my many inquiries over several years.

This situation presents any scholar of Le Corbusier's thought with a puzzle. Jean Petit has stated that *Mise au point* was meant as a "spiritual testament," which its author had been planning to publish since 1963.

In a letter to me dated 28 July 1992, Petit claims that he had sent a copy of the final version to its author at Cap-Martin in August 1965.[15] And Robert Rebutato, an assistant in Le Courbusier's studio and son of the owner of the property where Le Corbusier's *cabanon* at Cap-Martin is located, admits to having carried the manuscript from Cap-Martin to Paris that same August.[16]

Only a one-page sample of the handwritten manuscript appeared in the original French version (1966, 8). However, Petit himself did not hesitate to alter the text slightly in the second French edition (Les Editions Archigraphie, 1987), splicing into it additional fragments of Le Corbusier's handwritten legacy. We find four additional samples of Le Corbusier's manuscript appended in this second edition (and reproduced here), whetting our appetite for more, especially since the character of the manuscript is more or less consistent and legible.

The only documents extant at Fondation Le Corbusier in Paris that attest to the architect's intent to publish this pamphlet-sized text with Jean Petit are two sheets of paper entitled "La ligne irrécusable" (The irrefutable line)—which, it turns out, is also the title of one of the final chapters in *Mise au point* and a phrase used to divide in two the only illustration in the book. In his artistic scribbling on these two sheets, Le Corbusier also linked *Mise au point* with another short text, *L'Urbanisme est une clef*—and Petit did in fact include both short texts back-to-back in his centennial edition of 1987. Beyond the evidence of these two sheets, the precise role and extent of Le Corbusier's participation in these publishing plans are difficult to determine.

Other areas are also problematic. The text of *Mise au point* contains pages that Le Corbusier appears not to have intended for inclusion, although they are in his

hand. For instance, parts of a cover letter from Le Corbusier to Jean-Jacques Duval in 1961, concerning the sending of a certain manuscript, are reproduced with this introductory comment: "In 1961, . . . I wrote a little text which I sent to my friend Jean-Jacques Duval, at Saint Dié" (*Mise,* 90). There follows an extract from the letter: "I am sending you a first copy of my text '*The Irrefutable Diagram.*'" Elsewhere in the text of *Mise au point,* Le Corbusier states that he had begun "the writing of this text with an entirely random incident: the little revolution in the pharmacy, brotherly and motherly, and the obliteration of Monsieur the Apothecary." This text, with a three-part title, "'Le graphique irrécusable,' 'La ligne irrévocable,' ou 'La fin du potard'" (The irrefutable diagram, the irrevocable line, or the end of the apothecary), was written in 1961, was sent to Jean-Jacques Duval on 12 October of that year, and is found in the first edition of *Mise au point.* Another variant of this text, a somewhat shorter manuscript Le Corbusier entitled "Page qui tourne . . . ," dates from 14 September 1961.[17] Who was the intended audience or recipient of these interrelated but discrete segments? The "definitive text" is conflated with bits of its own history.

Quite clearly and correctly, Jean Petit considered *Mise au point* too short to be a commercially successful book after its original publication as a pocket-sized booklet. Lacking any scholarly apparatus, it remains too disjointed for a reader unfamiliar with the rest of Le Corbusier's written and unbuilt oeuvre and is therefore unknown to many scholars. The very brevity of *Mise au point* might be one reason why Petit combined it with *L'Urbanisme est une clef* for the 1987 edition, to make a combined (still pocket-sized) volume of 122 large-print pages. In his own biography-collage *Le Corbusier lui-même* (1970), Petit further complicated the matter by incorporating long paragraphs from *Mise au point* into his own text, both with and without quotation marks, and in most cases without referring to their source. Clearly, then, the text of *Mise au point* was not presumed to have any special authorial integrity.

In a slightly expanded Introduction to the centennial edition, Petit provided an enhanced but rather impressionistic "history of the text." He states, for example, that *Mise au point* was planned in 1963 as one of a series of booklets Le Corbusier intended to publish on various themes—Sun and Architecture, Architecture and Mathematics, Notes and Drawings for the Open Hand Monument. Only three ultimately appeared in this series: *Textes et dessins pour Ronchamp* (1965), *L'Urbanisme est une clef* (1966), and *Mise au point* (1966). Petit also indicates that *Mise au point* itself was worked out in stages. Le Corbusier had gathered various unpublished notes and memoranda, including "'Le graphique irrécusable . . .'" of 1961.[18] Another stretch of text from 1965 was added—and then, we read, Le Corbusier drew up the final text. The portion of the manuscript dating from 1965 has not surfaced, so we cannot yet isolate all the parts with absolute authority. In a personal letter, however, Petit has intimated that the text was the same as the one published in 1966.

In summary: It could well be that *Mise au point,* despite its provocative title, philosophical ideas, and literary references, is fated to be a text *without* a sharp focus and without an easily reconstituted history. The responsibility for this is not all Jean Petit's. The exquisite, self-conscious stylistic tradition of French writing—journalistic as well as belletristic—would intimidate any but the most gifted or arrogant apprentice writer, and Le Corbusier's genius lay, after all, in visual and spatial artistry. But early in life he had been seized by a desire to capture in words all the images that he knew he could capture so well

conceptually or in his sketchbooks; he was continually frustrated by his inability to "get it right" in writing. As he confessed in Pompeii in October 1911, "I wanted 'to commit myself,' to be obliged to pursue it to the very end. . . . [But] these notes are lifeless; the beauties I have seen always break down under my pen; there were murderous repetitions. That would bore me and torment me for hours, disheartening hours of vexation, of despair. . . . During my hours of gold, ivory, and crystal, there were flaws, stains, and cracks—because of these notes that I so wanted to write! I didn't know my own language, I have never studied it!"[19]

This juvenile confession of commitment and disillusionment leads to an important insight. First, in spite of his enormous achievements in modern art and his absolute confidence in matters of spatial creativity, Le Corbusier–Jeanneret retained a Romantic attitude toward words. As the Romantics had preached, poetic inspiration is volatile, something that begins to die as soon as the poet senses its presence; the best a poet can do is to capture its trace, its memory—one can never recreate the moment of epiphany or the blinding sense of the perfect poetic vision. Most readers today would agree that *Journey to the East* is full of evocative poetry, but Jeanneret tormented himself over the verbal precision of his memories. Even then, in 1911, when the editors of the local paper in Jeanneret's native La Chaux-de-Fonds edited these "travel notes" for publication while he was still traveling, the young author was offended.[20] Throughout his life, whenever he attempted to transcribe his personal or spiritual sentiments as opposed to his theoretical or polemical declarations, Le Corbusier retained this sense of the inadequacy of language. Ultimately, perhaps, the struggle for the right word, begun early in life, gave way in later years to an appreciation of silence, of resignation and reconciliation. When, in *Mise au point,* Le Corbusier turns to the Bible, he refers to a phrase from Revelation 8:1: "There was silence in heaven for about half an hour." What a blessing that would be, if at the end of the world—and Le Corbusier sensed that his world was ending—he could be blessed with a perfect suspension of words, a perfect silence, as it were, in the heavens at the critical moment.

Yet at the same time, if "nothing is transmissible but thought," as Le Corbusier wrote in his opening sentence of *Mise au point,* there must be some vehicle for these thoughts. In *Mise au point,* the reader senses Le Corbusier's urgency at what he knew was the approaching end of his life—and also his disappointment, in part with that unfulfilled life but perhaps also to a degree with his inability to sum up that life in words that would both elevate and transcend it. The sea itself was to play an important role. Le Corbusier admitted that after years of traveling across continents he had become a man from everywhere, but that he had only one deep attachment: the Mediterranean. Jean Petit describes a scene he once witnessed at Cap-Martin. Le Corbusier was trying to regain the land after his daily swim. After several attempts, each time being thrown back by the waves, Corbusier finally gained a foothold—and his breath. "You see," he said to his friend, "The Creator is always there to remind jokers like me that they are so insignificant, and it is precisely there that one must react, and must fight."[21] Much has been said about Le Corbusier's combative spirit—and Le Corbusier himself often reminded his audience: "Forty years of research and forty years of combating the forces of inertia that invade the world."[22] And yet the final summing up of his life was tentative and poetic. Here is how he put it in the closing paragraph of *Mise au point:* "All this happens inside the head, formulating itself, passing through an embryonic stage, little by little in the course of a lifetime that flies by in a vertigo, whose end one reaches without even realizing

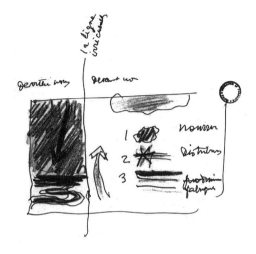

La Ligne irrécusable, earlier version. This is the only illustration included in *Mise au point,* 1966. Courtesy FLC, Paris.

it." Le Corbusier knew the value of capturing a transient thought, even though he could not always bring it into steady focus.

Major Themes and Resonances

Although *Mise au point* is a collage of manuscripts, documents, laments, declarations, reminiscences, and occasional platitudes, certain themes recur with some regularity. Although almost all of the fifty or more books Le Corbusier published during his lifetime are profusely illustrated with convincing images (in fact, the "iconic" component is often even more important than the text), *Mise au point* has only one double-image diagram, in a disturbingly dramatic tone. Its two parts, labeled "Behind us" and "In front of us," are highly schematic. To the left is a vertical line, a black area, a descending arrow, the trajectory of a catastrophe, of atomic war; to the right of the vertical line, an arrow soars upward into the sunlight, toward the destiny of Le Corbusier's *Three Human Establishments* (*Mise,* 94). As we shall see, the symbols that fill Le Corbusier's final years became increasingly schematic, polarized in significance, and powerfully stylized.

From Balkan Pots to the Open Hand

For all his great enthusiasm for the ways of the industrial world and its products, Le Corbusier had an enduring fascination with the hand, literally and symbolically. It expressed itself in his passion for handmade objects, for manual labor, for the imprint of the human hand on architecture and decorative arts, and it symbolized qualities far beyond the merely anatomical and personal.[23] In early letters to friends in La Chaux-de-Fonds in 1911, Jeanneret was already writing about peasant potters, observing: "Fingers unconsciously obey the rules of an age-old tradition. . . . Their fingers do the work, not their minds or their hearts."[24] In *Mise au point,* Le Corbusier reflects on his early experiences with what became his calling, the building trade, writing: "At seventeen and a half, I built my first house. . . . at the site, I picked up a brick and weighed it in my hand. Its weight frightens me. I am petrified. Thus one brick . . . then millions of bricks laid one upon the other" (85–86). At twenty-four, in *Journey to the East,* Le Corbusier wrote about his hands in contact with the product of other hands in an unmistakably erotic

tone: "You recognize these joys: to feel the generous belly of a vase, to caress its slender neck, and then to explore the subtleties of its contours. To thrust your hands into the deepest part of your pockets and, with your eyes half-closed, to give way slowly to the intoxication of the fantastic glazes."[25] Throughout *Journey to the East,* young Jeanneret, accompanied by his traveling companion, the future art historian Auguste Klipstein, was on the prowl for the vernacular, for handmade objects: rugs or pots.

Mise au point displays an equivalent passion for the manual symbol. In that later context, however, the hand becomes a public project and not a private object, and the aesthetic or erotic element that governed the young Jeanneret's appreciation of Balkan vases is replaced in the mature Le Corbusier by a much larger and more comprehensive vision: the Open Hand Monument, planned for the city of Chandigarh, India, against the backdrop of the Himalayas. (Le Corbusier's cousin Pierre Jeanneret was serving at the time as chief architect and town planning adviser to the government of Punjab and supervising the construction of Chandigarh. Were this site to fall through, Le Corbusier had selected an alternative location in India: crowning the 740-foot-high (220 m.) Bhakra Dam, then under construction.) The monument was intended to crown the public meeting place "Fosse de la Considération" (Pit of Contemplation) in Chandigarh as a giant weather vane and inspirational symbol of humanity unarmed, fearless, and spiritually receptive. Le Corbusier spoke about it with Prime Minister Jawaharlal Nehru on his second visit to India in 1951: "'Since 1948, I have been obsessed by the symbol of the Open Hand. I would like to place it at the end of the Capitol, in front of the Himalayas,' . . . to which Nehru smiled and nodded in approval."[26] Indeed, the project remained for the architect closely connected with Nehru: when, in 1964, on the occasion of Nehru's seventy-fifth birthday, Le

Chandigarh: first project, 1951. As seen from the Palace of Justice (High Court), *from left to right:* the Assembly Building, Governor's Palace, and Open Hand Monument. Courtesy FLC, Paris.

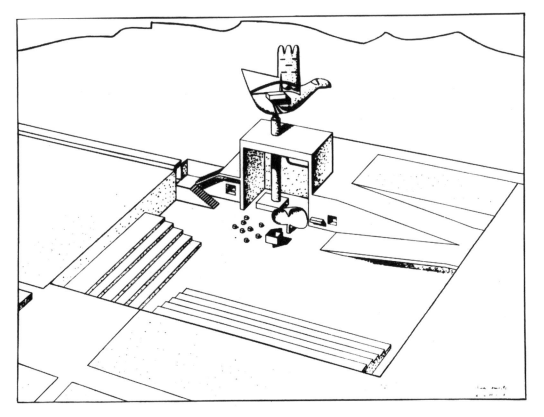

The Open Hand Monument and "La Fosse de la Considération" at Chandigarh, drawing, 1954. Courtesy FLC, Paris.

Notes from the first meeting with Prime Minister Jawaharlal Nehru, with sketches by Le Corbusier; Nehru and the Open Hand. 22 March 1951. Courtesy FLC, Paris.

Corbusier was invited to contribute to a celebratory volume, he immediately annotated the letter of invitation with sketches of the Open Hand and returned the document as his contribution.[27] It was a long-standing dream. "The Open Hand Monument has preoccupied me for six years now," Le Corbusier wrote as early as 1954, "and each day it takes more concrete form, from the subconscious it passes into the conscious; the material and power of the symbol will elevate itself to affirm ideas, inventions, which the Open Hand will receive and distribute and ex-

change without limit, either material or spiritual. . . . The Open Hand, twenty-six meters high, will turn with the wind and will gleam with colors: yellow, red, green and white in front of the mountain chain."[28]

To realize this project would have been a joy and satisfaction for Le Corbusier. In April 1965, a few months before his death, Corbusier impatiently wrote to Jean Petit, "For days now I have been trying to reach you to ask you to call me. There has been total silence. I don't find it very friendly, and I plead with you to contact me as soon as possible."[29] He was inquiring about progress on the Open Hand—not the monument but a little booklet, which Petit was to publish, entitled *La Main ouverte,* explicating its model and its site.

The Open Hand was not only a work of art, a sculpture, but a personal symbol for the architect; above the sketch he wrote, "La fin d'un monde" (see his sketch of 27 July 1950).[30] Despite Le Corbusier's enthusiasm, worldwide fame, and personal connections, it was not easy to guarantee the funding or installation of this utopian symbol of peace and reconciliation in a poor and remote though spiritually rich province. As we read in *Mise au point,* on several occasions Le Corbusier appealed for help to André Malraux, as well as to his friends and associates. At one point in 1958, he wrote Malraux: "My proposal is that France make a gift of 'The Open Hand' at this moment, just as the last phases of the work on the Capitol Complex at Chandigarh are being completed."[31] In March 1965, he wrote anxiously in a private letter to his cousin Pierre about the final model: "I count on your friendship to watch over the sheet-metal work in the factories of Nangal so that it is made according to plans. . . . I think that you especially, along with Prabhawalkar and Malhotra (all three authentic artists), you can be proud of making this for Corbu, who is now in his seventy-seventh

Design for the Open Hand Monument, with text addressed to Nehru (in English) read at the opening of the Palace of Justice (High Court). November 1954. Courtesy FLC, Paris.

year, having created this Open Hand, which is no doubt the expression of an intense moment in the life of modern society. It is not politics, it is modern 'history.' This thing standing up against the sky of the Himalayas is worth doing and must be done. I count on you."[32] Le Corbusier stopped short of saying, "You owe it to me" or "Do it for me," though on another occasion he wrote, "I would like to know if you are friends of mine or if you are rebels against me." As the founders of the city decreed, the erection of any personal statues in the city or district of Chandigarh was forbidden. "Commemoration of persons shall be confined to suitably placed bronze plaques."[33]

In spite of these supplications, only twenty years after Le Corbusier's death, in 1985, was the memorial finally realized. The Open Hand was erected next to the location that had first been planned for the governor's residence and was later replaced by Le Corbusier's Museum of Knowledge. And thus the plea that Le Corbusier had entered into *Mise au point* was answered: "This Open Hand, which marks for père Corbu a deed, a certain distance covered."

How might we understand the role of the Open Hand monument in Le Corbusier's own retrospective of his life? As usual with his proclamations and declarations, this final project is open to various interpretations. In a letter to his close friend Eugène Claudius-Petit in September 1964, Le Corbusier wrote: "I never did politics (all the while respecting those who do it—the good ones); but I made one political gesture, that of the Open Hand. The day that one of the two parties dividing the world in the interests of two different natures made me choose sides, as a moral duty. On the plane to Bogota, at that moment in 1951, I drew 'The Open Hand.'"[34] Much research has been done on its symbolism; in particular, Mary Patricia May Sekler associates the Open Hand with the tree, with rejuvenation, and with hopes of peace.[35] André Wogenscky, long-time collaborator of the architect, wrote a short book entitled *Les Mains de Le Corbusier,* and in an interview with me reiterated the profound moral topography of the flattened, stylized, upward sweep of the hand that was ultimately built at Chandigarh.[36] There seems to be an additional possible subtext to the Open Hand in Le Corbusier's own final testament, however, especially if viewed in the context of André Malraux's funeral oration of 1965, which celebrated that great, and at the time still unrealized, "Hand of Peace" on which the birds of the Himalayas would come to perch.[37] This cluster of symbols and images evokes the biblical story of Noah and the Flood.

After forty days, Noah released a bird to see if the waters had subsided. The first bird released, a raven (*corbeau*), returned, for there was no dry place upon which it could land. Seven days later, Noah released a dove, and she, too, returned to the ark, "for the waters were still on the face of the whole earth (Gen. 8:9). But when Noah released her again seven days later, she returned in the evening, . . . in her mouth a freshly plucked olive leaf (Gen. 8:11). Noah stretched out his hand, caught her, and brought her into the ark. Le Corbusier must have seen European culture as if it were a world after the Flood: devastated by two world wars, ravaged by the arms race (in *Mise au*

point he refers to the new spirit of threat and confrontation in the early 1960s), yet still capable of recovery—in fact, more capable now than ever. His Chandigarh monument was to be testimony to that faith. The Open Hand thus had to be built even on that dry Indian terrain, as long as the dove would need a place to perch upon. At some point the dove would come back with an olive leaf, and then she would not need to come back at all. And by that time, Le Corbusier himself would have performed his last geometric calculation and would have reunited himself with the waters.

Pierre Jeanneret and Sancho Panza

Long before André Wogenscky became Le Corbusier's friend and collaborator (from 1936 to 1957), the architect had another close, almost constant companion. Pierre Jeanneret's role as adviser, intercessor, and intimate support system throughout Le Corbusier's career and the more difficult moments of his life is probably unmatched by any other fellow associate.[38] The two cousins complemented each other in a number of ways. Pierre, born in 1896, was Le Corbusier's junior by nine years. He distinguished himself at the Ecole des Beaux Arts, where in 1915 he received first prize in painting, sculpture, and architecture. Like his illustrious cousin, Pierre left his native Switzerland (which he considered a country of cowherds and bankers) for France; he, too, worked for Perret Brothers in Paris.

The two men collaborated on the journal *L'Esprit nouveau*—although overall Pierre left few traces of his writing and Le Corbusier perhaps too many. For twenty years, architectural projects were signed by both men (Pierre had an academic architectural degree, whereas Le Corbusier did not). Of the two, Pierre was the more sociable, Le Corbusier the more solitary; as Alfred Roth, one of their collaborators in

Le Corbusier's drawing "Chandigarh, Birth of a Capitol." Birds are flying against the backdrop of the Himalayas. Courtesy FLC, Paris.

The Open Hand Monument at Chandigarh, built in 1985. Photo © Deidi Von Schaewen.

"Leading the way with Rabelais." Panels on the right read: to battle windmills (*top*), to sack Troy (*middle*), carriage horse at the end of the line (*bottom*). Cap-Martin, 9 August 1955. Courtesy FLC, Paris.

the late 1920s, recalled, Pierre Jeanneret assumed the role of project architect with confidence, friendliness, and loyalty and "was always disposed toward cheerfulness and telling jokes."[39] It is plausible that in *Mise au point* the figure of Pierre Jeanneret was the inspiration for some of Le Corbusier's more affectionate raids into literature, primarily into the great works of Cervantes and Rabelais. "The most beautiful reading for a man engaged in battle," Corbu writes, " . . . One takes cover from brutishness, one laughs. Thank you, Rabelais and Cervantes" (99).

What do these two authors and their novels have in common with the relationship between these two cousins? A commitment to create against all odds, even if it means idealizing the task and perhaps even tilting at windmills; a willingness to struggle and to laugh at defeat (that is, a belief that defeat is real but that laughter will transform it and strengthen the person who has been defeated); and a robust attach-

Pierre Jeanneret with his inseparable cousin Charles-Edouard Jeanneret (Le Corbusier). Courtesy FLC, Paris.

ment to the crude things of this earth, which are vital and regenerative. If Don Quixote is beautiful, utopian, idealistic—one side of Le Corbusier himself—then his earthy Rabelaisian companion Sancho Panza is no less essential, for it is he who keeps the body and soul of Quixote together. "Panza gets through, always survives it . . . He is always right" (*Mise*, 99). At times, a crudeness of appetite is even desirable when confronting the world. "At the other end," Corbu writes, "Panurge and Friar John carry on their discussions and commentaries beyond the limit of politeness" (99).

These literary references in *Mise au point* might be read as a coded tribute to the loyal cousin who was so often willing to act the practical Sancho Panza to the genius of Le Corbusier's idealistic dreams. Pierre was also willing, for the most part, to remain in the background, which is surely one reason why he remained relatively unknown—and perhaps why he lasted with Le Corbusier as long as he did, for two decades.

Their relationship began early. From 1922, when Le Corbusier, at his cousin's suggestion, founded the professional office in Paris that was known until his death in 1965 around the world simply as "L'Atelier du 35 rue de Sèvres," Pierre Jeanneret was an indispensable part of it. The projects listed in the first three volumes of *Oeuvre complète* and the first part of the fourth carry joint credit. Separation occurred only at the beginning of World War Two (December 1940), when the Atelier was closed until Le Corbusier returned to Paris in 1942. The real reopening of the office occurred only after the Liberation. In that year, Le Corbusier received his commission to build the Unité d'Habitation at Marseilles. In that second phase of the Atelier's activity, other collaborators—such as André Wogenscky—took the place of the faithful, pragmatic, and completely professional Pierre Jeanneret. But the special intimacy between the two cousins continued. "Pierre Jeanneret a été le meilleur ami," Le Corbusier wrote, and throughout his life he asserted that, for all their differences in character and ideology, his cousin was his closest personal collaborator and friend.[40] Friendship, he often remarked, was what counted most in life; and his cousin would reassure him, "Don't worry, you don't

Le Corbusier and André Wogenscky at 35 rue de Sèvres. Ca. 1947. Photo courtesy André Wogenscky.

have enemies around you, and anyway our solidarity gets stronger when it's under attack."[41]

Architectural accomplishments for which Le Corbusier took primary credit were often the result of close teamwork among a number of collaborators, but especially between the two cousins. In 1950, when Le Corbusier was asked to build Chandigarh, the new capital of Punjab, the French minister of reconstruction, Claudius-Petit, suggested that Pierre Jeanneret also work on the project. While Le Corbusier was to design the layout and major monuments of the capital, Jeanneret would join the couple Maxwell Fry and Jane Drew, members of CIAM (Congrés Internationaux d'Architecture Moderne)

Maxwell Fry and his wife, Jane Drew, with Le Corbusier in India. Wrote Fry, "When Le Corbusier came to do the plans for Chandigarh, they were finished in four days and nights by four people of our team." Courtesy FLC, Paris.

from London, to work on-site and direct its construction. As it happened, Pierre actually designed and built many of the city's buildings: residential structures, schools, hotels, theaters, town halls, the library, and commercial centers. Le Corbusier himself was getting old and could not travel to India as frequently as would have been desirable; Pierre was there to supervise. Over time, the cousins corresponded less frequently; in June 1965, the last summer of his life, Le Corbusier complained to an Indian architect that Pierre "had the habit of never saying anything of what he thought or did."[42] That year Pierre left India for good because of ill health; he died two years later in Geneva.

The Open Hand Monument and Pierre Jeanneret's participation in its construction runs like a leitmotif through portions of *Mise au point*. Early in both men's careers, Pierre was his cousin's practical and critical conscience; Le Corbusier was the source of ideas and

As the construction of Chandigarh began in 1952, Le Corbusier drew a "family portrait" of those credited with the success of the project. He, of course, is the raven (*corbeau*). We might speculate that his cousin Pierre Jeanneret, beak to the ground, is the cock, which leaves the husband-and-wife team of Maxwell Fry and Jane Drew filling the role of the larger pack animals. Courtesy FLC, Paris.

syntheses, whereas Pierre was the realist. According to the British scholar Tim Benton, Pierre Jeanneret played a role that was both functional and artistic.[43] He was the one who resolved technical and organizational problems—plans, elevations, sections—and eventually he was called on to work out the theoretical implications of his cousin's formal concepts.

This sketch of 1952 was realized in 1962 in a final version of the Enamel Door for the Palace of the Assembly at Chandigarh. Signed: Le Corbusier and Jean Petit. Courtesy FLC, Paris.

Pierre Jeanneret was, in short, the indispensable pragmatist laboring in the shadow of the idealist and utopian master.

As early as his adolescent response to *Les Grands Initiés,* Le Corbusier had expressed a fondness for prototypical historical personalities, and he had eagerly sought in them models and inspiration for his own life's path. When he first read *Don Quixote* as a young man, he was greatly impressed by the depth and universality of its characters. Throughout his life he returned to the book, annotating his two-volume copy in the margins. His last handwritten notes date from

6 August 1963 in volume 1 and 6 August 1956 in volume 2. It is tempting to speculate that by the time Le Corbusier was assembling *Mise au point,* he had come to see himself in the role of Don Quixote—and his cousin Pierre as the Don's faithful, intelligent, and indispensable companion.

Le Corbusier seem to have found in Don Quixote's often absurd but exhilarating nobility and beauty of character a justification for his own inherent idealism and crusader's zeal, which was frustrated time after time. But Sancho Panza held just as much appeal. For he was the emissary of common sense, the ser-

Enamel Door, exterior. Palace of the Assembly at Chandigarh. Photo by Weld Royal.

vant who was wiser than his master in the ways of the world, the man who could administer successfully and make things "work" because he was of a temperament and physical build that always kept the ground, not the heavens, in view. What Cervantes suggests by his famous and inseparable literary pair, perhaps, is that a successful life can be realized only when *idealism coexists with pragmatism;* the rights of both sides must be respected. And this might well be what Le Corbusier wished to acknowledge when he wrote, both admiringly and ruefully, that "Panza is always right." Could this be a final tribute to Pierre Jeanneret, without whom so much inspiration would have remained unrealized? Or perhaps even more apropos, is it a reference to Le Corbusier's own double identity—that is, to the Jeanneret/Panza in his own nature?

Vulnerable as he was to biographical models, Le Corbusier must have been inspired not only by the idealism of the fictional Don Quixote—an idealism so stubborn that at times it could alter the very perception of reality—but also by the heroic and unfortunate biography of Cervantes himself. Le Corbusier's library contained a biography of Cervantes, and some of the architect's marginal notes in this copy make it clear that he related events from Cervantes's sixteenth century to his own projects and beliefs.[44] Indeed, a remarkable letter by his elder brother, Albert, a musician, testifies to the power this novel held over Le Corbusier. A year after Le Corbusier's death, Albert Jeanneret wrote to the administrator of the estate to request his brother's annotated copy of *Don Quixote*. In the letter Albert confessed: "I discovered Christ late in life; for Le Corbusier, Don Quixote was a Christ-like figure. He noted his reactions in the margins. By reading *Don Quixote* and his annotations, I, his brother, would be able to follow, confidently and in a deeply intimate way, this legacy from one

departed, and yet still present, to one who is still alive."[45]

Quixote Embittered

As early as 1948, Le Corbusier began to write about himself in the third person singular. In this outside voice he hurled insults and miscomprehension at his own first person: "A painter who does architecture!" "An architect who paints!" "The mind of an engineer!" "Poet [as an insult] . . . artist!" "And from the first: 'Bolshevik!' . . . and since 1933: 'Fascist' or 'Communist,' according to taste!"[46] He seemed equally to resent and to relish such epithets. Le Corbusier thought grandly, in terms of the heroic and the martyred. But the frequent irritation one meets in the pages of *Mise au point* as well as the evidence of the final interview of 1965 suggest that the architect was forever being surprised by how the world reacted to his visionary projects and dismayed at the number of blows he received. An entire support staff of Sancho Panzas could not make that fact easier to bear. It is often difficult for us to remember today that for most of his professional life Le Corbusier, though world famous, was not given the work—and especially the government commissions—that he felt he deserved. In his final decade, he reminded his audience of this fact at every turn. A sense of injury and vexation mixed with his invigorating bravado. In the final interview, Hugues Desalle asked Le Corbusier: "Have you been discontented by many things?" To which the architect answered: "Discontented, never. Me, I'm the kind of guy . . . who is used to getting punched in the nose and to punching back, too."[47]

Certain punches hurt especially. And the passing of time did not mellow Le Corbusier's emotional recollection of them. Perhaps the best known, and certainly the most painful, were the disqualification of his winning design for the League of Nations Palace in Geneva (1927) and the scandal he created over the design for the United Nations Headquarters in New York City (1946–47)—in the case of the U.N. Headquarters, a set of misunderstandings that prefigured the troubles he had with UNESCO a decade later. During the final year of his life, in February 1965, Le Corbusier was contacted by the New York writer Abel Sorensen, who in the mid-1940s had been a member of the U.N. Secretariat Commission and two decades later was writing a book on the history of the United Nations building. In his letter, Sorensen remarked that his account would not be complete without Le Corbusier's current "views and comments" of this matter, by then eighteen years old. In response, Le Corbusier wrote Sorensen: "What I can say today is that the behavior of the U.N. people toward me was simply scandalous. They let me design the plans for the U.N. such as it was built, and paid me for it. Wallace K. Harrison took hold of my plans, realized them without modification, and it was he who signed his name to it, in publications all around the world. . . . Such dealings can happen only in the U.S. . . . [because] the feeling of 'basic truth' which still exists in Europe is an indifferent value in the U.S. *Business is business, time is money.* I confess I was scandalized by Harrison's behavior. . . . These are not technical details I am giving you. . . . It is simply a human story."[48]

What really happened with Corbusier's United Nations design, known the world over as Scheme 23A? This is not the place to recount the complex sequence of events in full detail, but because *Mise au point* does allude to this "betrayal" and exhibits a bitterness toward the United States that might be said to begin with this project, the issue deserves some attention. At the base of the United Nations fiasco was an inflammable mix of pride, generosity, faulty memory, collaborative creativity, discipleship, miscalculation, and perhaps covert dealing. George A. Dudley has carried out a close and highly detailed analysis of Le Corbusier's United Nations sketchbook, concluding that the relevant entries there were *not* sufficiently similar to Scheme 23A and that none of Le Corbusier's sketches closely anticipated Oscar Niemeyer's later winning design.[49] Niemeyer was a disciple of Le Corbusier's and his junior by twenty years. The two men had first met in Brazil in 1929 during Le Corbusier's lecture tour; later they had worked together on the Ministry of National Education Building in Rio de Janeiro. Niemeyer had been chosen this time as a member of the U.N. Commission representing Brazil. His account of the misunderstanding goes as follows.[50]

Le Corbusier had phoned Niemeyer in New York City on Niemeyer's arrival in 1947: "Oscar, j'ai besoin de vous . . . pouvez-vous m'aider" (Oscar, I need your help . . . can you assist me?). The older architect explained that his preliminary designs for the United Nations were causing polemics and controversy and asked Niemeyer to work with him as a partner. Niemeyer claims that he could not refuse, out of admiration and respect for his master. So they worked on the project together—until Wallace K. Harrison, director of planning for the United Nations Headquarters, found out, called Niemeyer in, and reminded him that he—like the other nine board of design consultants—needed to produce his own project. Niemeyer hastened to inform Le Corbusier, who replied, "Don't worry, that will mess things up . . . stay with me." Issues of professional integrity and personal loyalty had become dangerously interwoven, a pattern that we see richly and fatally reflected in the angers underlying *Mise au point;* but Niemeyer continued to work on the joint design with his mentor. Then, one day, Le Corbusier advised Niemeyer

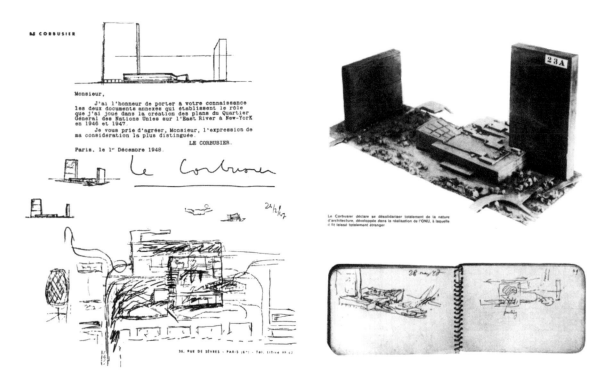

Drawings, sketches, and model of the United Nations Headquarters known as "Scheme 23A." Le Corbusier always maintained that these documents, produced between 1946 and 1947, served as the pivot of the work done in the planning office and that this fact demonstrated the primacy of his role in the overall design. Courtesy FLC, Paris.

that unless he presented his own separate project as well, there would be problems. Niemeyer quickly returned to work and produced his own project, somewhat different from the one he had been generating with Le Corbusier.

The day the jury was to meet, Le Corbusier saw his younger colleague's project for the first time and remarked, "Ah! Il est grand!" and one of Le Corbusier's collaborators approached Niemeyer and whispered in his ear: "You did it better than he did." Wallace Harrison agreed. He told Niemeyer that he would recommend his project officially as the best of the contestants. After this was done, matters began to darken. Niemeyer recalls that when his winning project was presented, Le Corbusier rose and insisted in defending his own project before the final decision was made. Le Corbusier claimed that his solution was "fantastic," admitting only one fault: "inadequate drawings." And he stressed his faithful adherence to technical and scientific principles.

This irrational behavior confused and embarrassed Niemeyer, whose project, after all, had been judged

United Nations Board of Design, *left to right:* Sven Markelius (Sweden), Le Corbusier (France), Vladimir Bodiansky (special consultant, France), Ssu-Ch'eng Liang (China), Oscar Niemeyer (Brazil), Wallace K. Harrison (director of planning, partially hidden), Gyle A. Soilleux (Australia), Nikolai D. Bassov (USSR), Max Abramovitz (deputy director of planning), Ernest Cormier (Canada), Ernest Weissmann (special consultant, Yugoslavia), Matthew Nowicki (special consultant, Poland). Courtesy United Nations, D.P.I.

the best. Le Corbusier again sought Niemeyer out and the next morning insisted on making certain changes in the winning design of his younger colleague, such as moving the U.N. General Assembly Building to the middle of the site. Niemeyer conceded (although he later regretted this compliance); together they created a joint variant of the two projects. When Harrison was presented with this architectural hybrid, he was furious at Niemeyer for allowing himself to be taken advantage of so easily. In the end, the hybrid proposal was accepted. Le Corbusier later refused to acknowledge that any conversation about "changes in the design" had ever taken place. But several years later, when the two architects met over lunch in Paris, Le Corbusier looked Niemeyer straight in the face and said, "Oscar, vous êtes un type généreux" (Oscar, you are a generous person).

The design for the United Nations Headquarters raises complex questions of coauthorship and, more broadly, of "idea-ownership." Most scholars would agree, of course, that Le Corbusier's principles influenced his disciple: after all, the whole idea of a vertical city began with the Contemporary City (1922) and was followed by the Radiant City in 1930; the elevated vertical slab also has its precedent in the Swiss Pavilion in Paris (1930), the Ministry of Education in Rio de Janeiro (1936), and the Algiers skyscraper (1942); and the general concept of combining a free-standing slab (the vertical city, the U.N. Secretariat) with a low, free-standing form (the U.N. General Assembly) is clearly Corbusian. But many specific designs could be generated from these basic principles, and as Niemeyer became painfully aware, Le Corbusier was reluctant to grant those individual designs autonomy from his own more encompassing vision. Max Abramovitz, then deputy director of planning, remembered the incident thus in 1991: "Of course the man who tried to dominate everything was Le Corbusier. He was really trying to run the whole thing. . . . Actually what happened is that when Corbu saw Niemeyer, he expected him to be his yes-man—he expected him to work for him. Harrison tried to keep everything under control."[51]

Le Corbusier also stubbornly resisted the sealed, climate-controlled environment that American technology was foisting on its urban buildings and that Harrison fully endorsed. Le Corbusier wished to wrap his design with his beloved *brise-soleil* (sunbreaker)—which, in addition to making (in his opinion) good environmental sense, would have made the building obviously Corbusian. But Harrison installed air-conditioning and applied a veil of heat-absorbing glass, which created a mirrorlike shimmering effect—thus realizing, after a fashion, the dreams of those "poets of glass" of the 1920s, like Ludwig Mies van der Rohe. Le Corbusier's reaction to this "cellophane veil" of heat-absorbing glass can be ascertained from a marginal note he scribbled in his copy of the November 1950 issue of *Architectural Forum,* which contained an article and photos on the U.N. complex: "sepulchral repression."[52]

Although the U.N. Headquarters as built was a modification of this "joint" U.N. design, Niemeyer came to consider the design not "his" but a compromise arrived at to please Le Corbusier. From that moment on, Niemeyer writes, his relationship with his mentor deteriorated. Le Corbusier continued to claim the project as his own, proclaiming loudly for years afterward that it had been stolen from him. He appears to have forgotten that Abel Sorensen had written him in 1947 to the effect that "strong attempts are being made to give this 'Board of Design Consultants' a maximum of decisive power in regard to the design problem, in order to secure the very best results rather than a one-man job by Mr. Harrison. You will, however, understand that he . . . . has been given extensive powers."[53]

Joint variant of the two projects by Le Corbusier and Oscar Niemeyer. Drawing by Hugh Ferriss. Courtesy Drawings and Archives, Avery Library, Columbia University, New York.

Wallace Harrison, clearly infuriated by Le Corbusier's intrusive behavior, undertook to expunge him from the history of the U.N. competition and construction. One example will suffice. Harrison formally presented the U.N. project in 1951 at the invitation of the Royal Institute of British Architects (RIBA).[54] In his official retrospective, he depicted it as a cooperative effort of architects and engineers from fourteen countries speaking ten languages who disagreed and struggled with one another but who in the end came together—entirely in the spirit of the international organization they had housed. His account paid tribute to each contestant, detailed their biographies, and described the specifics of such technical problems as lighting, plumbing, and wind bracing. Aside from a single mention in an impersonal introductory

Bird's eye view of the United Nations Headquarters. A fragment of Le Corbusier's Radiant City facing the East River. Courtesy United Nations, D.P.I.

list, the names of Le Corbusier and of his engineer Vladimir Bodiansky, both representing France, were not mentioned by Harrison. And in the discussion that followed Harrison's speech, not a single British architect inquired about Le Corbusier's contribution or invoked his name. Little wonder that, at the bottom of Abel Sorensen's letter of invitation to Le Corbusier in 1965, seeking his "views and comments" on the distant event, the old man had written: "Harrison—pirate." However, in his formal relations with Harrison after the United Nations incident of 1947, Le Corbusier remained cooperative, polite, and re-

Le Corbusier explains his drawing to Henri Troyat, French writer and biographer, and Jean Benoit-Levy, chief of United Nations Films and Visual Information, Section D.P.I., on 8 June 1947. Adding his signature to that of Vladimir Bodiansky, Le Corbusier has just dedicated this drawing to Benoit-Levy. Courtesy United Nations D.P.I.

strained.[55] But in his other forums, among which we must number *Mise au point* and the impulsive response to Abel Sorensen, Le Corbusier continued to feel persecuted and misunderstood in this matter, right up to the moment of his death.

After the fiasco, Le Corbusier harbored a deep resentment not just against Harrison but also against the United States. Kept in check in official publications, this bitterness overflows in the personal correspondence. One graphic example occurs in an exchange with Jean-Pierre de Montmollin, personal lawyer and friend from Neuchâtel, to whom Le Corbusier penned the following handwritten note in January 1962: "My dear Jean-Pierre, your dealings with these cattle-traders in the U.S. make me shudder. The Americans are unscrupulous, dishonest, perfidious and disingenuous. I have known the greatest (they are repulsive) and their lackey, the U.N. (it is appalling). The U.S. will undergo another terrible crisis (remember 1928 [sic])and you can be sure that your dealers' stock will lose their horns! A friendly warning: Watch out! Why add a jolly 'Hello, boy!' to your 70th year."[56] It is hard to know, of course, how much of this anti-Americanism is a standard European reflex against the crass, pragmatic "cowboy culture" of the New World and how much is Le Corbusier's own exquisite personal animus. At the bottom of this note, Le Corbusier drew a rudimentary sketch. Europe is to the right, North and South America are to the left; five strong vertical lines over the Atlantic divide the two sides. Across Europe we read: " a) One sort of morality"; across the United States: "b) Another kind of morality." "This is obvious," Le Corbusier appended to the bottom of the sketch. "The eyes of the world are open to it."

This rancor against the United States often took petty form. Among the material Le Corbusier was compiling in 1961 for the filming of "Paris demain," for example, is a full-color photograph of the United Nations building, published in the journal *L'Oeil,* no. 75, into which the architect had inserted a note on a sheet of paper that read: "Gratte-ciel ONU volé, photo couleur. Sans Corbu" (U.N. skyscraper, stolen, color photo. Without Corbu).[57] Even the planned film—never realized, as it turned out—was to be a polemical forum for reviving old injuries.

This anger began to be mollified in the early 1960s, when Le Corbusier was offered prizes and honorary degrees from such famous institutions as Harvard, Columbia, and the American Institute of Architects (AIA). There is some indication that the aging architect perceived his rising official status in America as possibly helpful in emphasizing his worth to his adopted homeland, France—which he also often accused of ingratitude and insufficient attention.

But Le Corbusier played cat and mouse with the American institutions that wished to honor him. The AIA wished to award Le Corbusier a gold medal, counting on five thousand designers in attendance. At the same time Columbia University wished to bestow an honorary doctorate of humane letters; somewhat earlier, Harvard University had hoped to grant an honorary degree. Harvard was never accommodated (Le Corbusier declined to visit the campus, and honorary degrees were never conferred in absentia), but the Columbia and AIA ceremonies were arranged. Although he later boasted proudly of these honors, to bring the architect in person to the United States was a herculean task of diplomacy, patience, and compromise.

Le Corbusier coyly evaded the Columbia School of Architecture's dean, Charles R. Colbert, the university's president, Grayson Kirk, and James M. Fitch, chairman of the elaborate series of celebratory lectures entitled "Four Great Makers of Modern Architecture" (March–May 1961), all of whom were working together with AIA president Philip Will to accommodate the recalcitrant architect. At times Le Corbusier claimed to be too busy; at another times he insisted that he could not return to the United States on principle but suggested that he might "write something that might be read," since at the proposed time he was planning to be in India for the inauguration of his Parliament building and the Bhakra Dam project. There, Corbu added with apparent malicious delight, "I am fighting the hostile idea of one American engi-

In his Sketchbook L-48, May–July 1957, Le Corbusier made an entry referring to pages 168–69 of his book *Modulor,* which featured both the Palace of the Soviets (1931) and the United Nations (1947). Le Corbusier's notes read: 1930 USSR = rejected. 1947 USA: stolen [crossed out] "absorbed" without saying: thank you." Courtesy FLC, Paris.

Le Corbusier in front of the United Nations Headquarters after its completion, comparing notes for his proposal and Harrison's execution. Courtesy FLC, Paris.

neer, a consultant. . . . If you wish that I express my-self in drawing, I will give you a copy of a drawing that I made at Cambridge University, where I spent two hours in 1959 [receiving another honorary de-gree]. . . . I should add that my most recent biogra-

pher has said that I'm not handsome and that I have a poor voice, so there is no special loss for my Ameri-can friends."[58] Suspecting a no-show for the "Four Great Makers" lecture series—which also featured the still-living Walter Gropius and Ludwig Mies van der Rohe as well as the recently departed Frank Lloyd Wright—Dean Colbert finally wrote in exasperation to Le Corbusier, "Your absence from the honors we

Le Corbusier drawing for architecture students and faculty at Columbia University, 28 April 1961. "'I prefer drawing to talking. Drawing allows less room for lies,' he said. Regional Planning and the evolution of the city for the Machine-Age civilization are his primary concerns: 'The city has become an absolute drama,' Le Corbusier said while sketching." *Time*, 5 May 1961, 36. Courtesy Geysa Sarkany, Jr.

ness against a monolithic adversary: American Offi-cialdom."[60] He points out further that were it not for his friendship with José Luis Sert, then dean of Harvard's Graduate School of Design, Le Corbusier would have turned down the commission to design what was to be his only building in the United States, the Carpenter Center for the Visual Arts at Harvard University.[61] And even then, when offered the commission, Le Corbusier is said to have remarked: "Such a small commission from such a big country." When asked if there might be any particular problems working with Le Corbusier, who had a reputation of being somewhat strong-willed in design matters, José Luis Sert replied simply: "He is an unusual man. . . . So was Michelangelo."[62]

But the United States was not the only focus of bitterness during Le Corbusier's final years. In France, his adopted homeland, there were other terrible disappointments. Only in 1963 did France bestow its highest honor on the architect. Most painfully, Le Corbusier had not been invited to exercise leadership in the postwar rebuilding of Paris—even though he had worked out schemes for wholesale rational city planning starting in the early 1920s and continuing until his death. Paris would never see a major project by Le Corbusier. In fact, his conception of the modern metropolis was being held up to scorn. When he advocated that the "urban slate be wiped clean," that debris and accretions be cleared away, that the "town is a tool" and the city "a grip of man upon nature,"[63] he fell afoul of the new generation of conservative, at times reactionary preservationists, who accused Le Corbusier of encouraging monumental urbicide.

How is all this reflected in *Mise au point?* On the theme of city planning as on so many others, Le Corbusier is not of a single emotional piece. He presents a mixed image of arrogance, bitterness, pride, and

wish to bestow could negate the effort of years for some of us. Progress leans on small support. I wake each morning feeling like a donkey too. But please do not make us all look like donkeys for working for you. . . . Please do not destroy our hopes."[59] Le Corbusier did eventually visit the United States, for two and a half days, stayed at the Plaza Hotel, and was chauffeured between New York and Philadelphia on dates different than those announced on the posters for the Columbia University series.

Curtis and Sekler have attributed Le Corbusier's often petty but deep-seated anti-Americanism to a "bitter-

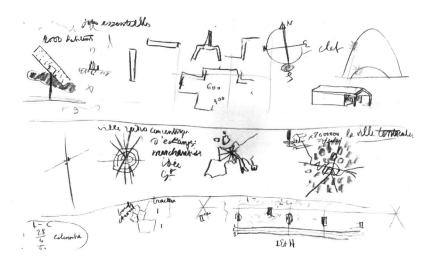

The primary topics discussed and illustrated for his audience at Columbia University were the Three Essential Joys and l'Unités d'Habitation (*top*); the Radioconcentric City of Exchanges (*middle*); and the Three Human Establishments (*bottom*). Courtesy Drawings and Archives, Avery Library, Columbia University, New York.

"These roads follow the old roads of history, all the way to China. And at the end of these roads . . . to show the context and continuity, I shall draw the building of Columbia University. . . . I shall finish this talk and my sketch with these two hands, one opposite the other. . . . They represent a friendly dialogue, a brotherly dialogue from beginning to end." Signed: Columbia, 28/4/61, a grateful LC. Courtesy Drawings and Archives, Avery Library, Columbia University, New York.

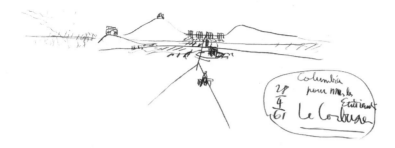

Le Corbusier's gift to the students of Columbia University. The drawing shows Paris with one of his visionary proposals to rebuild the Right Bank. Courtesy Drawings and Archives, Avery Library, Columbia University, New York.

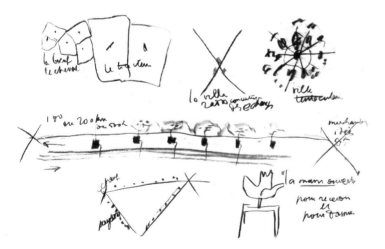

When presented with an honorary doctorate at Columbia in April 1961, Le Corbusier sketched and described his concept of the Three Human Establishments: the Agricultural Unit, with its ox, horse, and tractor; the Radio-concentric City of Exchanges, which began as a simple intersection of two roads and developed into a tentacular city; the Linear Industrial City of Exchanges extending along three routes: waterways, railways, and roadways. He concluded: "I shall finish this sketch with a picture of the Monument of the Open Hand, which is my only political statement in fifty years. The Open Hand, to give and to receive." Courtesy Drawings and Archives, Avery Library, Columbia University, New York.

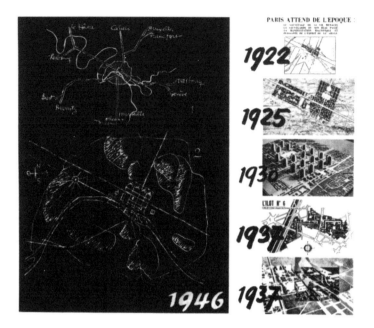

Le Corbusier proposed many plans for Paris from 1922 to his death in 1965. "I haven't built a single apartment in Paris for thirty years," he admitted bitterly and repeatedly in his final years. Courtesy FLC, Paris.

modesty, and above all of an absolute lack of diplomacy. Ever since 1922, when he first conceived his inspirational proposal for Paris as "A Contemporary City for Three Million Inhabitants," and followed by his "Plan voisin" (1925) and "La Ville radieuse" (1930), his sense of social mission had grown, and plans for regional solutions had become visions of global solutions. On one level, like every true innovator, Le Corbusier understood that he was merely a carrier of ideas that were larger than him. In *Mise au point* he reminds us, "I am not a revolutionary. I am a shy person who does not interfere in what does not concern him, but the basic elements are revolutionary" (89). Yet on other levels he felt his personal exclusion keenly. After three years of designing the city of Algiers, for example, Corbusier wrote in *La Ville radieuse*: "I have been expelled, the doors have been shut in my face."[64]

After Charles de Gaulle was elected president in 1958, the Paris region underwent huge changes. A major administrative reform took place in 1961 with the creation of the Paris Region District. Hoping to make Paris a great modern metropolis, de Gaulle later approved major projects within the capital, including Montparnasse, Porte d'Italie, Hauts de Belleville, Front de Seine, and the most ambitious of all, La Défense across Pont Neuilly, a new district in the west of Paris. In 1964, one year before Le Corbusier's death, seven new departments were created outside Paris to better coordinate economic and interurban development. All this fostered ambitious schemes and presented enormous logistical problems: highways, bridges, and overpasses had to be built, parking resolved, the RER (Réseau Express Régional) extended, and offices expanded; the Central Markets had to be moved out and a whole new series of satellite towns and suburbs had to be planned to house the masses. There appeared to be plenty of work for

years to come — for Prime Minister Michel Debré designated the Paris region a national priority. Not since Baron Haussmann's developments in the mid-nineteenth century had the French capital seen plans on such a scale.

Le Corbusier was convinced that only one man was fit for a task of this magnitude, and that was himself. He had written about it, warned of its problems if undertaken carelessly, and demonstrated his readiness and ability to undertake the challenge and even to coordinate the task. For example: in July 1958, Le Corbusier wrote a two-page proposal to André Malraux entitled "Sort de Paris" (The fate of Paris). In it he proposed the creation of a tripartite, temporary study group for the center of Paris, to be made up of urbanists, researchers, and engineers. He would lead the first group, and assigned reading for his section would be his own *Les Trois Etablissements humains* of 1945 and *Les Plans de Paris* of 1956. "Good urbanism makes money," he wrote André Malraux. "Bad urbanism ruins the community and enriches parasites." The proper revitalization of Paris, he wrote, would "bring about transformations, a source of wealth, and stimulate tremendous vitality."[65] And yet Le Corbusier was not only not asked to lead in this reconstruction; he was not included in it at all. Scholars like Jean-Louis Cohen have suggested that Le Corbusier's failures resulted in part from his being outside the elite circles (what Cohen calls "the court") and in part from poor timing; in spite of heroic efforts to be avant-garde, he was "out of focus and out of step" with contemporary movements.[66]

From the beginning, Le Corbusier assumed that eventually his ideas would receive the support he had so long sought. Indeed, there was some indication in the early 1960s — from France and from the United States — that such recognition was at last forthcoming, which made the ultimate disillusionment all the more painful. In spring 1962, Michel Debré appointed Paul Delouvrier chief executive in charge of a regional planning program for Paris and the greater metropolitan area. On 7 April, immediately after he had been confirmed in this post, Delouvrier wrote to Le Corbusier asking for his help in preparing an official report: "I have taken the liberty of coming to you to ask for your precious contribution to this document. . . . I thought it would be a privilege for us to see you make your point 26 years after *The Athens Charter*."[67]

The invitation was apparently rather routine, and routinely polite. The report was to have a multitude of contributors from many fields, including the presidents of Parisian banks and the chamber of commerce, university professors, and well-known writers, among them André Maurois of the Académie Française. But Le Corbusier clearly interpreted the letter as the invitation to him in a special, personal sense. He was extremely busy at the time, on the verge of leaving for India to supervise the construction of Chandigarh. But he nevertheless promised to send a contribution from that distant place in a month's time and in fact did produce the essay, using himself as a benchmark: "Where are we, 26 years after *The Athens Charter?*"[68] What happened to this contribution, which had been quite routinely solicited, is a painful mix of etiquette, formal rhetoric, and misplaced trust. The correspondence around it forms an exemplary psychological document in Le Corbusier's mental preparations for writing his final testament.

On receiving the invitation from Delouvrier, Le Corbusier wrote back that he would be "happy to speak to him about it and remained available." Delouvrier responded politely that the report was to be published later that year. But then he included the seductive sentiment "No one could be better than you for finding the proper solutions to reverse a somewhat conformist mentality and for bringing aware-

ness of the future's new dimensions."[69] From that point on, naively misled by what looked like a sign of special trust, Le Corbusier kept Delouvrier abreast of his general urban projects for other European cities, sending him many unsolicited documents to prove his worth. He forwarded to Delouvrier a copy of the letter written to the mayor of Venice; he reminded him of a huge retrospective exhibit opening at the Museum of Modern Art in Paris featuring his plans for the center of Berlin (which were disqualified without appeal); and he ended his cover letter with the self-pitying comment that had by now become something of a leitmotiv: "I haven't built a single apartment in Paris for thirty years. . . . This is simply background information, not at all to grumble."[70] Through all this we see the painful moves of a master at the pinnacle of his career, seventy-five years old, putting himself in situations where he is almost begging and yet who remains supremely confident in the rightness of his vision. This exclusion lasted until the year of his death in 1965. In 1964, the influential paper *Le Figaro littéraire* organized a great debate on Paris in the year 2000. Five important figures were invited to participate, among them three architects—but not Le Corbusier. Instead, one of the five was Corbu's longtime associate André Wogenscky. Asked about ideal urban solutions for increasing density while decreasing built surface, Wogenscky—who must have felt the awkwardness of the situation keenly—hastened to reply: "I worked with Le Corbusier. He proposed solutions . . . which would preserve urban density . . . the Marseilles prototype."[71]

Le Corbusier's twenty-seven-page contribution to the District of Paris project of 1962, "Where Are We, 26 Years after *The Athens Charter?*" was among the last solicited position papers written in his own voice. In tone and scope it bears comparison with *Mise au point*. The text curiously blurs the private and public

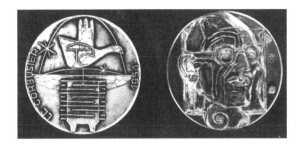

The medal honoring Le Corbusier on the completion of l'Unité d'Habitation at Marseilles in 1951. The National Mint, Paris, Lallement. Courtesy FLC, Paris.

Pablo Picasso visits l'Unité d'Habitation at Marseilles with Le Corbusier, 1951. Courtesy FLC, Paris.

voice, mixing bitter "first-person" accomplishments, grudges, and disappointments with a still-vigorous sense of social responsibility. It touches on all manner of angers. Le Corbusier invokes the assaults on him during the building of the Unité d'Habitation at Marseilles ("five years of unimaginable attacks, hatred, and stupidity"); he recalls the distant oldest and deepest wound, the League of Nations competition of 1927; he details his activities that continued even while Hitler was occupying Paris ("I established AS-CORAL [Association des Constructeurs pour la Rénovation Architecturale] even though I had not been commissioned to realize a single square centimeter of my urbanism, nor build a centimeter of reconstruction. I devoted an entire year to it "). Just as Le Corbusier lashes out against government-issued diplomas in *Mise au point,* so does he jump at the chance to lash out in his submission for the District of Paris report. "The present era breathes only through diplomas," he wrote. "It is legitimate, but disastrous. Those great diplomas: 'Ecole supérieure' . . . 'Ecole nationale de . . .' . . . 'Ecole des hautes études' . . ." A self-made man (with the additional assurance of knowing he was a genius), Le Corbusier believed strongly that a good elementary school education was all that was needed.

Did Le Corbusier's bitterness in this document blind him to the fact that the other contributing members to the report, numbering ninety-one in all, were largely the product of these same official institutions, sponsored by the government, with identities tightly bound to their diplomas? In the end, the published version of the report did not include Le Corbusier's contribution—and perhaps for this very reason. Its personal tone and irascible content were completely out of place. In the words of Siegfried Giedion, writing about Le Corbusier several years earlier: "He has not tried to be politically shrewd. His mind just doesn't work this way and he burns his hands every time he tries."[72]

Indeed, Le Corbusier was almost triumphantly deficient in political sense. Having inconvenienced his American enthusiasts with his hard-to-get tactics concerning the AIA medal and the honorary degree from Columbia University, he now tried to employ those very honors to lend authority to his next major battle, the Gare d'Orsay project, and to increase his competitive edge in further honors. In personal correspondence, he attributed his lack of success to various "cabals" mounted against him—even as he reserved for himself the right to mock most other schools and institutions.[73] Thus Le Corbusier was kept at the sidelines, allowed to chip away at major projects in the rebuilding of Paris but without lending his hand or his vision to the whole.

His only involvement in major projects at this time came at André Malraux's invitation to design a museum of twentieth-century art. Through this window of opportunity, Le Corbusier attempted to gain recognition for his more ambitious ideas in urban planning, worked out decades earlier but never applied; as he noted in his sketchbook for 1962, "LC to send the book 'The Three Human Establishments' to President de Gaulle and Malraux.'"[74] The museum project was begun about 1962, with an ambitious program that included four art schools (music, architecture, cinema and television, and decorative arts); it seemed to offer Le Corbusier a chance to articulate the global vision that came so naturally to him. But the project was delayed, the program and the site were changed many times, and when Le Corbusier insisted on a more central location within Paris as late as 1965 in the area of Les Halles—where some building did take place a decade later—de Gaulle was not interested. Finally the site was fixed at Nanterre, adjacent to La Défense; but ultimately no museum was built at all under de Gaulle.[75]

For Le Corbusier, the La Défense district remained a special sore spot and in *Mise au point* became the node of a lifetime of cumulative anger. Focusing on the CNIT (Centre National des Industries et des Techniques) building, Le Corbusier noted: "They did not hesitate to repeat the mistake; they did not hesitate to redo it at La Défense, the largest vault in the world. . . . the so-called avenue Triomphale is being redone by real estate agents" (92). (Le Corbusier laments further: "Never has the word gr-r-rand been used so tragically" [92].) In these remarks, one hears the frustration of one whose many ideas were taken and applied around the world but who remained an unsung and unsought-out hero in his adopted city, Paris.

Private dwelling was always an issue close to Le Corbusier's heart. Finally, in 1946–52, he had had a chance to apply his revolutionary theories to the most celebrated and controversial project in Marseilles, an innovative housing solution in the form of a single concrete slab for a community of sixteen hundred people. New commissions were not coming his way in this period, and so Le Corbusier invested tremendous energy in the design of this Unité d'Habitation. An entire community was to be housed in a single block, containing twenty-three types of units depending on the size of the family and twenty-six services provided within the building. Yet each unit was to preserve what Le Corbusier considered minimum criteria for quality of life: maximum privacy, easy access to communal facilities, and close contact with nature. Called by some critics a "cottage-cooperative" and by others "La Maison du Fada" (a loony-bin), the Unité d'Habitation remains one of the world's most innovative attempts at mass housing. But neither the public nor the authorities were impressed. In *Mise au point,* we read about various reactions, bitterly repeated by Le Corbusier: "Slums to make you knock your head against walls," "a hatchery for mental illness." In his response to these accusations, the beleaguered architect paraphrased the president of the medical association, who declared: "Mr. Le Corbusier is going to multiply the number of the insane in France, in their promiscuity and up-roar."[76] Although there were signs of success in the images of children at play on the rooftop nurseries, swimming pool, and other facilities atop this giant block, one month before he died, Le Corbusier wrote bluntly to Lilette Ougier, the director of the nursery school at the Unité who worked with these happy children: "They should create temples of patience and endurance for those who have received kicks in the butt all their lives!"[77] Little wonder, then, that in later years Le Corbusier reacted cautiously whenever the question of public housing was raised—as it was in the early 1960s, in yet another pretext for disillu-sionment.

A note in Le Corbusier's hand from the archives dated 9 October 1961 gives a taste of his attitude when he advocated the mass production and standardization of housing units by a major manufacturer: "Last year the Minister of Construction had a project to build 350,000 dwellings," Le Corbusier writes. "I went to introduce him to M. Myon, P.D.G. of Renault Engi-neering, and I told the Minister: 'I would like you to give me 5,000 units, in order to put into mass pro-duction the most appropriate ones I could dream of, appropriate not for me but for the country.' Monsieur the Minister got up and said: 'That would be awful,' etc., etc. All the heads of the department were there."[78] Further correspondence indicates that an order for two hundred apartment units, to be de-signed by Le Corbusier, followed this exchange.

In *Mise au point* we read the following line: "After the war, reconstruction; zero for Corbu" (86). It echoes personal correspondence to Delouvrier—"For thirty years, I did not build a single apartment in Paris"—even though he had been awarded an honor few dis-tinguished figures receive, that of Grand Officier de la Légion d'Honneur under de Gaulle (86).[79] We find this disillusioned comment in *Mise au point:* "The

dwelling had no chance to become the temple of the family. Rental boxes were made" (92).

In 1961, Le Corbusier took part in a competition for the Gare d'Orsay site. It involved a hotel and cultural center in the heart of Paris but would have meant tearing down the old Beaux-Arts style railroad sta-tion. Again Corbu devised an ambitious scheme: in addition to a thirty-four-story hotel, there would be an exhibition hall and space for music shows and conferences.[80] It never got beyond the early planning stages. And again his bitterness appears to be a mix-ture of the personal, the professional, and the artistic. How he responded to this loss, however, and why some details of his project might have discouraged his potential clients, explain a good deal about the "embittered Quixote" tone that we sense throughout *Mise au point.*

Le Corbusier thought grandly, in large blocks. Ever since his *Journey to the East* in 1911, he had considered the art of building to be a sacred one to which few were called. To be a builder was to be a person apart, a person with wider visions and ascetic discipline. About the collapse of his cultural center project, he wrote: "Only if the promoters of this project love Paris fervently can this goal—attainable though lofty—be reached."[81] He readily admitted that his early conceptual scheme required "months of work," but hastened to assure his clients and Minister of Culture Malraux of his absolute honesty and rigor. His goal was "to bring about a decisive manifesta-tion of architecture at a time when Paris is in danger of being milked by profiteers or by persons altogether lacking in spirit."[82] By late 1961, Le Corbusier was in-formed that the commission would not be his. But he continued to insist that his project be presented, even after his client and financial backer had withdrawn their support. He sought advice from a fellow archi-tect about hiring a lawyer. Then, in a final embarrass-

Model of the Orsay Cultural Center, Paris, in its context, with the Musée du Louvre and the Tuileries in the foreground. Across the Seine, the block, 125 meters (410 feet) high, was to replace the Gare d'Orsay. "A work of total rigor, complete accuracy, and absolute honesty, " wrote Le Corbusier to André Malraux. Courtesy FLC, Paris.

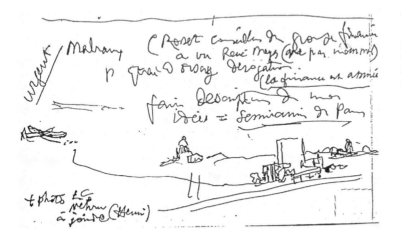

"Urgent/Malraux . . . describe my ideas = Semiramis of Paris. Append the photo of LC and Nehru," wrote Le Corbusier in his pocket-sized diary over his Orsay Cultural Center sketch. Courtesy FLC, Paris.

Left: President Charles de Gaulle and Le Corbusier at the reception celebrating Le Corbusier's promotion to Grand Officier of the Legion of Honor, Paris, 19 December 1963. Courtesy, A.F.P. Paris.

Le Corbusier with the model of the Orsay Cultural Center, Paris. "Le block d'Orsay est un block inerte qui tuerrait Paris," wrote Yvan Christ in *Les Arts,* 10 January 1962. "Le projet confectionné par Mr LC est un monstre" (The block of Orsay is an inert block that would kill Paris. . . . The project assembled by Mr. Corbusier is a monster). Courtesy FLC, Paris/Apis-Henri Bureau.

Beaux-Arts building of 1900, celebrating the fin-de-siècle "bourgeois excess" that Le Corbusier would have torn down, now recycled and known as the Musée d'Orsay. This recent preservation and restoration, in which two French presidents took a genuine interest, is a great success with the public. But it could also be seen as the ultimate slap in the face administered to such a vocal anti-academic as Le Corbusier.

One detail of Le Corbusier's aborted plan is worth noting, however. For the Hôtel d'Orsay, he proposed that a select number of the hotel rooms be 183 centimeters (seven feet, six inches) wide, similar in size to ship cabins or—more accurately—to a monk's cell. This idea was poorly received by the American partner, International Hotel Corporation (IHC), which was accustomed to providing rather lavish rooms with every comfort, marked by the most conspicuous consumption. Le Corbusier's insistence on a spartan environment of limited size was a result of his commitment not only to the proportional system of the Modulor but to his early attraction to monasticism, asceticism, and a solitary existence. As he jotted down on a sketch in 1963, "Certains me dénomment 'Le Sanglier solitaire'" (Some call me "The Lone Boar").[84]

But what can one say, finally, about a plan for a quality hotel in the heart of Paris that had beds appropriate for monks? For Le Corbusier, a hotel room should be a place of contemplation and recuperation. He genuinely believed that he could persuade the world of this piety. In a letter of 1961 to Malraux's assistant for artistic affairs, he expressed the hope that the 183-centimeter-wide hotel room, "ship-cabin or airplane style," could become the norm, as opposed to the "very banal" Hilton style.[85] Discipline within its borders would teach discipline in the larger society: "Un homme = une cellule; des cellules = la ville." Several times in his book *The Radiant City,* he embed-

ing gesture, he sent a letter to his former financial backers enumerating his recent honors and accomplishments and listing the foreign-language editions of his best-selling books—hoping to persuade them to change their minds.[83] Meanwhile, the Gare d'Orsay grew ever more dilapidated.

On that site today stands a popularly acclaimed nineteenth-century museum inside the shell of the ded a formula for happiness in a little frame that read: "the key = the cell = men = happiness." As he put it in an unpublished essay, "Everything is in the value, the efficiency and the integrity of the cell. In the matter of human habitat: urbanism (cities and country), streets, houses and dwellings, the cell rules."[86]

Le Corbusier's research into the cell was not limited to large projects or to orthogonal geometry. In his "Roq" et "Rob" project of 1949 and while designing two houses for the Jaoul family in Neuilly in the 1950s, for example, he pursued this "cell prototype" as a module, making it applicable both to the vernacular form of a catalan vault and to the bourgeois dwelling, which could expand as a module.[87] Le Corbusier advocated standardized "cells" produced by industry, which he considered to be efficient, aesthetic, and humanizing. The same commitment to the cell was reflected in other projects, built and unbuilt, and in certain spatial solutions he encountered throughout his life: the Carthusian monastery he had visited at Galluzzo near Florence in 1907 and 1911, the Unités d'Habitation, the transatlantic liners, the Venice hospital. Multiple dwellings are inevitably communal enterprises, and Le Corbusier believed that shared functions should be provided in each. But the essence of Corbusian design was the human being, detached and alone. "Home" was above all the place of "intangible and sacred solitude."[88] In his essay on Dwelling, which discussed the primordial functions of urbanism according to *The Athens Charter,* Le Corbusier wrote, "The home is the basic social cell containing that inestimable side of life, intimacy, the feeling that one is master, king of one's domain, dependent not on others but on one's self alone."[89] The tiny cabin built toward the end of his life as a hermitage at Cap-Martin on the French coast—with no kitchen, no telephone, and no access road—exempli-

fied this principle. An intensely autonomous and creative personality, Le Corbusier understood that all communal or clustering activities are more or less interruptions in a schedule of essentially solitary and contemplative action.

Indeed, père Corbu's genius was contradictory and contrary. He rebuked society and yet expected to be honored by it; he felt every rejection deeply, wished to be courted and featured, and yet stressed the need to withdraw; he wished to lead the world and yet he identified, in his favorite literature, with noble eccentrics and misfits. Two characteristic anecdotes catch this side of the man, both concerned with the preservation of the master's legacy by the media. In November 1962, Le Corbusier wrote a letter to Robert Bordaz, director of the Radiodiffusion-Télévision Française. Ultimately he was sensible enough not to send it. "One of yours (a reporter) used and abused me last evening, making a long recording about the problems of Paris," Le Corbusier wrote. "I gave him important ideas, but all of a sudden I remembered that scissors are at work in your place as elsewhere— and that from this long recording, only a few words would remain, made as banal as possible, and that the remainder would find its way into the wastepaper basket of lost memories." Le Corbusier proceeded to request that a full recording be made for his personal use, remarking that his request "had nothing excessive about it." To be sure, if everyone asked for such favors, it might be difficult. He then added: "Mais je ne suis pas un Monsieur quelconque . . . ."[90]

A year earlier, Le Corbusier read over a film scenario written by Michel Bataille, inspired by his book *Creation Is a Patient Search,* which featured the architect and his best known concepts.[91] One innocent scene depicted the old master sitting in an airplane engaged in casual discussion; the script read: "LC et M.X. dans avion. La conversation s'achève." Over this passage Le Corbusier scribbled, "Non. L.C. toujours seul . . . lisait Orphée, Rabelais, Cervantes" (No. L.C. is always alone. Reading Orpheus, Rabelais, Cervantes). Real-life confirmations of this scenario are plentiful. In his memoir of Le Corbusier's visit to New York City in 1946, Constantino Nivola recalled that "seated alone at a table for two in the corner, Le Corbusier, the master, was modestly eating lunch. All of the newspapers had just announced his second visit to the United States, and I was shocked to find him by himself. I would discover later that this was typical of his way of living."[92]

Le Corbusier and the Academy

Le Corbusier's irritation at unresponsive bureaucrats and the indifferent public was matched by his distrust, and often scorn, of the official academy—and especially the Ecole des Beaux-Arts. In *Mise au point* he writes: "I repudiate all treatises. But I declare war, war on Vignola (and Company), which always smells to me of dead bodies" (88). Givers of form must be inventors, not imitators. The three orders of the architect Giacomo da Vignola were to him vestiges of past civilizations, false witnesses. In what might seem like a paradox, Le Corbusier, so enamored of technology and its potential, had the values of an old-fashioned humanist: he insisted that for the solution of modern-day problems only one measure was acceptable, that of the human being. He perceived the academy as hostile to this human measure. In his first lecture in Buenos Aires in 1929, "To Free Oneself Entirely of Academic Thinking," Le Corbusier proclaimed: "Today I'm considered a revolutionary. I shall confess to you that I have had only one teacher, the past; only one education, the study of the past." He concluded the lecture with the advice, "One must no longer think academically."[93]

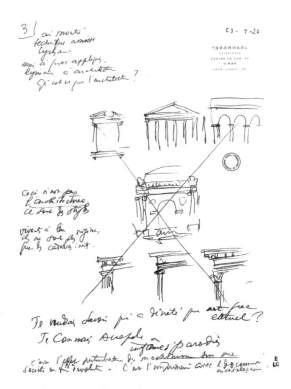

According to Le Corbusier, the givers of form must be inventors and not imitators. The three orders of Vignola and the past styles are the remains of past civilizations still maintained, and against all reason. "This is not architecture, these are styles," he wrote above, and x'ed them out. A similar drawing produced during his third lecture at the Faculty of Exact Sciences, Buenos Aires, 8 October 1929. Courtesy FLC, Paris.

There was a biographical side to the prejudice. Le Corbusier was proud that he had never received a formal architectural education. Although he was constantly and passionately engaged in the search for cultural knowledge through foreign travel, visiting libraries and museums, attending concerts and operas, viewing art exhibits, and making his own referential notes and drawings in sketchbooks, Le Corbusier had a deep dislike of institutions, "schools," and class-rooms—whose purpose, he believed, was to turn out professionals according to a standardized mold. At the end of his life he was as stubborn on this point as he had been as a young man. In 1965, he wrote: "I practiced architecture without professional lectures, without school, without diplomas. I set out on a road across Europe: Paris, Constantinople, Asia Minor, Athens, Rome. I looked, saw, observed, discovered. Life belongs not to those who *know,* but to those who *discover.*"[94]

A half-century earlier, in June 1910 at the age of twenty-two, he had written, "I think it is almost ten times easier to obtain an architectural degree in a polytechnic than not to want to do it."[95] That October he was invited to be part of Peter Behrens's office in Berlin. In a letter to his parents he rejoiced that "out of the thirteen architects who work for Behrens, not one has a professional degree!"[96] Also among those office assistants were Walter Gropius and Ludwig Mies Van der Rohe. At that time, none of the three could imagine that they would change twentieth-century architecture forever.

In this question of academic legitimization, however, Le Corbusier was ambivalent and stubborn—as he was on any matter that required compromise between the public reception of his work and the sanctity of his inner vision. One example from the war years is especially telling. After the German occupation began, Le Corbusier's atelier was closed. He moved to Vichy and then to Vézelay, before returning to Paris in 1942. After his return, a group of students at the Académie des Beaux-Arts became interested in setting up an "atelier libre" taught by Le Corbusier; over the objections of the director of the academy, they approached the famous architect with this in mind. (One of the coordinators for the Beaux-Arts splinter student group was Roger Aujame, who later

worked for many years as a collaborator at the atelier at 35 rue de Sèvres.)

Seeking support for this plan, in January 1943 Le Corbusier wrote to the chief of the cabinet of the Ministry of National Education at Vichy. His letter demonstrated a genuine interest in setting up an "academy" that would permit him to grant a diploma ("diplôme des hautes études architecturales"), but he posed several conditions. "Le Corbusier suggests that his atelier be authorized to grant the degree 'diplôme Le Corbusier.' But only a jury of a disposition similar to his would be qualified to grant such a diploma, a jury that brought together people similar to those who had gathered before 1939 in the 'l'Union pour l'Art' led by Auguste Perret." Further, Le Corbusier had no problem with "state-granted diplomas" as long as they did not imply a monopoly of the "academic tendency"—which, he intimated, would be a disaster for the future of architectural education in France, because the official Society of Architects "satisfied only one aspect of the mind."[97]

Le Corbusier was willing to make his atelier at 35 rue de Sèvres available to students who wished to pursue advanced training under his supervision. The Beaux-Arts students sought support for this plan from their professor of theory, Michel Roux-Spitz, who was also president and director of the Ecole des Beaux-Arts; not surprisingly, no support was forthcoming for an "atelier libre" at 35 rue de Sèvres. External studios were common practice in the Beaux-Arts tradition, but they were always staffed by insiders. The Vichy government was thus caught in a dilemma, one Le Corbusier had hoped to play to his advantage. Vichy wished to accommodate a world-famous architect who was willing to be authorized by the regime; and yet, Vichy could not alienate the Beaux-Arts regulars, who saw this latest "rebellious" move by Le Corbusier as both capricious and divisive.[98] Ultimately,

Atelier 35 rue de Sèvres, Le Corbusier standing in the foreground facing the camera, January 1962. Courtesy FLC, Paris.

Atelier 35 rue de Sèvres, Le Corbusier and Jullian de la Fuente (October 1960). "Once upon a time we were forty here; it was crazy and everyone had the right to say what he thought; it was a civil war. Now we are four, it works better. . . . Do you want to work for me? (from a phone conversation he had with two young architects, P. Langley and G. Maurois, recorded 16 November 1963). Courtesy FLC, Paris.

no atelier was approved, and Le Corbusier spent the war years seeking work and writing.

More than a decade later, in January 1956, an attempt was made to recruit Le Corbusier for membership in the Académie des Beaux-Arts. As he described the incident in a confidential memo written the following day: "Yesterday, January 3, 1956, Mr. X, a member of the Institute, requested an immediate meeting. Fifteen minutes later he was in my office.

'Will you agree to be a member of the Institute?" he asked. My response: 'No, thank you. Never!'" He wrote further that his name would be used as a banner to cover the actual progress of the Ecole des Beaux-Arts, which would never be more than a "superficial modernism." According to Le Corbusier, the Ecole was now sick: unable to move forward hon-

Left: Atelier 35 rue de Sèvres, around 1957. *First row, left to right:* Iannis Xénakis, Olek Kujawski, Jeannette Gabillard (secretary), Jeanine Dargent (secretary), Arvind Talati, Jeanne Heilbuth (Le Corbusier's secretary), Le Corbusier. *Second row, left to right:* Jacques Michel, Mr. Sachinidis, Mr. Mériot, Kim-Chun-Up, Augusto Tobito, Henri Bruaux, Roggio Andréini, Jacques Masson, André Maissonnier, and Fernand Gardien. Courtesy PARIS MATCH/Rizzo.

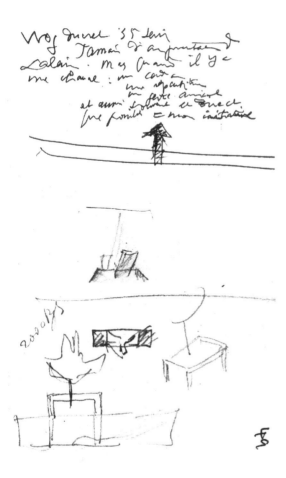

"Never a raise in salaries. But when there is a chance: a gift, a distribution, a friendly gesture, and as often and directly as possible = my initiative." Sketchbook H 34 (1954), 49. Courtesy FLC, Paris.

estly, still feeding its young students Vignola, the Paris Opéra, the Grand Palais, and Orsay, it had nevertheless departed from the directions that had earned it glory in the past. "Alas, dear Mr. X," Le Corbusier concluded. "Thank you for your offer. But I must remain on the firing line, where one receives blows and where life is tough."[99]

Le Corbusier's individualism and anti-academicism had a militant, somewhat aggressive accent, especially in his later years. Even in the architect's own atelier, which he considered a cooperative endeavor where everyone contributed proportionally, when a few of the longtime members demanded special status (the right to sign their names to projects they designed and a pay increase to keep up with other professionals in the field), Le Corbusier could not reconcile himself to the request and locked some of them out, telling them, "I set you free."[100] These associates had put in long, often quite faceless years of service. Although there were individual instances of gratitude and the master did, under pressure, acknowledge collaboration, Le Corbusier apparently could not detach himself from the image of the master-disciple relationship; he resisted any notion of the disciple growing into a master in his own right within the confines of his atelier.

What happens, however, when the solitary warrior grows tired? Where does he turn for support? Here, too, there are inconsistencies and vacillations. Le Corbusier never concealed his disdain for the products of institutions. During his trip to the United States in 1935–36, for example, he reacted against the French academic tradition practiced at all major universities, including Columbia, Yale, and Princeton—where, he said, instruction was timid, full of reservations, and based on "Vignolesque" principles that had killed architecture and lacked the spirit of modern times. As we have seen, he refused the Académie des Beaux-Arts's invitation to become a member in 1956 and to have the "atelier libre" he had been denied in 1943. Yet in the last years of his life, he accepted honorary degrees from Cambridge University in 1959 and Columbia University in 1961, the Royal Institute of British Architects (RIBA) Gold Medal in 1953 and the American Institute of Architects Gold Medal in 1961. Toward the end, he attempted to modify his harsh

The United States honors Le Corbusier. Reception at the United States Information Service, Paris, 2 July 1953. Le Corbusier, *at left,* holds the scroll of the National Institute of Arts and Letters Award. To his right are Marc Connolly, president of the National Institute of Arts and Letters, and U.S. Ambassador to France C. Douglas Dillon. Courtesy FLC, Paris.

position on honors and institutions by placing himself, as it were, permanently in the learner's realm: "Daily life is made up of perseverance, courage, modesty and difficulties," he remarked on receiving the AIA Gold Medal in Philadelphia. "I am like St.

Thomas, but without the sanctity. . . . Values change from one day to the next. The world is bursting forth. I, for one, still live the life of the student."[101] But it was not just living "the life of the student" that he coveted as a self-image. Also precious was the

Le Corbusier, Doctor of Laws Honoris Causa, Cambridge
University, 11 June 1959. Le Corbusier sketches a caricature
of himself in front of Henry Moore, among the distinguished
guests, and writes: "Down with the Academy!" *Le Corbusier
Sketchbook* N 57 (1959), 51. Courtesy FLC, Paris.

The Modulor Man is a token of appreciation from Le Corbusier for the great honor of being awarded the Gold
Medal of the American Institute of Architects for 1961. The Gold Medal citation read: "Architect, planner, sculptor,
painter, author, poet, teacher, visionary, and, most of all, man of principle, who, often misunderstood but always
respected, has by his tenacious insistence on seeking truth and beauty for the human environment, by his great
works, by his discoveries, and by his motto that 'Creation is a patient search,' led and inspired the dawn of a new
architecture." Courtesy American Institute of Architects Library and Archives, Washington, D.C.

Philip Will, Jr., F.A.I.A., as president of the AIA in 1961 presents the Gold Medal to Le Corbusier. In his brief acceptance speech, Le Corbusier was quite gloomy: "There is no 'wing of victory' in this room. There is no 'wing of victory' in life. . . . If you will excuse me, I am going to become very vulgar. . . . It is Le Corbusier who cleans the toilets of 35 rue de Sèvres, and that's why he's the boss." Courtesy American Institute of Architects Library and Archives, Washington, D.C.

He again complained about not receiving state commissions; he reiterated his major failures since the League of Nations in 1927; and he made certain that his audience knew how much he disliked being called "a poet" and "a dreamer." He was—as one of the architects honoring him pointed out—a worker, a fighter, a "Don Quixote" battling the "substantial windmills" of bureaucracies and academies. But Le Corbusier could provide only a litany of losses and failures. How indeed could this have been received by a group of admirers bestowing on him the highest professional honor on behalf of the queen of England?

In a paradox that is common to many sages of simplicity from Henry David Thoreau to Leo Tolstoy, this embittered outcast and permanent student Le Corbusier was not at all averse to the public role of moral pedagogue. As he addressed the academy: "What should I teach? A philosophy of life? The philosophy of a seventy-year-old?"[103] Correspondence between Le Corbusier and André Malraux suggests that the master architect was indeed eager to influence architectural education in a formal way—but only on his own terms, as a personal example and charismatic model, and distinctly separate from any institution that might constrain or limit him. In February 1960, he lectured at the Sorbonne before 3,500 enthusiastic students and another 1,000 crowded in the street. The lecture was on themes dear to him that were to surface again in *Mise au point:* "l'homme et la femme," the human being with sensibility and heart, materialism versus the satisfaction of one's conscience.[104]

Le Corbusier's philosophy of life was a curious mix of utopian idealism, Mediterranean vitality, Swiss skepticism, and work-ethic Calvinism. Perhaps unexpectedly, it involved a serious theory of play. "Mountain climbers, rugby players, card players, and gamblers are all frauds because they do not play." Le Corbusier had remarked to his cousin Pierre Jeanneret. "Yes, the rule has been to play the game . . . and men have

Quixotic image of himself as humiliated, beaten up, a mixture of abuse and spiritual purity. In his speech to RIBA on 31 March 1953, after having been praised by Britain's most distinguished architects, Le Corbusier presented himself as a "cab-horse" who had been working for forty years, "receiving many blows."[102]

forgotten how to play" (*Mise au point,* 88). To "play the game," apparently, meant to follow others' rules, to conform to schools and institutions, or perhaps to observe no rules at all; creative freedom for the artist, in contrast, means to *play one's own game,* "the rules of my game . . . the game of this house, of that arrangement whose order emerged at the moment of its creation and developed, proved correct, became dominant. All within the rules! Nothing outside of the rules! Otherwise I no longer have a reason for being" (88). Mountain climbers, rugby players, card players, and gamblers are frauds, Le Corbusier intimates, because in their quest their goal is too clear and precise; they are not seriously at play *at their own game.* In this concept of the creative process and play, he reconfirms himself as a Romantic.

Le Corbusier naturally thought in a broad context, across wide stretches of space and time. For him, "urbanism" was always a large-scale commitment. It was not just erecting a fountain, building an isolated square, or planting a row of trees. To him, city planning meant a total change from the past, a new environment for the new urban dweller, and like all such visions of utopian scope, it did not allow for sentimental or undisciplined human habits. Even "total change" had its limits, of course; in his most radical proposals, when applied to Paris, Le Corbusier would have never touched such historic landmarks as the Louvre and Tuileries gardens, the Tour St. Jacques, St.-Germain-l'Auxerrois, le Châtelet, l'Hôtel de Ville, and, in the distance, Sacré-Coeur. He targeted areas that were in decay, such as the central area of Les Halles, which he would have pulled down and replaced by 220-meter-high (729 feet) skyscrapers, cruciform or "patte de poule" (hen's foot) in shape, spaced far apart and bathed in greenery. Le Corbusier would have killed the traditional street—but in compensation, Paris would have become a greener, and

denser city. This ideal had never before been realized in a major metropolis and would have combined the best of rural and urban.

Le Corbusier's passionate desire to instruct the French in the ways of proper building for the modern era had a certain rancorous aspect and specific focal point: the Grand Palais in Paris. This exhibition hall, opened in 1900, was a frequent target of his attacks.[105] In *Mise au point* he continues the barrage: "This palace was the mortal enemy of all exhibitions" (92). The Ecole des Beaux-Arts had inspired this sort of architecture, and Le Corbusier considered it the exemplar of everything insipid and pompous. Along with the Petit Palais and later the Gare d'Orsay, he wanted the Grand Palais torn down—and he had made similar proposals for other sites in Paris since 1922. Renewal or urban removal would be the ultimate retaliation against the academic thinking that produced these buildings. Le Corbusier's deeply felt conviction that the Grand Palais was inappropriate for exhibits, and his sustained attacks on it over many years, never persuaded the authorities to pull it down or to find a more fitting use for it.[106]

Le Corbusier's fortunes in Paris appeared to change suddenly near the end of his life. By the early 1960s, the French capital could no longer compete with other European metropolitan centers in accommodating great exhibitions of modern and contemporary art. The Ministry of Culture began to reevaluate existing museums (the Grand Palais, Petit Palais, and Musée d'Art Moderne on avenue du Président-Wilson) and laid plans for new exhibition spaces in Paris: the Musée National des Arts et Traditions Populaires in the Bois de Boulogne, the Musée des Sciences et Techniques, and a Musée du Vingtième Siècle (Museum of the Twentieth Century). The new museum was needed, but there was no readily available site. Some planners favored the new district of

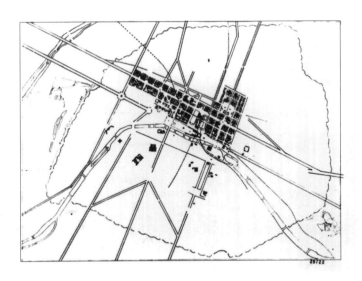

Plan Voisin for Paris, 1925. In this proposal for the Right Bank of Paris, Le Corbusier would have torn down the slums but preserved all the major monuments. Courtesy FLC, Paris.

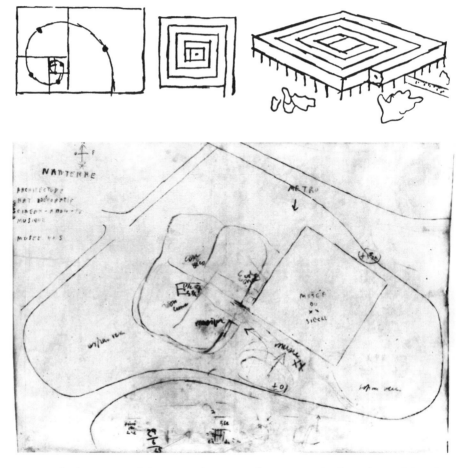

Prototype for the Museum of the Twentieth Century: the Museum of Unlimited Growth based on the square spiral (*top*); the Museum of the Twentieth Century planned for Nanterre, adjacent to La Défense district, as late as June 1965 (*bottom*). Courtesy FLC, Paris.

La Défense, which was being developed as an office and commercial zone but also slated for cultural institutions, such as a branch of the University of Paris at Nanterre. As mentioned earlier, when André Malraux contacted Le Corbusier and asked him to undertake to build a Museum of the Twentieth Century, which would include music, film, radio and television, architecture, and decorative arts, Le Corbusier fell to work on it with abandon. This was his first authentic commission for the national capital in forty years.

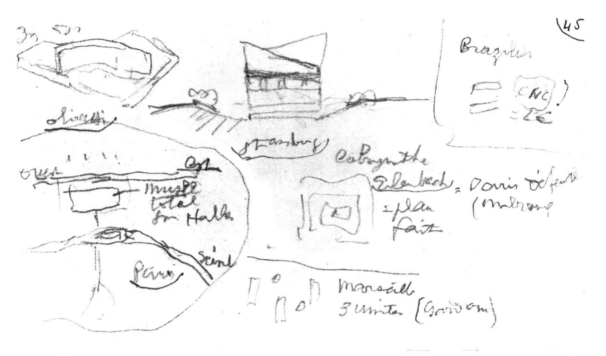

A page from Le Corbusier's sketchbook, with major projects under way in 1963: Electronic Laboratory for Olivetti, Milan; Palace of Congresses for Strasbourg; Embassy of France for Brasilia; International Art Center (with Twentieth-Century Museum) for Erlenbach, near Frankfurt; "Total Museum" for Les Halles District of Paris and three Unités d'Habitation for Marseilles. *Le Corbusier Sketchbook* T 69. Courtesy FLC, Paris.

Since the early 1930s, Le Corbusier had been developing a twentieth-century museum prototype known as the "Museum of unlimited growth" (Musée à croissance illimitée), in the shape of a square spiral. Three versions of it had already been realized: two in India (Ahmedabad, 1952–57, and Chandigarh, 1960–65), and one in Tokyo (1952–57). The prototype is dynamic and designed to grow as the need arises; obviously, the best site for such a museum is reasonably open and unconstricted, rather than an inevitably limited or constricted urban site in the center of

Paris. On receiving the commission from Malraux, Le Corbusier's stubborn, contradictory mind set to work: he wanted a central, as well as centrally accessible, location in the heart of Paris that offered the possibility of unlimited growth on a potentially open site. The Défense district, he felt, was possible but too far away; he preferred a site along the Seine—more precisely, the site of the odious Grand and Petit Palais. Again, a single building had massive implications for the entire city; and once again, Le Corbusier's genius as an architect of individual structures seemed inseparable from his visionary projections as city planner. But most of all, *he wanted to build*. And by this time he seemed willing to take on whatever was necessary to leave his mark on Paris.

Le Corbusier began to work with the two associate architects designated by the ministry, Jean Dubuisson and his long-time colleague André Wogenscky. In 1963, after various plans had already been aired in the papers, Le Corbusier received a letter from a group of young architects, nineteen in all, expressing their support for a Museum of the Twentieth Century in the heart of Paris. But they were astonished that Le Corbusier was willing to associate his name with Dubuisson, an established "academic" architect and winner of a Prix de Rome. Le Corbusier granted this group of students a telephone interview to discuss the matter on 16 November 1963, in which he emphasized that he had, after all, been studying possibilities for a "museum of unlimited growth" ever since 1930; that he was now seventy-six years old and this would be his first official commission from the Ministry of Culture; that "Dubuisson was a serious young man, he is a Prix de Rome but even a Prix de Rome can be intelligent"; that André Malraux, "himself a serious and intelligent individual," had suggested this; and that he himself, Le Corbusier, would take the matter very seriously, adding, "For months I think things over without touching a pencil" and "I always try to do my best." The students assured him that they were all his admirers; they had traveled as far as Chandigarh and Tokyo to see his buildings; their sole concern was that he not compromise his strict principles. For once, Le Corbusier found himself in an awkward position. "Once upon a time I was attacked by the old guard," he observed; "and now it is the young. . . . I worked for the U.N. and UNESCO," he added, "Zehrfuss said that he did UNESCO, since I wanted to work alone, I was a recluse, I was not very sociable. . . . It was my ideas they built, and they built them without me."[107]

The admission is significant. As an old man taking stock of his past, Le Corbusier was apparently convinced that his best ideas had been taken and often "built without him." Now he was determined to *build his ideas,* one way or the other. Thus his advice to the group of students was ironic and pragmatic, not his usual rebellious, impractical, quixotic, often heroic bravado. At the end of the interview he counseled them not to believe what they read in the papers and that a crusade would lead them nowhere. "If you wish to do battle, take up your lances and set off for Jerusalem; but you will probably die en route. Voilà!" This scene between Le Corbusier the aging rebel and these earnest Parisian students is in fact eerily reminiscent of the end of Cervantes's *Don Quixote*. On his deathbed, Quixote renounces his chivalric fantasies; it is Sancho Panza who begs him to carry on with his idealistic missions, even though to many they appear as madness. The beauty of those visions, Panza insists, is of great and necessary value to the world. "If it's beatings you are dying of," the faithful squire says, "put the blame on me. . . . For the maddest thing a man can do in life is to be finished off by his own melancholy."[108] Again we should remember that Le Corbusier was re-reading Cervantes's masterpiece weeks before he died.

The Corbusian project was never built. And the idea of a dynamic, changing museum was eventually real-

Right: The selection board for the design of UNESCO–Paris. In the foreground, seated: Walter Gropius (USA) and Le Corbusier (France), surrounded by, *left to right,* Ernesto Rogers (Italy), Bernard Zehrfuss (France), Benjamin Wermiel (UNESCO official), Marcel Breuer (USA), and Sven Markelius (Sweden). Paris, 1955. Courtesy UNESCO, Paris.

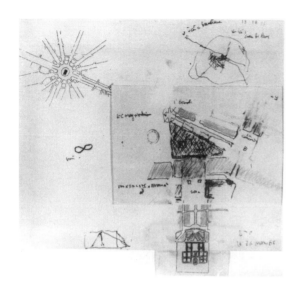

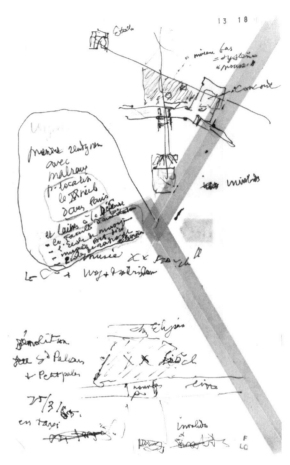

Le Corbusier's last project for Paris: the Museum of the Twentieth Century for La Défense or, preferably, the heart of Paris, 26 March 1965. The drawing shows the area between the Arc de Triomphe/Place de la Concorde and the Esplanade des Invalides, where ample open space would be available. The architects to be associated with Le Corbusier were André Wogenscky and Jean Dubuisson. The sketch was made on the front side of an envelope. Courtesy FLC, Paris.

ized in the 1970s in a quite different vocabulary at Plateau Beaubourg, known today as Centre National d'Art et de Culture Georges Pompidou.

In connection with the twentieth-century museum, Claudius-Petit has told this revealing story of Le Corbusier's attempt, in his last year, to give Paris something on a scale worthy of the grand city: a new plan for the section of the capital across from Les Invalides. Le Corbusier's purpose was to make the district more contemporary and above all to fit his proposed Museum of the Twentieth Century into this central location, rather than into the Défense district.

The Museum of the Twentieth Century for Paris, 25 March 1965, sketched in a taxi. Le Corbusier's notes read: "Urgent: arrange a meeting with Malraux to locate the Museum of the 20th century in Paris, and leave at La Défense the School of Architecture, School of Music, Museum of Decorative Arts, School of Radio and Television. Tear down Grand Palais + Petit Palais." This sketch was made on the back side of an envelope. Courtesy FLC, Paris.

Right: Le Corbusier and Eugène Claudius-Petit at a reception in the Elysée Palace. Courtesy Archive Photos.

Returning in a taxi one day from La Défense through the central district, he was struck by inspiration. In that taxi, he sketched on the back of an envelope the center of Paris from L'Etoile to the Esplanade des Invalides, adding a few touches of color. He signed and dated the sketch "26 March 1965," adding a note: "Urgent: arrange a meeting with Malraux to locate the Museum of the 20th century in Paris, and leave at La Défense the School of Architecture, School of Music, Museum of Decorative Arts, School of Radio and Television." Below the note he scribbled, "Tear down Grand Palais + Petit Palais." The following day, from the atelier at 35 rue de Sèvres, Le Corbusier called his influential friend Eugène Claudius-Petit (who was, incidentally, a defender of the Grand Palais), urging him to contact Malraux right away about this ultimate proposal for "a majestic space." Claudius-Petit agreed to act. But immediately Le Corbusier called back to say: "Claudius, n'intervenez pas, ne faites rien, je ne veux plus me battre" (Claudius, don't intervene, don't do anything, I don't want to fight any more).[109] It might well have been a matter of embarrassment to Le Corbusier that he could not stand alone, that his superior talent, name recognition, and all the honors bestowed on him were not sufficient to persuade the world to accept him, to come to him—in short, that intervention was always necessary to convince the authorities of his abilities, and that even then, neither the chance to prove himself nor success itself was guaranteed. These are melancholic reflections reminiscent of the old, tired Don Quixote in his own final testament.

The Law of Life: Death

As many who knew him have pointed out, Le Corbusier suffered a deep loss with the death of his wife, Yvonne, in October 1957, that was worsened by the death in February 1960 of his mother in her 101st

year. As he writes in the opening paragraph of *Mise au point*: "All the passionate quests of the individual, all that capital, that experience so dearly paid for, will disappear. The law of life: death" (83). But for all his Romantic concentration on the creative self, Le Corbusier also possessed a modernist's stern and unsentimental perspective. "Reposer s'étendre dormir—mourir. Le dos au sol" (To rest to lie down to sleep—to die. The back to the ground), he wrote in *Le Poème de l'angle droit*.[110] We sense that Le Corbusier, as builder, mathematician, and geometrician, was *theoretically opposed* to fearing death, and the strength to resist that fear derived from his respect for the balance of nature and for spatial calculation, for the geometry of the right angle. It is not surprising, then, that Le Corbusier came to terms with death through a complicated series of metaphors and consolations. "Nothing is transmissible but thought": over and over, this is his refrain—that if there is any survival at all, it must come through the energy of one mind on other minds.

Death was indeed terrible and arbitrary in its way. But it remained a law of life; one could count on it, calculate with it, even reduce it to a geometric absolute. Whatever is born must die. On the death of André Wogenscky's father, he wrote these lines to his faithful associate: "La mort est la porte de sortie de chacun de nous. Je ne sais pas pourquoi on veut la rendre atroce. Elle est l'horizontale de la verticale: complémentaire et naturelle" (Death is the exit door for all of us. I don't know why it has to be made so atrocious. It represents the horizontal of the vertical: complementary and natural).[111] "L'angle droit est un 'pacte avec la nature'" (the right angle is a "pact with nature") Wogenscky wrote in 1989 in his introduction to Le Corbusier's *Poème*.

In the weeks preceding his death, Le Corbusier's correspondence with his elder brother, Albert, then age eighty, is full of optimism about his vigor and good health. Le Corbusier was playfully defiant of his housekeeper and his doctor, who advised diet and rest. "They are coddling me like sugar candy," he wrote. The day after he arrived at his cabanon at Cap-Martin, he wrote his brother, "My moral stand: in life one must act, which means to act with all modesty, precision, uprightness . . . that is the atmosphere conducive to artistic creation." But then he added, "For me in life I have this hope, expressed by an impolite term: 'On crèvera bien un jour' [One fine day I will drop dead] . . . words of hope, which summon us to choose, in life on this earth, the dignified side (for oneself, for one's conscience)."[112]

The loss of his wife and closest companion, Yvonne, in October 1957 had profoundly affected Le Corbusier. In her youth Yvonne Galis had been an artist's model, very beautiful, generous, always a bit eccentric. Le Corbusier called her "l'ange gardien du foyer" (the guardian angel of the hearth) and after her death said, "Thirty-seven years of perfect happiness, thanks to her."[113] But in the final years, according to Yvonne's physician, Jacques Hindermeyer, Le Corbusier had grown accustomed to concealing a great deal in his private affairs. Yvonne had chronic gastritis as well as a drinking problem, and most probably suffered from osteoporosis; disabled and disfigured, she could not walk. She led a reclusive life near the end. When asked about this, Le Corbusier remarked that Yvonne's withdrawal from society gave him more time to immerse himself in creative work. But her illness caused him great anxiety and pain, although only a few close friends knew of it and until recently none have chosen to talk about it.[114] It is possible that Le Corbusier's meditations in *Mise au point* on the geometric ideal versus the unjust "grotesquery" of death were inspired by this decline and passing of his closest life companion. Of this, too, he tried to make a challenge and attempted to transcend. As he wrote of Yvonne's last hours: "I was

Yvonne Le Corbusier, ink drawing by Le Corbusier, 1955. Courtesy FLC, Paris.

with her . . . for eight hours in the hospital . . . she left life with spasms and muttering all night long. . . . She departed before the dawn. And on this calm day, I think that death is not repugnant."[115] Years later, in September 1964, when his friend and business adviser Paul Ducret died, Le Corbusier wrote, "I don't pity those who die, death is a beautiful thing when you've lived an active life."[116]

In spite of these brave observations by Le Corbusier, however, accounts by close personal friends on his general health and state of mind that last summer are more generally pessimistic, though they do vary widely. Jean-Pierre de Montmollin, longtime friend and lawyer in charge of the legacy, wrote to his fellow members of what would become the Fondation Le Corbusier at the end of March 1965: "The last meet-

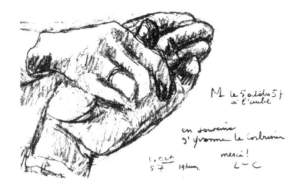

The death announcement of Yvonne Le Corbusier. Le Corbusier included this drawing, which he had made three days before her death, her hand in one of his. Courtesy FLC, Paris.

Yvonne Le Corbusier, 5 October 1957, 2 A.M. "She died two hours later, her hand in mine, in silence," wrote Le Corbusier. Courtesy FLC, Paris.

ing I had with Le Corbusier, on March 18, wasn't good. He was very tired . . . impatient to be left alone, even aggressive. He couldn't understand anything of our actions. . . . it is as if he deliberately forgot it all."[117] In the same concerned spirit, the son of the landlord and innkeeper-neighbor at Cap-Martin, Robert Rubutato, reported on Le Corbusier's health to Dr. Hindermeyer in mid-August: "Le Corbusier is in terrible shape; on our side, we are following all instructions coming from Paris."[118]

A theme that runs like a leitmotiv through *Mise au point* is Le Corbusier's preparations for his death. Like so much else in his life, they were contradictory. On one hand, true to his Romantic view of creativity and in keeping with the great sages and prophets who so inspired him when he read Schuré's *Les Grands Initiés,* death was an abrupt cut-off of one person's unique potential—and as such unacceptable. On the other hand, death was a law, whose simple impersonal application to all living things was an absolutely normal

event. Le Corbusier's solution, it appears, was to approach death as a spiritual exercise that involved increased compression, isolation, self-sufficiency, and self-discipline. The most tangible mark of this "solution" was, of course, Cap-Martin itself, the monastic *cabanon* where Le Corbusier lived and the barrack next door where he worked, its walls hung with sketches on variations of the Open Hand.[119] Le Corbusier wrote to a friend in June 1965 that "in August he had to undergo a treatment of silence and solitude."[120] For those who knew him intimately, this was a well-known and recurring ritual. In a letter to his brother on 23 July 1965, Albert Jeanneret sensed that just such a "treatment" was needed: "Look after yourself in all respects, food, bathing, relax 100%, not always with a book in your hand," he wrote, ending the letter, "Long live rest, solitude, silence at Cap-Martin."[121]

The solitude that Le Corbusier had cherished all his life and had attempted, paradoxically, to "encode"

Left: Le Corbusier and Yvonne Le Corbusier at Cap-Martin. Photo by Lucien Hervé.

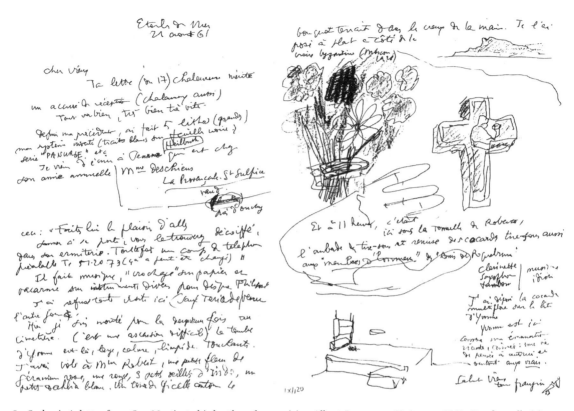

Le Corbusier's letter from Cap-Martin to his brother, the musician Albert Jeanneret, 21 August 1961: "I refuse all visits except that of Tériade [the publisher of his *Le Poème de l'angle droit*]. . . . Yesterday I went up to the cemetery for the second time. It is a difficult climb. Yvonne's tomb is there, broad, calm, clear, moving. I had stolen from Mme Rebutato some geraniums, one rose-colored and one red, three little French marigolds, and one little white dahlia. A piece of string around the bouquet kept in the hollow of the hand. I placed it flat next to the Byzantine cross (Moscow 1928). . . . I put the multicolored cluster down upon the bed of Yvonne, Yvonne is here like an emanation, smiling, loved; a life of caring for others and especially for the *true ones*. Greetings, your brother" (signed with a crow sketch). Courtesy Bibliothèque de la Ville, La Chaux-de-Fonds / FLC, Paris.

into the rooms of the Unités d'Habitation and commercial hotels, became imperative in his old age. Remembering the Carthusian monastery at Galluzzo near Florence and the twenty monasteries and sketes on Mount Athos, which he had visited as a young man during his travels in 1911, Le Corbusier came to see creativity, even of the most globally visionary sort, connected with withdrawal and contemplative silence. "Monks' cells . . . secret gardens . . . an infinity of landscape . . . a tete-à-tete with oneself. A sensation of extraordinary harmony comes over me," Le Corbusier wrote of that monastery in an unpublished

silence. "In the final account, the dialogue is reduced to a man alone, face to face with himself, the struggle of Jacob with the Angel, within man himself! There is only one judge. Your conscience—in other words, yourself" (85).

Yet the actual circumstances of his death that same summer have never been satisfactorily resolved. Le Corbusier was about to return to Paris to begin another year's cycle of work. He was proud of his physical fitness: "Je fais encore mon kilomètre tous les jours" (I am still doing my kilometer every day), he had boasted of his routine exercise in the sea.[123] About this he had argued with his doctors, who recommended no swimming at all. But he finally agreed to take only *one* and not two swims a day (once at noon, before lunch, and skipping the swim at 7:00 A.M.). "You couldn't dictate to Le Corbusier," Dr. Hindermeyer remarked in 1994, recalling that summer thirty years earlier. "You had to make compromises." Le Corbusier had confessed to Hindermeyer during the final year: "I don't want to die now, but if something happens to me I do not want to be reduced to a . . . wheelchair with you behind me, pushing it . . . . Can you imagine that?" Both men painfully remembered Yvonne's crippled years, although there had been a pact of sorts between them not to discuss her helpless condition.

The cabanon had in fact been built as Le Corbusier's birthday gift for Yvonne in 1952. During her final years, Hindermeyer recalled, "She couldn't move; an entire compartment of the night train from Paris to Vintimille had to be reserved for her and the domestic accompanying her. Once arrived at Cap-Martin, she had to be delivered down the little path to the cabanon in a wheelbarrow; that was the only solution."[124] For Le Corbusier himself, that final disfigurement, helplessness, and loss of human dignity had to be avoided at all cost.

mône Corbu

2 moines momifiés
le souhaitent le
bonne année
et se serrent
la main   Niam 63

mône Claude

Le Corbusier carried on a correspondence with a young monk, Claude Ducret, the stepson of his longtime associate Paul Ducret. The above sketch is an exchange of greetings for the holiday season 1963, Friar Corbu and Friar Claude. Courtesy FLC, Paris.

memoir half a century later.[122] Similarly, in *Mise au point* he writes, "Finding myself alone again, I thought of that wonderful phrase from the Apocalypse: There was silence in heaven for about half an hour" (100). Looking back on a long life, in *Mise au point* Le Corbusier works all the bitterness, disappointment, and triumph into this final compressed

Le Corbusier at the window of his cabanon. In an interview with Brassaï in July 1952, he admitted, "I feel so good in my cabanon that without a doubt I will meet my end here." Courtesy FLC, Paris.

During his last summer, even while complaining playfully about having grown old, Le Corbusier was quick to share (with casual strangers and passers-by) his disappointments, which in these last years seemed to spring more readily to mind than his accomplishments. In a revealing oral account of 1995, Henry Pessar reminisced about his meeting with the old master thirty years earlier—and eight days before the end. "I was starting my career as a young journalist, writer, and photographer," Pessar recalled:

Between Monte-Carlo and Cap-Martin, there is a small beach and a beautiful villa, which at the time belonged to Dino de Laurentiis; he lived there with the actress Silvana Mangano. The whole family left the beach that day on a motorboat, and I shot half a reel of film with my Pentax.

Suddenly, a young man came up to me. "As a photographer of movie stars, Le Corbusier probably does not interest you?"

"He fascinates me! Could you tell me where he is?"

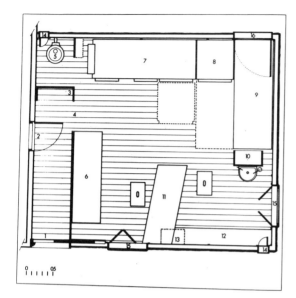

The plan of Le Corbusier's cabanon: (1) entry from outside; (2) entry from the inn "L'Etoile de Mer"; (3) closet; (4) access to living space; (5) toilet; (6) wardrobe; (7) bed; (8) low table; (9) bed; (10) plumbing stack; (11) table; (12) low shelves; (13) high shelf; (14) vertical opening for ventilation; (15) window; (16) window. All needs provided for, almost all functions built in: this was his ideal "palace." Courtesy *Parenthèses*. Drawing by Bruno Chiambretto.

"He is swimming in front of you, right this minute!"

I was so excited that I waded into the water toward him with my trousers on, taking two pictures. Then I asked permission to take some more. "Don't take the trouble with an ugly old man like me," was his response. "It would be better for you to take pictures of Princess Grace, just behind that rock, or Brigitte Bardot at Saint Tropez."

"I don't want to bother you, but could you spare me a few minutes to talk, later?"

After ten minutes Le Corbusier came back. I took three more pictures of him before he walked up onto the beach. He stood up on the stone stairs and began to stare at a man who was smashing against a rock a small octopus that he had just harpooned. Le Corbusier then said, "You told me that you appreciate me. But you must understand that for most of my life, I have simply been smashed down. Many people were so jealous, they wanted to destroy me, to crush my head just like that octopus."

"But you were so successful, with Chandigarh and the Cité Radieuse [at Marseilles] . . . and André Malraux was so fond of you!"

"None of that means anything. Even André Malraux was obliged to follow the barking crowd." Then he shook my hand and walked away, following the tiny footpath climbing to his small "cabanon"; he seemed so bitter and so lonely.[125]

A week later, on 27 August 1965, on his way down to the sea for what would be his final swim, Le Corbusier exchanged a few words with his neighbor, Madame Schelbert. "You know, I'm an old blockhead, but I still have plans for at least a hundred years," he jested. "So see you later!"[126]

Most people who knew the old warrior do not believe that he explicitly decided to take his own life. But they do concede that Le Corbusier desired to have a say in this final geometric calculation, the last that was his to perform here. Kenneth Frampton, by contrast, has speculated on Le Corbusier's final swim as a "sacred suicide," known as *endura* in the Albigensian tradition, a "virtuous act whereby spirit is liberated from matter"—and he quotes Jerzy Soltan, once a member of Le Corbusier's atelier, who recalled Le Corbusier's comment: "My dear Soltan, how nice it would be to die swimming toward the sun."[127]

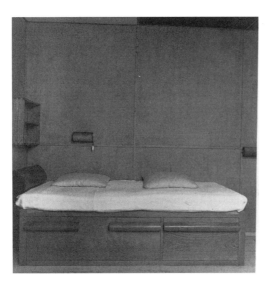

The interior of the cabanon: *at left,* the sleeping area, single bed, lamp, and shelf; *right,* the living area: table, stools, and shelves. The stools are Ballantine Scotch whiskey cases fished from the sea and refinished. Courtesy Hughes Bigo.

Le Corbusier in the doorway of his work room (chambre de travail); behind him is his residential cabanon. One for work, the other for rest. Courtesy FLC, Paris.

The work room, or chambre de travail, installed in July 1954 at Cap-Martin. Two years after moving to his residential cabanon, Le Corbusier wrote in a letter dated 15 April 1954: "15 meters from my cabanon I have built myself a construction-site barrack, 4 m × 2 m. I live like a happy monk." Courtesy FLC, Paris.

Le Corbusier, the "happy monk," at work in his "chambre de travail," its walls hung with sketches of the Open Hand. Courtesy FLC, Paris.

Le Corbusier at Cap-Martin, painting the murals of the neighboring Villa E 1027, by Eileen Gray for Jean Badovici, where Le Corbusier spent his vacations before building his own cabanon. Courtesy FLC, Paris.

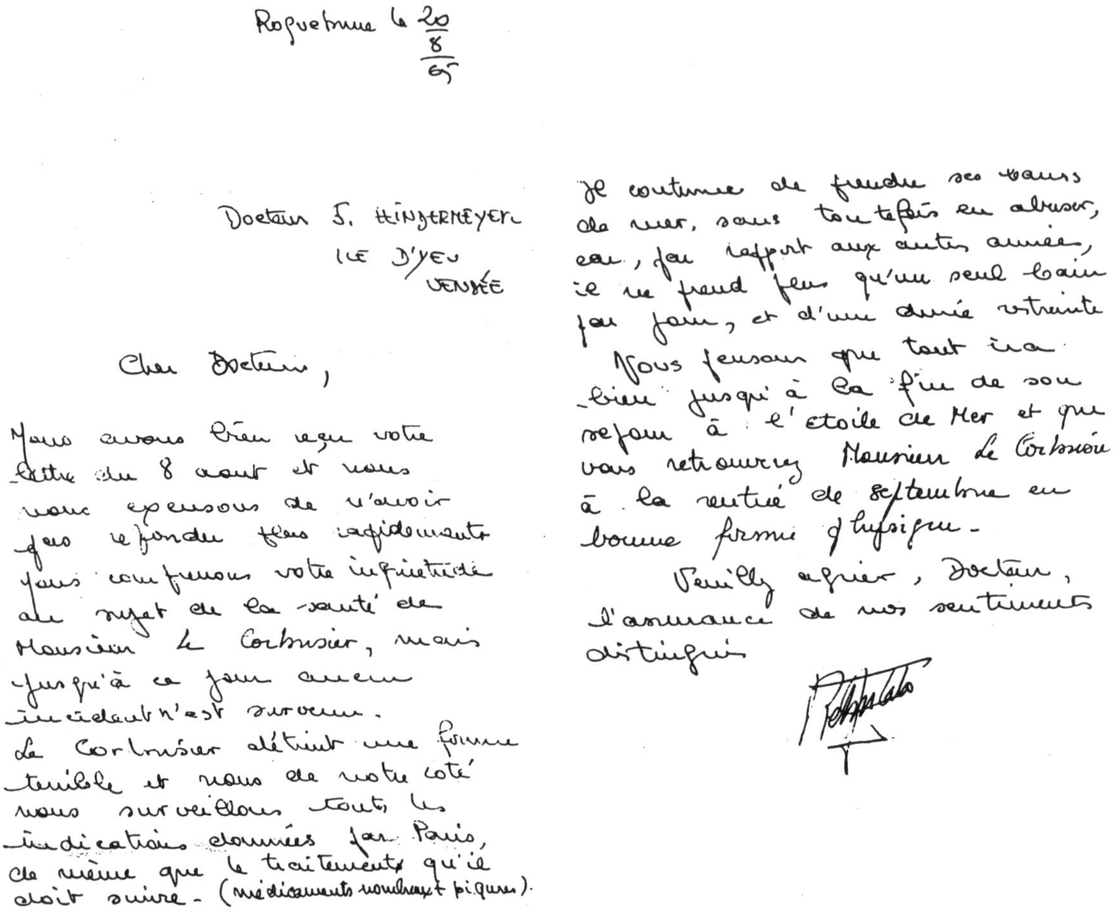

Roquebrune le 20/8/65

Docteur J. HINDERMEYER
ILE D'YEU
VENDÉE

Cher Docteur,

[handwritten letter in French]

Letter from Robert Rebutato to Le Corbusier's friend and doctor, Jacques Hindermeyer in Paris, written from Cap-Martin 20 August 1965, one week before Le Corbusier died by drowning: "Dear doctor: We confirm your anxiety concerning the health of Monsieur Le Corbusier. . . . Le Corbusier remains in terrible shape; on our side, we are following all the instructions coming from Paris. . . . He continues to swim without, however, overdoing it . . . one swim a day and of limited duration. . . . We think everything will work out until the end of his stay at L'Etoile de Mer." Courtesy Dr. Jacques Hindermeyer and Robert Rebutato.

"Don't take the trouble with an ugly old man like me. . . . It would be better for you to take pictures of Princess Grace, just behind that rock, or Brigitte Bardot at Saint Tropez," Le Corbusier said to the young photographer of this last sequence. Photos by Henry Pessar.

View of the Mediterranean at Cap-Martin, from the cemetery where Le Corbusier and Yvonne Le Corbusier are buried. The arrow in the distance marks the location where Le Corbusier was swimming before his fatal seizure on 27 August 1965. Photo by author.

Left: Le Corbusier in the Mediterranean, the sea he never ceased to love and where he finished his last geometric calculation. Photo by Henry Pessar.

Simon Ozieblo and Jean Deschamps, friends from Douai, who were swimming nearby when Le Corbusier went for his final swim around 11:15 A.M, 27 August 1965. Eight minutes later he had the seizure that cost him his life. "We were about 20 meters from the beach. . . . The swimmer gave the impression of struggling and not being able to move forward. All of a sudden he was no longer moving. His body was floating, but he wasn't making any movement. He was inert. Then a lady shouted. I rushed. . . . I took him by the arm and brought him to the beach. Then the forensic pathologist Dr. Bernard arrived at the scene and attributed the cause of death to a heart attack and not to drowning, as was initially thought." Courtesy Agence France Presse, Paris.

Surely Le Corbusier felt that his exquisite sense of proportion and geometry should not be excluded at this final important moment. For *ars moriendi* could be acceptable only as part of *ars vivendi:* the art of dying was part of the art of living. Most important, each was an art. The alpha and the omega were now joined. Appropriately, this encounter took place in the sea he so loved, the Mediterranean, which he had discovered in 1911 during his *Journey to the East* and which had captivated him ever since, the sea he called "the queen of forms and light." *Mise au point* was Le Corbusier's final attempt to transmit the only thing transmissible—thought—but through words, that medium he so admired and yet always felt was inadequate to his vision of the world. Here is his ultimate and highly conflicted testament.

A crowd of Parisians gather in front of 35 rue de Sèvres as the mortal remains of Le Corbusier arrive at his atelier for a final visit, 1 September 1965. Courtesy Archive Photos.

9:00 P.M., 1 September 1965. Le Corbusier's coffin, escorted by torch-bearing soldiers, arrives at the Cour Carrée of the Louvre for the state funeral, to the accompaniment of Beethoven's funeral march. Courtesy Archive Photos.

Left: At the end of the long corridor of 35 rue de Sèvres, which led to the atelier of the master, Le Corbusier lies in state, 1 September 1965, in front of his tapestry *Les dés sont jetés* (The dice are cast, 1960). The French flag drapes the coffin; in front is the cross of a "Grand Officier de la Légion d'Honneur." Courtesy Archive Photos.

André Malraux gave the official government eulogy to Le Corbusier at the Cour Carrée, concluding, "And finally, here is France, who has so often misunderstood you, whom you carried in your heart when you chose to become French again after two hundred years, who says to you, in the voice of her greatest poet: 'Je te salue au seuil sévère du tombeau!' (I salute you, upon the severe threshold of the tomb!)." Courtesy Archive Photos.

Right: In the foreground, Albert Jeanneret, Le Corbusier's eighty-year-old older brother, with his daughter Kerstin Rääf, at the Crematorium of Père-Lachaise, Paris, 2 September 1965, while Olivier Messiaen's music played. Le Corbusier's ashes were flown the next day to Cap-Martin for burial next to Yvonne. Courtesy PARIS MATCH/Melet.

Le Corbusier's burial in the little cemetery up the hill from his cabanon, 4 September 1965. Pallbearers included his faithful associates Alain Tavès, Fernand Gardien, and Robert Rebutato standing to the left of the grave, and Roggio Andréini standing on top of the concrete slab. Courtesy PARIS MATCH/Sartres.

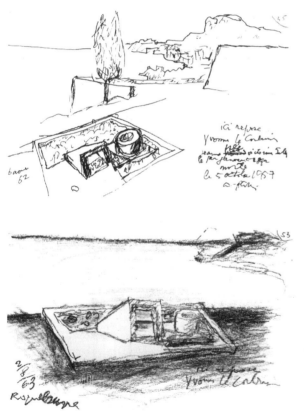

Le Corbusier's sketches of Yvonne Le Corbusier's tomb. Before her death, he went to look for a plot, and after she was buried, he made frequent visits to her tomb, *carnet* in hand. Courtesy FLC, Paris.

Cemetery at Cap-Martin, tomb of Le Corbusier and his wife, Yvonne, overlooking the Mediterranean, the sea he called "the Queen of forms under light." Photo by author.

Courtesy FLC, Paris.

Mise au point

The text of this little book was written by Le Corbusier in July 1965. Now that Le Corbusier is no longer with us, one can doubtlessly find some resonances in it and attach certain meanings to them. But make no mistake. This text is one of struggle, a series of thoughts and conclusions dictated by experience. It is fitting therefore to read them as though Corbu were still among us, and in fact he is.[1]

Nothing is transmissible but thought. Over the years a man gradually acquires, through his struggles, his work, his inner combat, a certain capital, his own individual and personal conquest. But all the passionate quests of the individual, all that capital, that experience so dearly paid for, will disappear. The law of life: death.[2] Nature shuts off all activity by death. Thought alone, the fruit of labor, is transmissible. Days pass, in the stream of days, in the course of a life . . . .

Everything is harmony, relationships, presences. And also thundering synthesis, an unleashing, a trigger, a flash of lightning for the sight, intervention, catalysis. *Raison d'être:* that which is impassably permanent in the midst of, beyond, above, below certain events, certain elements throughout everything.

There are presences: the eternal aspect of that which is permanent. Scientists claim to have arrived at knowledge! But how can one justify, how can one explain the existence of shellfish, lizards, dogs (good fellows), and others, elephants, men and women. . . . Those who dissect but do not see: knowledge through reason, through intervention. Coexistence: the context, the fluid which passes on. Unity demonstrated in a personal act of humanity: understanding. Illumination. Between the why and the how: gradations, the whole range of various minds.

Observe! Where are the observers? To know that ants have radar, all right. But to know why they exist and why they share such a fate. Life weaves its web and never turns back . . . .

From my early youth I had harsh contact with the weight of things. The heaviness of materials and the resistance of materials. And men: the diverse qualities of men and the resilience of men. My life was to live in their midst and to offer daring solutions to the weight of materials . . . but they stood up! And the knowledge that men are of one sort or another. To be amazed sometimes, and still today to be sometimes dumbfounded. But to recognize it, to admit it, having

83

Ma vie fut de vivre dans en la
campagne. Et de proposer au poids
des matériaux de solutions réputées
téméraires — mais qui a terme. Et
de savoir que les hommes sont tels ou
tels. D'en être étonné parfois, et
encore aujourd'hui, — D'en être étouffé
parfois. Mais de le reconnaître, de
l'admettre, l'expiant un, la voyant.
Et de faire mon humble partie en
travers les vents et les soleils. Et de
n'avoir jamais été amer, si ce n'est
de l'avoir pour tel parfois, devant
les journalistes, et surtout ....
devant leur philosophie qui
pour l'ennui à plein tous, m'a mis....
ensuite, appui de ....

seen it, seeing it . . . and to play my humble part throughout hard times. And never to have been bitter, except when occasionally I have appeared to be so facing . . . the media and especially their photographers who, with their more or less average minds, ask you (and manage to get) your own masquerade by their numerous mistakes, absentmindedness, fecklessness, conformity, etc. . . . And this form of activity rhymes with journalism; it is based upon the day to day (its name makes that clear) and on the notion: all that is, but for a single day.

"One must burrow into life again in order to put on flesh."[3]

It is not I but Henry Miller who utters those timeless words, yet it seems to me that I had already thought them. Burrow into life again . . . resist war, abundance over the whole earth . . . metamorphosis through equipment: machines and minds for the yellow, the black, and the white. Then there will be the general awakening of civilizations. Then there will be death to Wall Street, and the fruits of the earth conquered.[4] What remains is to plunge into what is divinely human: sufficiently to find in it the great deed of universal significance.

Life is a strange adventure. One is a ball, a sphere. And that molecule, that star, slides, strikes, shatters, we please X or Y. One is in one's own sphere and this shapes one's own destiny.

I am seventy-seven years old and my philosophy could be summed up in this way: in life one must act, that is, one must act with modesty, correctly, with precision. The only possible atmosphere conducive to artistic creation is steadiness, modesty, continuity, perseverance.[5]

I have already written somewhere that constancy is a definition of life, since constancy is natural and pro-

ductive. In order to be constant one must be moderate, one must persevere. It is a mark of courage, of inner strength, an essential quality of the nature of existence.[6]

In life there are those who act and those who let things happen. Thus all sorts of consequences come about. Look at the surface of water. . . . Look at the blue sky, filled with all the good works that men will have created . . . for after all everything returns to the sea. . . . In the final account, the dialogue is reduced to a man alone, face to face with himself, the struggle of Jacob with the Angel, within man himself![7] There is only one judge. Your conscience—in other words, yourself. Thus: very small or very large, but able to ascend (small or large) from the disgusting to the sublime. It depends on each individual from the very beginning. One can choose the honorable side for oneself, for one's conscience, but one can also choose the opposite: profit, money.

All my life was filled with discoveries. It is a matter of choice. One can drive a magnificent Cadillac or Jaguar, or one can be passionately devoted to one's work. The quest for the truth isn't easy. There is no truth in extremes. The truth, a thin streak of water or the mighty mass of a tumbling river, flows between two banks . . . and every day different . . . .[8]

And we live in a world of bureaucrats closed in upon themselves, incapable of making a decision. There are assemblies . . . councils. . . . It's good that the fools take their turn to speak, because we others might forget the weight of stones and the sweat necessary to move them.

At seventeen and a half, I built my first house. Already I was taking a risk against the advice of the wise. A daring concept: two corner windows. Early on, at the site, I picked up a brick and weighed it in my hand. Its weight frightens me. I am petrified.

Thus one brick . . . then millions of bricks laid one upon the other.

The advice of the wise, of our bureaucrats? It doesn't matter. I recall a conversation I had with Maurice Jardot around 1953.[9] We were talking about Picasso. Picasso had asked Jardot: "My exhibit in Rome was a success, wasn't it?" and so on. I replied to my friend Jardot: "If you had said 'No, the exhibit was a flop,' Picasso would have said to you, 'I don't give a damn, I am right, your opinion makes no difference to me.'"

I was sixty years old when they gave me my first and only government project, and that, without a doubt, was for laughs! Everywhere the world was warned. The spirit: as it was in the Middle Ages. After the War: reconstruction; zero for Corbu. All my commissions are due to private enterprise. A great number of really good projects, let's be modest enough to admit it, were torpedoed by the bureaucrats. Once, while they were bestowing on me an eminent honor in order to keep me out, I admitted that I was a total failure.[10] It is true, insofar that not all my projects were realized; it is true in the sense that later, after I am dead and gone, the times of the horse and buggy will continue. Gentlemen Naysayers, you will be always lying in wait, always against. Mediocrity will prevail, idiocies will always be written, spoken, or proclaimed . . . obstacles will always be set up . . . my dear colleagues . . . the authorities . . . the professional associations, the state boards. . . . Do you remember those words, those punches below the belt? for l'Unité d'Habitation at Marseilles, for example:

"slums to make you knock your head against walls . . . ." And that psychiatrist, the president of the French Medical Association:[11] "A hatchery for mental illness . . . ."

And also: "Against the laws of hygiene . . ." (from the Chief Council for Hygiene and Public Health).

I could tell you a true story: where are the dregs? It's too easy and smells bad. . . . The boxer knows that he must get a bloody nose and the rugby player knows that he must dislocate his shoulder or knock his knee out of joint. . . . I am saying here that the problem is not how to make money, the problem is how to accomplish something (to produce, to create, to organize, to supervise, etc.). It is the only way to find happiness. Happiness is inside, and I spare myself the drudgeries of Palm Beach or girls and the ostentation of "Petits Lits Blancs."[12] You have to know, to see everything, to predict everything, etc., and then above all to make allowances and take into account the unforeseen: that is what it means to feel, to smell the fruit of a talent, of an experiment, of a life that one builds on daily.

At the age of thirty-two, with *l'Esprit Nouveau,* I was full of eagerness, loyalty, boldness, but also of courage, taking risks. *Towards a New Architecture* was written at the age of thirty-two, a clear vision and affirmation of a sense of reality (including the risks). When the roots were laid down, they took hold. Youth is toughness, intransigence, purity. Yet the spring stretches, has stretched. That is man's fate, his destiny. From childhood to the age of thirty what an intense uproar, what schemes, what accomplishments! He[13] never knew, the little fellow. He went his way, the same way one sees ranks of boys (with their crewcuts) in Paris, going to the swimming pool with their class in the morning, or to the seashore on vacation, an intensity in their gestures, their remarks,

their looks, their walk, the friendly gestures toward their friends. How much will remain of this vast potential, of so much purity? . . .

The pattern of behavior of today's young people, who follow the example of their elders, does not necessarily seem to me to be the discovery of a transitory aestheticism but a profound, passionate, and intimate search for all the professional secrets they need to construct objects with precision, fit to provide tools for the new society that is being formed under our very eyes all over the world. Everything lies in the manner of doing (an inner labor) and not in the manner of being, which interests no one.

In Bogota in 1950 I had the feeling that a page was turning:[14] the end of a world, immanent, imminent. Nothing remains to be known but the length in human hours, seconds or minutes until that . . . catastrophe? No, my friends, until that deliverance. An ordinary circumstance without any solemnity: a business trip to Bogota filled me in only five days with a harvest of facts and findings, both personal and general, capable of affirming without anguish but indeed with the joy of tomorrow that a page was going to turn, an important page in human history, the history of the life of men before the machine and which the machine has shattered, ground up, pulverized. An example in the U.S.A., in New York with its fifteen million inhabitants, the horror of an affluent society without aim or reason. On Long Island, my friend Nivola, son of a mason, cultivates vegetables between the party walls enclosing spaces. U.S.A.: women, psychoanalysis everywhere, an act without resonance, without goal. Days pass by without results, except that of getting through them. People work twenty-four hours, without provision for the future, without wisdom, without plans, without stop. New York! That atrocious city, towering into the sky, bristling, without courtesy, everyone for himself! Land is sold by surface, by the square meter. You have the right to do as you please.[15] A city of "trade,"[16] nothing but manufacturing and selling to get out a day's work. People rush in all directions . . . without pity, without fun.

One evening at Chandigarh I said to Pierre Jeanneret: only those who play are serious! When Pierre objected, I went on: "Mountain climbers, rugby players, card players, and gamblers are all frauds because they do not play . . . ." They do not play. . . . Conformity and nonconformity. Everything one learns in school, in political clubs, in dance classes, makes up for each individual according to his character a constellation of fixed points forming an unalterable design, a fortress between free judgment and the free and proper use of things given to us by God himself, or the compromises offered by men. Montaigne was right: "Sitting on the highest throne in the world is after all still sitting on one's ass."[17] Yes, the rule has been to play the game. There was money to be used, then it enslaved us, and men have forgotten how to play. When my client fills my head with various little requirements of his, I accept, I accept, up to a certain point when I say no, impossible! For it is then beyond the rules of my game, of the game in question: the game of this house, of that arrangement whose order emerged at the moment of its creation and developed, proved correct, became dominant. All within the rules! Nothing outside of the rules! Otherwise I no longer have a reason for being. That's the key. A reason for being: to play. To participate, but as a human being, that is to say, within a clear and orderly system. But first of all one must have scrutinized, seen, observed. Only then can one separate sensations, perceptions, ideas. Metaphysics is but foam on the surface of a conquest, the downward slope, an action where the muscles have ceased to function. It is not an act, not a fact; it is an echo, a reflection. And it moves and affects particular types

of human beings: speakers in debates. They attribute to me powers of the occult, mathematics, numbers, etc.

I am an ass, but with a sharp eye. We are dealing here with the eye of an ass who has the capacity of feeling. I am an ass with an instinct for proportion. I am, and remain, an impenitent visual person. It is beautiful when it is beautiful . . . but it is according to Modulor! I don't give a damn about Modulor,[18] what do you want me to do with Modulor? And yet, no! the Modulor is inevitably right, and it is you who feel nothing. The Modulor elongates the ass's ear. (Here I mean the ass other than myself mentioned earlier.)

My travel sketchbook from Bogota, from '50 or '51,[19] contained some notes sent afterwards to Jardot, on 31 January '53. They will be welcome in this connection. Here they are: "Recurrence of proportion in the work of art," "the contribution of L. C."

1919: regulating lines (the proof: in Choisy). From now on: exclusively personal research. I repudiate all treatises. But I declare war, war on Vignola (and Company),[20] which always smells to me of dead bodies.

Corbu before: 1922. A contemporary city for three million inhabitants. The townhouse apartments (discovered in 1910 at the Carthusian monastery of Ema).[21]

1919: The will to accomplish the task has become clear, in painting, in drawing. And the spirit of the architect has joined in, has made itself felt. Since then, consistency in research: architecture, painting (in fact sculpture, because it is space and light upon the shape of a new ethic).

Until 1928, not objects, glasses, and bottles but supports for geometry, instigators of proportion. After '28, then, human figure and objects with a poetic response . . . .

At the end of 1951, in Chandigarh: the possibility of getting in touch with the essential joys of Hindu principles: a brotherhood of relationships between the cosmos and all living things: stars, nature, sacred animals, birds, monkeys, and cows, and in the villages, children, adults, and still active older people, the pond and the mango trees, all present and all smiling, poor but in proportion.

From the time of my first house, built when I was seventeen and a half, I continued my efforts amid adventures, difficulties, catastrophes, and, from time to time, success. Now, at the age of seventy-seven, my name is known around the world. My research, my ideas seem to be shared sometimes, but there are always obstacles in the way. My answer? I was always active and so I remain. I have always searched for the poetry that is in the heart of man. A visual man, working with his eyes and his hands, I am moved by revelations above all in the plastic arts.[22] All is in everything: cohesion, coherence, unity, architecture, and urban planning interacting; a single problem that demands a single profession.

I am not a revolutionary. I am a shy person who does not interfere in what does not concern him, but the basic elements are revolutionary: in fact, the events are, too, and one must contemplate these things dispassionately, from a distance. During my travels I see a lot of typical things. At one time ambassadors were indispensable; they were sent on a mission for two or three years, which they carried out in four-wheeled carriages—not with crossword puzzles but with coded messages. And they acted in the best interests of their employer, be it the king, the prince, or the republic. These days, when a problem arises you immediately take the plane and in ten hours, or twenty hours, you are there at the building site with the other party, you place a file on the table, you resolve the problem, and you go home two or three days later. This change is taking place throughout the management of world affairs and has extraordinary consequences. I was brought in to Bogota to draw up the plan for the city. I traveled by plane and, upon arriving, learned something remarkable. It is a city four centuries old, founded by the conquistador of Mexico who, with fifty horses, had conquered the Indians—who did not have horses. Going from Bogota to Barranquilla, the port, took twenty-five days; now you need just two hours and fifteen minutes. For twenty years they had schools; books arrived in that Hispanic city. All of a sudden, the people there said, "Ah! We can get out!" And they went and saw the world, where they told others whom they met: "You can come over to us, too, come and see, there are things to be done." People went, they found the riches underground, the fertile soil, and said, "We are going to build a city for a million inhabitants . . . ."

You have the facts before you, the ground moves under our feet, but in fact it is not the ground that moves. We are on a moving sidewalk, which is the evolution of our epoch. We are a machine-age civilization, so we must adopt a point of view. Sociability is a natural human phenomenon: Adam and Eve to begin with, and so it has continued. The end result is the human occupation of the whole planet. At the Ministry of Reconstruction there are always kind people (and others far less kind).

They took my "little joke" and called it regional planning. On television you can even see very serious people talking about it on Sunday evenings, to break through the doors that I myself opened at least forty years ago. Well, that's the price of friendship. . . . So I said, "Gentlemen, beware! Before planning one must occupy the land, and where is the land?" That's the problem of today. We must lay out the roads of the present day between the transforming, linear cities. Those are the prophetic, ancient roads of all time. Along these roads, linear industrial cities could spread their combined roadways, railroads, waterways across administrative borders.[23] If topographical routes cross borders, with manufactured goods and new methods of production, then it is no less true that the whole human race needs to be governed; yet it is impossible to administer everything. Universality is one of the great ideas of modern times, but some administrative restrictions will always remain so that orders may be given to specific groups and so that order can come from elsewhere. Instead of orders for cannon fire, there will be instructions about the need for global planning.

Governments maintain boundaries, whereas these are really determined by evolution. There were once fortifications, the boundaries of Paris. As Paris grew, there were five or six of them in succession. Then, after the war of 1914, those last boundaries were removed, because of the advent of the airplane. Roads cut across and animate the land. The earth is round and extends, everything is contiguous; it is poorly inhabited, uninhabited, and so much remains to be done to occupy the earth instead of going to the moon. It's like the Stavisky Affair, which so occupied public opinion.[24] The construction of roadways and supplying water could be the great civilizing tasks of our modern society. It could be done with extraordinary ease. If you fly over the earth you can see where the inhabitants are and you can see that an immense space remains—but without water. No water? It has to be brought in. No roads? They have to be built . . . .

In 1961, taking advantage of a few days of the flu, I wrote a little text which I sent to my friend Jean-Jacques Duval, at Saint-Dié. At that time I wrote:[25] "I am sending you a first copy of my text *The 'Irrefutable' Diagram*. It's a real 'job' for you. In your millinery business your father used to make heavy socks for country folk and underwear for sixty-year-olds. In 1961 your millinery has become the ultimate in elegance for the *zazous!*[26] Your socks are sheer poetry, and your sweaters, etc. You kept your machines, you kept your workers, your management, your accounting department. You've changed nothing except your program. There you have invented, created. You have thus restructured your business in keeping with social evolution, which was itself entirely independent of your will. My problem is the same. We make guns, atomic theories, agitate against unemployment, create a prewar atmosphere, build up a succession of preventive armament programs. Well then, today I propose: Let's draw a vertical line! To the left, cross it out. On the right, a new inventory is made—workers, bosses, social problems, the hierarchy of labor, industrial program, preparations for retooling machines, propaganda by a new workforce in favor of a new society visible on the horizon . . . ."

This text, which treats the question of urbanism, should, it seems to me, find its place here. Here it is.

"THE IRREFUTABLE DIAGRAM," "THE IRREVOCABLE LINE," OR "THE END OF THE APOTHECARY"

A charming little revolution in the pharmacy, a brotherly, motherly revolution, has again shut the door in the face of Monsieur the Apothecary; it has meant in each household a decisive reform. New facts, even better than that—a miracle accomplished, with all its consequences: longevity, in France, has made an amazing leap; in less than a century, the life span increased from twenty-eight to forty years, and today it is sixty-eight years. Illness is fought in the heart of families by "civilized" means; the twentieth-century pharmacy is born! At home, a page has been turned on the Balzacian atmosphere. I have explained here the qualifying epithets *brotherly, motherly, friendly* . . . .

Now let's talk about the "home" (a favorite theme of the talkative press), let's talk about the dwelling; the family, work, rest. Even better, let's talk about the "three human establishments," which lead to a harmonious use of land by the works of machine-age civilization.[27]

All is still confusion, obscurity, hostility, jealousy, ferocity, speculation, greed for money, displays of ignorance, a thirst for vanities; to tell the truth, a pure and simple ignorance of this essential, immanent phenomenon: the realization of works of peace. . . . The discussion takes place in a void, under threat of bombs. All you hear is Khrushchev, Mao Tse-Tung, de Gaulle, or Queen Elizabeth, Kennedy! So many "trustworthy men" entrusted with authentic mandates, honest, intelligent, capable, impassioned. But also so many adversaries occupying fortresses, confronting each other. There are so many pretexts for killing one another rather than understanding one another! Each on his own pedestal, the pedestal of a machine-age civilization, which has been specifically entrusted with the safeguarding of our spirit, our will, our goals, our ideals. . . . They all talk about the same thing and they all have kind and devoted hearts; and yet here they all are, polishing their weapons, bombs, and cannons. The world is going to collapse! They are going to blow it up! It won't misfire! And at the end of the race, why not?

I carry within me one consolation. I bring consolation like an honest donkey who has done his work and accomplished his task! I know that the horizon is free and that the sun is going to rise again. . . . Consider this anecdote: One day, a century ago, gas was installed in all the kitchens of Paris. . . . The morning after, the population "woke up alive." There were no dead bodies on every floor; there were no ambulances in the street to carry away the corpses. The firemen stayed home. What had happened? To warm up their evening soup people had turned on the gas knob, and then they turned it off until it was time for the morning coffee. And since then children have been told, "Don't touch the gas knob!"

Far from the hustle and bustle, in my den (since I am a meditative person, I have even compared myself to a donkey, out of conviction), for fifty years now I have been studying "Everyman," his wife and children. One preoccupation has concerned me compulsively: to introduce into the home a sense of the sacred; to make the home the temple of the family. From that moment on, everything changed. A cubic centimeter of housing was worth gold, as it represented potential happiness. With such an idea of dimension and purpose, today you can build a temple to meet family needs beside the very cathedrals that were built . . . in another era; you can do it because of what you will put of yourself to it. But the nineteenth and twentieth centuries have instituted professional degrees in architecture; they have defined the concept of architecture while entrusting its control to the Beaux-Arts Institute and giving it jurisdiction over this matter. . . . France, until its defeat in 1940, was the only country which did not require an official diploma from its builders, allowing new and free minds the possibility of inventing and building. France had its pioneers, France, country of inventors. . . . The first law enacted by the Vichy government was a law requiring a professional degree, a law that had always been rejected by the Parliament before then.[28] In the schools they were taught how to design all-purpose palaces instead of "family enclosures," "work enclosures," leisure enclosures, etc., that is to say, instead of premises. France's "town halls"[29] were built, and so were churches in various styles, and railway stations like Orsay where the trains from one fourth of France converge in a basement, under a ceiling 3.5 meters high, while above it a titanic nave, more spacious than the Baths of Caracalla in Rome, is left for the sparrows. They also constructed the nearby "Grand Palais," titanic as well, for exhibits. What was exhibited there? Things for men and women. But men are on the average 1.70 meters tall; the nave of the "Grand Palais" is 50 meters high![30]

For sixty-one years, lipsticks, benches 43 centimeters high, and 70-centimeter-high tables have been lost under these majestic vaults! This palace was the mortal enemy of all exhibitions: the paintings exhibited there had no scale, and the same goes for the statues. For sixty-one years (and several times a year) it has been necessary to undertake costly fittings in order to make the objects on display more presentable. Fortunes were spent there—billions and billions.

Life-long concessions were made for these yearly installations. Despite this unimaginable failure, despite this lesson taught over and over again for sixty years, they did not hesitate to repeat the mistake; they did not hesitate to redo it at La Défense, the largest vault in the world, "which can cover the place de la Concorde in a single span." But the place de la Concorde remains in Paris! And La Défense is twenty kilometers away. Under the dome of La Défense there will be lipsticks, chairs 43 centimeters high, and tables 70 centimeters high. "The greatest in the world,"[31] that's what they call this vault.[32] Magic word! But cars and pedestrians can neither get there nor return from there. So the Métro is being extended, the bridge at

Neuilly is being enlarged, and the so-called avenue Triomphale is being redone by real estate agents.

It (the avenue) will terminate at the Arc de Triomphe, which is presently already congested with traffic beyond measure, and the Obélisque de la Concorde; it will come up against the walls of the Tuileries. . . . There is already talk of running it under the Louvre, under Saint-Germain-l'Auxerrois; it will reach the Hôtel de Ville and will pass below it. Never has the word "g-r-r-r-rand" been used so tragically. Yet that's how the architecture of "modern times" has been created for Paris.

The necessary task is to give attention to places and buildings. That is the task of "builders." And the "builders" are precisely the new profession that must link in a tireless and friendly dialogue the engineer and the architect, the left hand and the right hand of the art of building.[33]

Under those circumstances, the dwelling had no chance to become the temple of the family. Rental boxes were made, and people were making their living by renting boxes. The notion of architecture was lopsided, because it did not obey any precise definition—that is, it did not try to create places and buildings for living, working, and recreation, it did not try to place its occupants in "the conditions of nature," that is to say, under the strict laws of the sun, our irrefutable master, since the alternation of day and night forever dictates the proper sequence of our activities. The sun (our master, friend or enemy) had not been taken into consideration. With the United Nations Headquarters the Americans woke up a bit late and decided to wrap it all around with glazing; but without the benefit of a "solar control device."[34] New York, at the latitude of Naples, was hit by the sun full force, through fixed glazing. They do no better for cultivating orchids. . . . They installed "air conditioning." Refrigerants are very expensive. The heat had not been sufficiently reduced? Out of enthusiasm and inspiration, they baptized these glass facades "curtain walls." The fashion seduced Paris. . . . The people behind the curtain walls faced cruel risks. And yet they persisted! Dear sun! . . . Dear sun, now the enemy of the inhabitant![35] Everything became so confused after the wars of '14 and '39 that we lost our minds! Laissez-faire, lack of conscience, and carelessness overflowed. Sprawling cities were born, developed, and reached their apogee: a scandal, a disaster. Here New York, twelve million inhabitants; here London, ten million; and here is Moscow, which is already at five million. . . . This year, 1961,[36] Paris is gloriously arriving at eight million inhabitants! It's done, they let it happen. Someone should have rung the alarm in time. . . . But no one did!

It's been one hundred years since industry was born, since machine-age civilization appeared. They didn't know that it was the advent of a civilization, the birth of a new society. Rather they thought that it was a curse, a plague, a bad makeshift . . . a machine to make money. It took one century to fit people into that infernal machine—bosses and workers, exploitation and ordinances. Revolt! A century of violence, of attempts at regulation, of proposed solutions for the harmonization of working conditions, of postulates to justify the existence of work! One day, to make work friendly.

On this round earth, two human establishments have existed since the beginning of time: an "agricultural unit" measured by the pace of a horse or an ox (four kilometers per hour) and by the strength of their hamstrings; and the "Radio-Concentric City of Exchanges," which appeared at the crossing of two roads, three roads, four roads automatically causing the gathering and dispersing of consumer goods (merchandise), of ideas (schools and universities), of forces of authority and administration (government). Sites of exchange.[37]

Through incompetence, the modern workplace was located haphazardly, by chance, around built-up areas and within built-up areas. This event is now ripe: the twenty-four-hour day is completely distorted by uncoordinated and totally arbitrary distances between the home and work place.

Man began to live on wheels: suburban trains, suburban buses, bicycles, motorcycles, individual cars. The sun continued to turn impassively every twenty-four hours, dividing the solar day in two: day and night. And it was an insane expense: the squandering of modern times.[38]

Then they cried out, "This is a total disaster. From now on we must disperse industry!" It was not a valid answer.

They should have said, "We must localize industry," and discover the meaning of the term "to localize."[39]

By studying this same problem of the equipment, of machine-age civilization, in all countries and under every kind of climate, I happened to discover (as one suddenly perceives a flying saucer or a sputnik, in other words, with amazement) that machine-age society did not have an industrial human establishment, did not have Industrial Cities at its disposal. And I also discovered that the essence of this third and new human establishment,[40] the "Linear Industrial City," was a necessary and redeeming form for the solution of problems that had preoccupied reformers of good will, of all points of view, even the most opposed.

The "Industrial City" is "linear," shaped by the three routes—water, land, and railway—bringing in raw

DERRIÈRE NOUS...

LA LIGNE IRRÉCUSABLE

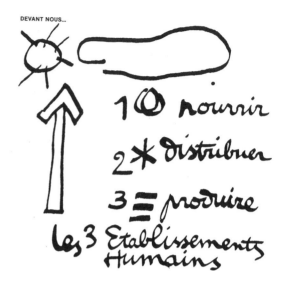

DEVANT NOUS...

1 ⊙ nourrir

2 ✳ distribuer

3 ≡ produire

les 3 Etablissements Humains

materials and shipping out manufactured products. The water, land, and rail routes have a common destiny determined by topography: the slope of thalweg[41] along which mountain waters flow down to the sea—through wide or narrow valleys or wide plains. These three routes are interconnected, or can be interconnected, by the topography.

A fundamental innovation occurs: "transshipment," an invention of modern times. The means of distribution along these routes of water, earth, and rail were, until now, "branchings" by water, on roads, or on rails. These branchings (especially for railroads) required unloading on the ground, sometimes over immense surfaces, causing giant congestions (the switchyards of large cities are an example). The innovation is the "transshipment," which replaces the "branchings." From now on people will assemble, transship and distribute goods by "overhead cranes" set up perpendicularly to the three routes on land, rail, and water, and overhead, in the air. This is of

fundamental importance: it is the articulation of the solution.

"THE IRREFUTABLE LINE
THE IRREVOCABLE GRAPH"

I can therefore sketch this figure:[42]

A vertical line. To the left of this vertical line, a black area, a descending arrow, the trajectory of a catastrophe, of atomic war (everything will be destroyed, including the newly rich of this adventure).

To the right of the vertical line an arrow soars upward toward the light bearing the fate of "The Three Human Establishments."

Two books appeared. One[43] at the time of the Liberation, signed by ASCORAL (Association of Builders for Architectural Renovation, created during the war and comprising eleven study sections), was entitled "The Three Human Establishments." The small format required only one and a half metric tons of paper for six thousand copies, paper that had been denied for three years. This edition was entirely sold out without anyone particularly needing to attend to it.[44] Twelve years later, in October 1959, Jean Petit, publisher of Editions "Forces Vives," reprinted this work in a different format, supplemented by many clear illustrations.[45]

Everything was being built then. Everything was being set up. The program was set up punctually and the "reconversion of work" seemed possible; from then on it turns its back on the nuclear race, on unemployment. A reconversion of work dedicated to the common good, to people: a program for a machine-age civilization.

I began the writing of this text with an entirely random incident: the little revolution in the pharmacy, brotherly and motherly, and the obliteration of Monsieur the Apothecary. A modest invention had intervened, the creation of plastics,[46] whose beginning had been a childish invasion of the children's toy market, with inflated dolls, all naked; one of its outcomes, in the modern pharmacy, has brought about the unparalleled longevity of man on earth, a lifespan carried into the sixties. A law governing insurance triggered the event, a generous law that stipulated: Let us help all our brothers irrespective of class. The status of the physicians was thrown into confusion and henceforth fixed: medicine was literally put into the service of man. . . .[47] Medication became as natural as eating for everyone: its precision, its cleanliness, its effectiveness, etc. Out of it, a new industry was born; from that point on it became the accepted state of things. The author of these lines ventures modestly to turn the reader's attention to this event, to the credit of modern society . . . .

Let us move on to the main theme: "The Three Human Establishments." Frontiers at gunpoint, social hatred, class hatred, the madness of competition; shameful abuses of business practices, "Struggle for Life,"[48] "Time Is Money."[49] . . . Let's shut the door on atomic war. Let's establish over the topography of the Good Earth, the Three Human Establishments, the first of which, the Agricultural Cultivation Unit, will be determined by the tractor and no longer by the pace of an ox or a horse. This is the impending, immanent innovation. The second establishment, "The Radioconcentric City for Exchanges," will be the setting into focus that will illuminate with a lightning flash the drama of sprawling contemporary cities and immediately find its solution in an exodus along the "Linear Industrial City." This third establishment, the "Linear City," faces up to conflicts, parries hatred and selfishness. Confronted by such a prodigious source of productive labor offered to modern society, the choice is between a night without hope (placed to the left of the irrefutable vertical line, drawn above) and complete freedom of action, an enormous range of programs, the boundlessness of solutions entrusted to modern societies (to the right of the vertical line): the construction of radiant dwellings (to live in), green factories (to work in), facilities for leisure (to cultivate body and mind), mobility!

This is not madness. No! Since 1933 it has been the prophecy of the "Athens Charter" of CIAM. These are the conclusions of CIAM, "The International Congress for Modern Architecture," which, in the course of thirty years (1928–1959), established in the modern world the basis of urban planning, of honest research—disinterested, persevering, detailed, and creative: its value is its honesty![50]

Urbanism, the human quest, honest and creative. Yes . . . laziness and the status quo must be shaken off. We must move beyond petty selfishness, beyond little things. We must try to discover life, to follow life. At least twenty years are needed for an idea to become known, thirty years for it to be appreciated, and fifty for it to be applied, when it then has to evolve. It is then that speeches resound over the tombs and commemorative tablets, and then it is too late, everything must be done over again. Why wait for misfortune or catastrophe to happen before taking useful decisions?

For my part, I devoted fifty years of my life to the study of housing. I brought back the temple to the family,[51] to the home. I restored the conditions of nature to the life of man. I could have never carried out this enterprise successfully without the wonderful assistance of the young people in my atelier at 35 rue de Sèvres—and without their passion, their faith, their integrity. I thank them all. Some fertile seeds have been planted, without a doubt, among all those who passed through rue de Sèvres. Perhaps some time in the future they will think of père Corbu who tells them today: "We must work according to the dictates of our own conscience. . . . It is within this realm that the human drama unfolds . . . ."

Soltan from Warsaw, a veteran of the atelier, wrote to me around 1954 (without dating his letter) these encouraging words, which are for me a sort of consolation: "The latest piece of news from you is the last Girsberger.[52] For a few hours I managed to hold in my hands the only copy of this book now in Warsaw. Of course you surely know that in Eastern Europe they reproach you for 'formalism and constructivism.'[53] Obviously these reproaches are silly, but when one looks at your recent work, what is striking is the great growth in the importance of content and subject. The 'Open Hand' in Chandigarh, for example.

"This importance of the poetry of the subject begins to give your work an extraordinary aesthetic value, completely pharaonic, although these values explore a sensibility and a subconscious that are really quite modern. (Indeed, that is the great contribution of these works.) To reproach you for formalism then becomes simply comic, were it not tragic! Tragic, because the authors of these reproaches build a great deal, but how? That's the tragedy! Personally I am absolutely certain that, even independent of the social and political future which awaits you, your ideas will triumph throughout the world. Besides, they do have a solid social base, do they not?

"The future triumph of Corbu's ideas throughout the world will come one day, but when will it come? Within the reach of a human life? Mine, for example?

"Will I be able to see you one day and speak to you about things I cannot resolve, problems that are particularly 'Eastern Europe': the accessibility of a work of art from the point of view of the consumer (for example)? The question of always being within the reach of the masses, etc. You certainly know those songs well. . . . But there are so many others. . . . Dear Monsieur Le Corbusier, friends who know me well laugh, saying that I always think of you when I work; I think that is very true, anyway . . . ."[54]

Such remarks allow one to hope that the efforts of père Corbu have not been entirely in vain . . . .

To Soltan, to all the others I can say: fellowship is an edifice where all is coherent, where one can find an entire range of interests indispensably present, some bringing shadow, others light. Light expresses the higher concerns of love, friendship, brotherhood. Shadow—material interests and selfishness. And depending on whether the light source is at point-blank range or at a distance, the view and quantity of the egoism or altruism will vary.

The Open Hand Monument, for example, of which Soltan speaks, is not a political emblem, not the creation of a politician. It is an architect's creation, it is the fruit of architecture. This creation is a specific case of human neutrality: he who creates something does so by virtue of the laws of physics, chemistry, biology, ethics, aesthetics, all bound in a single sheaf: a house, a city. This is different from politics in that the architect's equation requires physics, chemistry, the strength of materials, the law of gravity, biology—without which everything cracks, everything breaks, everything collapses. It is like the airplane: either it flies or it doesn't, and the verdict is delivered quickly. Thus in the relation of man to matter (the complexity of programs) we realize that everything is possible and that all conflicts can be diminished. All one needs to do is to be persuaded of this and to study the problem, to open one's hands to all materials, techniques, and ideas, to find the solution. To be content, to be happy. And not to be paid. Who follows me?

This Open Hand, a symbol of peace and reconciliation, must be erected in Chandigarh.[55] This symbol, which has preoccupied me and my subconscious for many years now, ought to be realized, to bear witness to harmony. We must stop preparing for war; the Cold War must cease to provide a living for men. We must invent, enact works of peace. Money is nothing but a means. There is God and the Devil—forces facing each other. The Devil is superfluous: the world of 1965 is capable of living in peace. There is still time to choose, let's equip ourselves rather than arm ourselves. This symbol of the Open Hand, open to receive the wealth created, to distribute to the peoples of the world, must be the symbol of our age. Before I find myself one day (a little later on) in the celestial spheres amid the stars of God Almighty, I shall be happy to see at Chandigarh, in front of the Himalayas,

which rise up straight upon the horizon, this Open Hand, which marks for père Corbu a deed, a certain distance covered. From you, André Malraux, from you, my associates, from you, my friends, I ask help in realizing this symbol of the Open Hand in the skies of Chandigarh, a city desired by Nehru, Gandhi's disciple.[56]

When asking me about these matters for his little booklets about Corbu,[57] Jean Petit wanted a survey of my ideas. . . . But I don't like to talk about myself. That should be left to journalists once I have been carried out feet first. However it is good to put on the table some ideas that can be useful. The other day a large gentleman, big and plump, came to see me.

"Monsieur Le Corbusier, how about a new recording!"

"So there has already been one?"

"Yes, several years ago . . . ."

"What! Are you kidding me?"

"No, it's true. Then it's all right?"

"Well, yes, but I forbid you to say a single word, or ask one single question."

"But to interrupt for a moment . . . ."

"No, this will be Corbu all the way . . . ."[58]

The other day they brought me copper plates two millimeters thick, which I am etching with a burin. A burin is a fierce tool. At the age of fourteen for a short while I used a burin. With great strength of arm and flexibility of wrist you carve a sharp track. You must go straight forward, neither to the right nor the left. A person who knows and can use the burin is led onto the path of clear-sightedness, straightfor-wardness, and honesty.[59]

It's all there, to be seen or to be looked at. The qualifications of men. Those who show off and display themselves only act in response to others' reactions, they become the superior "poets" of a humanity that itself feels superior in different ways. They are endlessly cutting off ties. Others, the architects worthy of their vocation, are identified with their work. The simple, true, propelling force of work. This force must rise up from physics, from imagination, from invention, courage, and risk. It is intense only when one takes risks. He risks it all: all his being, all his thought, his money, his family, and his job. He curses no one,

nothing except the obstacles themselves, the regulations, the craftiness of the ambitious, the dirty tricks of business people. He is in full combat, always exposed. He doesn't think of himself or his public appearance, nor of the impression he makes, but only of what is facing him: his work. It is not settled in a short sonnet or a play of free words, in a list of abuses or in arguments at the Café de Flore or at La Rotonde. It takes a period of a year, two years, five years for his work to be born and to be introduced, not within the pages of a book with its margins and white space, but in the public domain. Here all is responsibility, vigilance, a permanent state of alertness. Slow, slow, the painfully slow patience of expression

Au-dessus du bétail ahuri des humains
Bondissaient en clartés les sauvages crinières
Des mendieurs d'azur le pied dans nos chemins

and the vital impulse tirelessly knocking against physical and intellectual laws. Opposition, customs, and that immense No! unrelenting.

Some people think that one should proceed like a conquering god with a halo of blond hair, surpassing all that has been seen up to then and without hesitating to say "Shit!" to everyone and everything. Others think: to conquer and perhaps to be conquered, without blond hair, but with hair that has turned gray from persisting every morning in carrying out one's task, without being predestined, without any sign appearing from heaven, but because one wanted to risk adventure, because one had embarked on a ship, a plane, a chimera. . . . The moral lesson: honor to commerce and shit to industry. Gentlemen the creators, you are invited to buy yourselves a toothpick and to suck it publicly to get rich. You must; otherwise they will stone you.

Here, at this point, I must thank two men: Cervantes and Rabelais. The most beautiful reading for a man engaged in battle is the admirable Don Quixote of La Mancha. And life among these three companions, between Don Quixote and Sancho Panza, finds its explanation, if not its justification. Some are enraptured; others stand gaping and do not read the admirable Don Quixote of La Mancha. Don Quixote and

Panza show us man hammering away with the persistence of the tides, in the most optimistic outbursts: confidence, faith, love, a giving, a blossoming, a flowering, and an ecstasy, and their most precipitous falls clean and indisputable: punches in the nose preceded by spankings. Panza gets through, always survives it, and thinks of eating. He is always right. He knows how to accept (to offer or to thrash out a compromise). He lands on his feet. All this is extraordinarily true. At the other end, Panurge and Friar John carry on their discussions and commentaries beyond the limit of politeness, and rise above everything in the name of the wisest points of view, through the most laughable coarseness which welcomes them into the highest levels of the nobility. Shit, shit! . . . *braguette et balletron,*[60] old whores beautiful as goddesses, dypsode and werewolf, Homer and Pliny. Homeric, above and below, outside of pettiness, of the great words, the clash of battles and the cutlasses. One takes cover from the brutishness, one laughs. Thank you, Rabelais and Cervantes.

There are encounters, the permanence of existing facts, contacts . . . and thus Mallarmé:

> Gleaming above the bewildered human herd,
> Flaunting their uncouth manes and filthy rags,
> Beggars of azure skipped into our road.[61]

Il y eut dans le ciel un silence d'environ une Demi-heure

Apocalypse

. . . .

Recently I had to proofread the manuscript for a book written in 1911: *Le Voyage d'Orient*.[62] Tobito, a veteran from the atelier at 35 rue de Sèvres, had come to pay a visit from Venezuela to my apartment at rue Nungesser.[63] Jean Petit then arrived with the text of *Le Voyage d'Orient*. Together we drank pastis and spoke at length. I remember telling both of them that the line of conduct of little Charles-Edouard Jeanneret at the time of *Le Voyage d'Orient* was the same as that of père Corbu. Everything is a question of perseverance, of work, of courage. There are no glorious signs in heaven. But courage is an inner force, which alone can justify or not justify existence. I was happy to see Tobito again, to see that he had persevered, that he was among the faithful. When the three of us parted, I said to Tobito, who was planning on coming back to see me the following year: "Yes, in Paris or on another planet . . . " and I said to myself: "So, from time to time they will probably have a good thought for père Corbu."

Finding myself alone again, I thought of that wonderful phrase from the Apocalypse: "There was silence in heaven for about half an hour."[64]

Yes, nothing is transmissible except thought, the noble fruit of our labor. This thought may or may not triumph over fate in the hereafter, and perhaps it will assume a different, unforeseeable dimension.

Politicians, to be sure, leave no stone unturned and make the best of weaknesses in order to enlist support: they are bent on reassuring the weak and the doubting, the frightened. But life can be revived through plans—the potential life that lies in wait in the pastures and among the flocks, in these abandoned lands, in these sprawling cities that have to be pulled down, in the workplaces, and in the factories that must be made as beautiful as joy . . . outside the force of habit and jaded civil servants.

We must rediscover man. We must rediscover the straight line that joins the axis of fundamental laws: biology, nature, the cosmos. A straight line unbending like the horizon of the sea.[65]

The professional man, also, unbending like the horizon of the sea, ought to be a measuring instrument able to serve as a builder's level, as a datum line in the midst of flux and mobility. That is his social role. This role demands that he be clear-sighted. His followers have set up a perpendicular line in his mind. The moral: not to give a damn for honors but to rely on oneself, to act in accordance with one's own conscience. It is not by playing the hero that one is able to act, able to undertake tasks and to realize them.

All this happens inside the head, formulating itself, passing through an embryonic stage, little by little in the course of a lifetime that flies by in a vertigo, whose end one reaches without even realizing it.[66]

Paris, July 1965

The Final Year

A Transcription and Translation of Le Corbusier's Last Recorded Interview

Hugues Desalle conducted this interview with the master in Le Corbusier's apartment in Paris at 24 rue Nungesser-et-Coli on 15 May 1965. It was made into two 33-RPM records: *Le Corbusier revit son enfance, sa jeunesse, son aventure* (disque 17 A et B, 17 centimeters radius) and *Le Corbusier vit ses combats, le monde, son architecture, sa poésie* (disque 30 A et B, 30 centimeters radius) by Réalisations Sonores, Hugues Desalle, Paris, 1965. The records were part of a collection entitled "Français de notre temps, Hommes d'aujourd'hui," that was undertaken under the patronage of the Alliance Française. An earlier recording in the series, *Le Corbusier: mes pensées à 73 ans*, was made in 1961. Le Corbusier alludes to both recorded interviews in *Mise au point*, page 54. The recordings of 1965 carry the identifying number 27-8-65, the date of Le Corbusier's death. The jacket for the recording was designed by Le Corbusier's longtime friend Oscar Niemeyer and was dated 5 September 1965, a week after Le Corbusier's death.

In preparing the transcription and translation, I consulted, in addition to the tape of the interview, a French transcript entitled "Le Corbusier: Un inédit message dans une bouteille," which appeared in *Spazio e società* 6 (June 1979), 101–9, and an unsigned English translation that appeared as "Interview with Le Corbusier," in *Modulus,* the University of Virginia School of Architecture Review (1979), 65–75.

A HAUTE VOIX LE CORBUSIER UN GENIE
NOUS LÈGUE
SON TESTAMENT SPIRITUEL

Deux mois avant sa mort, chez lui, à Boulogne, dans la maison qu'il a construite — il est fier de sa terrasse où le vent a apporté le pollen de toutes les fleurs, plantes et arbres — détendu, confiant, spontané, extraordinairement vivant — « je serai bientôt dans les zones célestes » — nous reprenons un pastis — Le Corbusier se met à construire. Parfois sa voix peine, il pompe l'air de son grand cœur blessé. Puis il repart en force, en altitude. Je venais de lui dire que le nom de Le Corbusier ne faisait pas penser à un corbeau, comme il le pensait, mais à un oiseau aérodynamique qui, en vol plané, affamé de volumes, survole les chaînes, dévorant tout de son œil perçant, pour sa synthèse, du granit au lapin dans sa touffe.

« Le Président Kubitschek, qui fit surgir Brasilia des plateaux désertiques vous exalte, Le Corbusier, « visionnaire de l'architecture, avec vos disciples Niemeyer et Costa ». Niemeyer et Costa ne sont pas vos disciples, mais vos fils Niemeyer, l'architecte des palais d'État de l'Amérique latine, vient de dire : « Il fut le plus grand génie de l'architecture contemporaine ».

André Malraux,
écrivain, Ministre d'État des Affaires Culturelles

« Son combat fut difficile et parfois féroce. Le Corbusier a vécu sans concessions et ne sacrifie aucune de ses idées à des considérations autres que celles de son amour de l'art.

André Bloc,
architecte,
fondateur de « L'architecture d'aujourd'hui »

La photo de Le Corbusier, en août 1964, sans ornement, dépouillé, comme il émeut aussi, à Roquebrune-Cap Martin, qu'il aimait aussi. Un an après exactement, il y disparaître, plongeant dans la Méditerranée — malgré l'avis des médecins — dans sa mer grecque.

Oscar Niemeyer,
architecte de Brasilia,
vous a donné la joie
de dessiner la pochette
de disque de Le Corbusier.

N° 27-8-65
Le disque de Le Corbusier porte la date de sa mort

Disque 17 A et B
LE CORBUSIER
REVIT
SON ENFANCE, SA JEUNESSE,
SON AVENTURE

Disque 30 A et B
LE CORBUSIER
VIT
SES COMBATS, LE MONDE,
SON ARCHITECTURE, SA POESIE

Réalisations Sonores  **Hugues Desalle**

Un microsillon hors série de la Collection 17 cm. 30 t. « Hommes d'aujourd'hui ».

The record jacket (front and back) for the last interview Le Corbusier gave on 15 May 1965, marked 27-8-65 (the date of his death). It was designed by his longtime friend Oscar Niemeyer. Courtesy FLC, Paris.

Desalle: M. Le Corbusier, you have made your mark on our era. No one will be able to speak or write about architecture in the twentieth century without pronouncing or writing the name of Le Corbusier.

Le Corbusier: Thank you very much. . . . You are very kind. Today, in any case, you seem to be interested in my humble person. And, for whatever it's worth . . . you ask me to explain a little why I exist on this earth. I can't stand premature biographies. . . . Let's leave them for journalists to write later on, once one has passed feet first somewhere else . . . don't you agree? But there is one very simple thing about my life, which I can tell you now in all sincerity, and that is that I have never thought of being "somebody." I was born without fanfare. At school I was no more stupid than anyone else. My mother would constantly say, "Always playing in the streets without doing your homework, I want to know how you keep coming home with top grades. You must steal them . . . ." I used to say, "Of course not!" Life was very simple.

I was two years ahead of my classmates in school, because my parents had enough of me at home . . . and bundled me off to school at the age of four. I was two years ahead, so that when I left school at thirteen, everyone else was fifteen. And why did I leave school? Because I had been very interested by drawing ever since I could remember. I drew on the table, everywhere, nonstop. . . . One day my father told me, "Good, you'll go to the local Art School"—I went to the Art School, following a three-day exam, which took me only one day because that was long enough for me. . . . I came to art school. It was a school for engraving watch cases, which I realized once I was in . . . and it wasn't amusing. I said to myself, "What in the world am I going to do here, me, engraving watch cases? It didn't interest me in the least." . . . To begin with, I have nothing against people who en-

grave watch cases. But you must admit that I was lucky, because at that moment a technical invention intervened: the wristwatch, which meant that one didn't need to put watches in one's vest pocket any more with a watch charm on its chain. And consequently it was no longer necessary to decorate the watch cases because the back was on the arm in contact with the skin, where no one could see it. This was my first demonstration, no, not demonstration, but my first . . . my first experience with the rejection of useless ornament.

So I got into this school. . . . I learned fine-line engraving for three years . . . metal chiseling in fact. . . . I think the mean-spirited will say that this was what made me an insignificant little guy . . . precise, tedious, mechanical. I say no . . . when you have a burin in your hand and you're engraving, well! you've got to push your burin with the full strength of your arm: you've got to push it straight ahead, and follow where it goes, and there's no choice—left or right— you've got to push ahead. Now that forms a notion about how to draw, in a fellow who had no particular teachers.

I did have an excellent teacher who opened my eyes to the spectacle of nature. He would take us into forests, into meadows, among flowers, into greenery, and he would help us draw from nature—not landscapes, but elements of plants. He would push us toward an understanding of how things go together. That was very important for me, and I think that I responded well to his wishes. I was, without knowing it, his favorite student. I only found this out much later, when at one point I dropped engraving. I said, "I'm not going to do it any more. I shall try something else." So my teacher told me, "You'll do architecture." And I said, "But I hate architecture. . . . What are architects? . . . All that isn't droll and neither is architecture: so how can you expect me to go

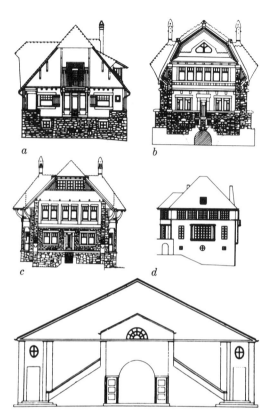

a   *b*

c   *d*

Le Corbusier's first constructions at La Chaux-de-Fonds: (a) Maison Fallet, 1906; (b) Maison Stotzer, 1908; (c) Maison Jacquemet, 1908; (d) Maison Jeanneret, 1912; (e) Cinema La Scala, 1916. Courtesy FLC, Paris.

into architecture?" "But yes, you'll see, Architecture," said Charles Blanc, in the *Grammar of the Arts.* Charles Blanc said, "Architecture is the foremost of the arts." I don't know if that improved my morale, but I passed through the gates of architecture anyway, and I set to it. I began by building my first house, right away, at the age of seventeen. I found a very good man, a decent sort, who was a member of the board of the art school where I was enrolled, and who told

me, "I am going to build myself a house." I told him, "You're going to build yourself a house. I'll build it for you." He said "You're crazy!" I said, "No, but I'll do it for you, by God!" So I wheedled him and I did his house for him; it got built with all sorts of charming details, romantic and well finished, impeccably designed and impeccably executed. I was a real watchdog on the building site. The contractors said to themselves, "This little man, we'll get him at every turn." But they didn't get me, I succeeded by putting my foot down on the construction site.

I left to go through Italy, to breathe, to look a little at things, at beautiful things for a while. I went to Vienna where Hoffmann was a luminary. Josef Hoffmann was a good man, but I didn't dare to approach him for three days. . . . I stayed on in Vienna several months, working on commissions I had.

Then one fine day we went to the Grand Opera of Vienna, which was a wonderful opera house—we went there once a week—and they were playing, not Wagner this time, but simply Puccini's *La Bohème.* And . . . this damned *Bohème* by Puccini made us believe it was Paris: they made the Parisians more Parisian than one usually portrays them, and it was admirably well done. They were very lively Parisians, very much at ease, very alert, like the Viennese know how to do it. And so, with the friend who was with me, we said to each other: "off to Paris." That was it. Three days later we were on the train for Paris.

We arrived in Paris on a rainy day in February. It was mid-Lent and raining as hard as it could, so I immediately went to find lodging in the Latin Quarter, on the rue des Ecoles, in a seventh-floor garret from which I could see all of Paris: Montmartre and the Arc de Triomphe . . . and I stayed here for thirteen to fifteen months. There I stood facing with Paris, and that's where I started looking at Paris, seeing Paris, studying it and loving it, loving it passionately. And I

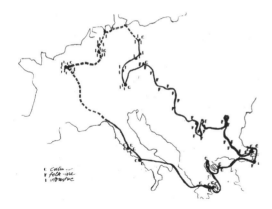

Itinerary of Le Corbusier's Journey to the East of 1911. Courtesy FLC, Paris.

Hagia Sophia, Istanbul, sketch by Le Corbusier, 1911. From *Journey to the East.* Courtesy FLC, Paris.

House between Muratli and Rodosto (today Tekirdag), Turkey, 1911. From *Journey to the East.* Courtesy FLC, Paris.

was lucky: I had nerve. I didn't know what to do to earn a living. I had to go to work in an architect's office, so I went to see Grasset, who was the author of the *Grammar of the Decorative Arts,*[1] a well-known work at the time. . . . I went to see him. He wanted to throw me out, so I showed him my drawings from Italy. He said to me, "Come in, it's all right, your

drawings are good. What do you want?" I told him. He replied, "A man who might be of interest to you, or rather men, are the Perret brothers, who do reinforced concrete. Reinforced concrete is, well, it's when you make wooden cases, put steel inside, and pour concrete on top . . . ." So I said, "All right, I'll go and see the Perrets."

I saw Auguste Perret, who received me graciously. I pulled out the drawings, which impressed him, and he hired me—on the spot. And that's how I began: in the best climate I could have dreamed of . . . that of Auguste Perret, who was an innovator, and who was young (every man is for a certain time). . . . He would yell through the office, "I do reinforced concrete!" This was something scandalous, something seemingly totally heretical, and he really loved this little bit of scandal. . . . "I do reinforced concrete!" . . .

And that's where I learned about reinforced concrete —by doing the working drawings for the Cathedral of . . . good God, where is that cathedral? It's in Algeria; I can't remember. . . . And so that's where I learned real drawing—working drawings—for a modern technique.

After that I wandered around Europe for a few years, for five or six years, then went to the Orient—I took

Le Corbusier at the Acropolis, 1911. Courtesy FLC, Paris.

a six-month trip on foot from Vienna to Asia Minor. There I was dumbfounded by the most anti-academic things possible, such as peasant houses, property enclosing walls that sloped with the land, slanting or tilted, depending on the slope of the land without the terracing that architects usually resort to when they have a sloping site . . . a method that has always revolted me. The wall followed the slope of the land: so beautiful, it struck me for life—that's the spirit of Truth.

And I saw Turkish art. The first example was based on Hagia Sophia in Asia Minor, an admirable work of art, with extraordinary power, an absolute masterpiece. . . . Then I saw Byzantine and Turkish art, and I really started to like the Turks, I found them very friendly. It was considered in bad taste at that time to say nice things about Turks.

Afterward I went to Athens and saw the Acropolis. I stayed there for seven weeks in daily contact, with a passion, a very great fervor. I discovered then that architecture was the play of volumes, the play of profiles, the play of, well, a total invention, depending exclusively on the creation of the one who designs it.

Charles-Edouard Jeanneret (Le Corbusier) with his brother, Albert, in Paris at 3 quai Saint Michel, 1908. Courtesy FLC, Paris.

I drew a lot, and decided that I, for sure, would never work in styles and would escape from the Vignolas . . . who had been directing architectural education for the past two centuries, or at least the entire nineteenth century. I left Vignola behind to the great surprise of those who knew me and who said, "But, after all, you have to study Vignola."

After that, I returned home to my country, to which I wanted to bring all of my youthful wisdom. They kicked my butt, saying, "You get on our nerves." And after a while I said, "All right, I'm leaving," and I came back to Paris. And from that moment on I began a fascinating life . . . eating once a day . . . (which can be enough when you're young) . . . and then doing what I wanted. I acquired an education by thinking and by going to museums, and then after I went to work. I opened a studio, an office, I got my first commissions. And that's how I became an architect without ever having read a single book on architecture, without ever having learned the seven orders of architecture—which I respected infinitely, but on condition that I didn't have to contend with them, you see, let's admit it—they are arbitrary, they were from now on obsolete in the light of the new times.

One day I was in my student room at quai Saint-Michel, my student room on the seventh floor, by the attic window. Suddenly I hear a terrific noise, I run to the window, and I see an airplane go by. It was the Count de Lambert's airplane flying over Paris for the first time. That was a shock. The Count de Lambert received a summons, of course; he wasn't allowed to fly over Paris, but he had done it anyway. And this was an event, an event in the history of mankind. Aviation was born at that moment, and was proving its potential.

And so I continued and I made a friend, you see, with whom I managed to quarrel later as often happens with friends; but for five years we worked together hand in hand. He was Amédée Ozenfant, who was an artist-painter, etc. . . . He had said to me, "You were born to be a painter. You have a painter's talent, etc."—because I had done quite a few drawings, watercolors, etc. . . . He started me off on research, which he himself called "Purism." Personally, I don't invent neologisms, others do it for me. Well, this Purism was serious research, serious if you will, in the midst of the confusion of Cubism, which . . . outside the great masters such as Picasso, Gris, or Braque, who were masters, very great masters, men of the greatest historical value . . . well, the others wriggled around a little in Cubism and Cu-cubism. So we decided to react against this and to come up with a style, a goal at least, for our efforts, an intention that would be commendable, and not only commendable but valid. In other words: treat objects in their genuine biologi-

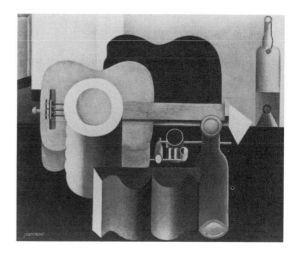

Nature morte à la pile d'assiettes (Still-life with a pile of dishes), 1920, oil on canvas. Signed: Jeanneret, 1920. Courtesy FLC, Paris.

cal form and with them compose the necessary distortions geometrically. . . . This later came to be called Purism according to Ozenfant.

I have kept my first Purist painting, which was hanging at the Museum of Modern Art. And the second one is also there. These were very intuitive works in which a man can assert himself as he is without knowing it, but also without cheating, you see. This is something I've observed: any individual at any age will not betray himself consciously but he will give himself away involuntarily. Either he is worth something or he is worth nothing.

So, from that practice of painting, which occupied me for several years, I went back once again to architecture after World War I. I opened an architectural office, where I began to think architecture, I received my first commission: a little house at Vaucresson. I had incredible difficulties with this little house, especially the toilet window, which wouldn't harmonize with the others, you see. That caused me considerable trouble. I even remember, as we were leaving one night to go to the Cirque d'Hiver, when all of a sudden in the elevator I said, "Aha, that's it! I've got it." It was the toilet window that was essential to my solution, because otherwise it was a window that didn't match. It sounds silly to say things like that, but it was crucial, that's the way it was. . . . So my window was finally in harmony with the whole.

And after that I had some adventures. I don't remember exactly. I left for the Orient . . . I left for the Orient . . . and I came back and spent five or six years in my native country, with no success. I wasn't after success. I had, above all—I must say this in all candor—the feeling that I was nobody. . . . Not for a minute did I have the idea that I was worth anything. . . . This I insist on saying here, because this is something crucial to my character, if not to that of many individuals who have left their mark: those who are not born with the idea of being somebody become so unintentionally, and by their work alone. To become somebody is indeed the Paris struggle: every man for himself [la foire d'empoigne], knowing how to scheme to succeed—all sorts of intrigues come into play. . . . I never did that.

Yvonne Le Corbusier and Pierre Jeanneret. Courtesy FLC, Paris.

What year are we at now? I can't remember. . . . I, I, I'll, what did I do, for God's sake, wait, I don't know. . . . OK, you know it's difficult to remember the dates . . . .

Desalle: But that doesn't matter—

Le Corbusier: Yes, I know that.

Desalle: Of course.

Le Corbusier: Yes. After that I opened an architectural office with my cousin, Pierre Jeanneret, who was a good man. He was ten years younger than I was. He was also fanatic about airplanes, even more so about cars. . . . He and Ozenfant would take cars apart. Ozenfant had a car that he spent all his time taking apart because he always heard noises in it. These were cars that didn't go very far because the noises alarmed them. . . . Anyway, all these tales of the beginnings of automobiles in the lives of men, of their use. . . . And after that . . . (I am referring to a few years later . . . when I came to Paris in '17), and I started with an architecture and business office. I launched myself into business ventures—I was an errand boy for a small company—and things went fairly well. Sometimes things didn't go well. I didn't come out looking like an idiot, or at least that's how I think it was. People always received me very nicely. But the money was not so good. I didn't have what it takes for that.

These were difficult years, very difficult. . . . That's when Ozenfant and I met Paul Dermée. Paul Dermée was a poet, and he suggested that we start a magazine, *L'Esprit nouveau.* From our first contacts, we realized that one thing, the title *L'Esprit nouveau* (The new spirit), was especially inspired. After the first two or three issues were published, we sort of took it over from Dermée, who was entirely involved in poetry. *L'Esprit nouveau,* which had such an attractive title, was able to justify itself because of the articles that

L'Esprit Nouveau Pavilion, Paris, 1925. Courtesy FLC, Paris.

Ozenfant and I wrote about painting. And then . . . came the appearance of a gentleman named Le Corbusier . . . who was, you see, all of a sudden baptized by Jeanneret . . . Jeanneret, me, Charles-Edouard Jeanneret, who announced: "If we must talk about architecture, I'm willing to do it, but I don't want to do it under the name of Jeanneret." I said, "I'll take the name of my maternal ancestors, Le Corbesier, and I'll sign my articles about architecture 'Le Corbusier.'"

So one day I wrote the first article. Then I was told, "You must write other articles. You have to go on, it's necessary." I had two days to do it. I wrote them in one stretch and signed "Le Corbusier." . . . It was published, and suddenly this name became venerated . . . a rallying cry, throughout the entire world. . . . It's really funny, isn't it? This article by Le Corbusier, which was called . . . was called . . . this is annoying . . . which was called "Towards a New Architecture . . . Plan, Section, and Elevation." I wrote three consecutive articles, which had the gift of attracting a vivid interest in countries everywhere among people who edited other journals, and among interesting artists who would come to Paris and say, "I want to talk to M. Le Corbusier." They were told, "There is no such

person. It's M. Jeanneret who takes care of these things." And after a while Le Corbusier was forced to take the name Le Corbusier even in his everyday life, because when he crossed a border his passport read Jeanneret, and the customs officials weren't too happy. . . . They would ask, "Who is this Jeanneret in your passport, your letters are all addressed to Le Corbusier?" So I said, "Jeanneret, otherwise known as Le Corbusier." And from then on I was definitely renamed.

So, once done, Le Corbusier began to follow a constructive line in the matter of architecture, and from his first ten or twelve articles that ran that year came the book, *Vers une architecture* (Towards a new architecture). So then, having finished the ten articles, the ten or twelve articles, I had to deliver a second series, and these articles were called "Urbanism." Urbanism was a new word, a new word whose meaning was still vague but to which the signature of Le Corbusier immediately gave breadth, an incredible intensity backed up by valuable articles, by valid arguments, of a revolutionary nature—unintentionally so, but revolutionary because the situation was revolutionary, because the age was revolutionary. And this is why Le Corbusier was born and had to put his jacket on and keep it on; so now I've been Le Corbusier for a long time.

Then, in the late twenties, I was invited as Le Corbusier around the world, to give lectures, to explain things. And then I adopted a technique of my own that was rather unique. . . . I never prepared my lectures. I had a little card, about twice the size of a business card; there were four or five lines on it, and I would improvise. Improvisation is an amazing thing, but I would draw. From the beginning I worked with chalk, with colored chalk, and a blackboard, when there was one. That caused me some mishaps at times. Once I was so hot, in a country I

don't remember, that after erasing my colored chalkboard, I wiped my face with the erasing rag, and the whole room laughed. . . . I, too, was happy.

Corbu left for all sorts of places, beginning with South America, Buenos Aires, where I was the guest of an extremely lively, kind, and intense population. So there I was quite a success with these lectures, which were published later from my drawings, the drawings that I would make on paper, on large sheets of paper measuring two meters by one meter forty. . . . I had about a dozen sheets of paper, and I would draw on them with colored chalk. . . . When one draws while speaking, and uses effective words, one creates something . . . and all my theory, my introspection, and my retrospection on the phenomenon of architecture and urbanism come from these improvised and illustrated lectures. I drew everything that was to be my future on these plans. . . . It's likely that everything was destroyed. There was once a wonderful incident . . . it occurred in the United States, at Yale, I think. Before an audience of bright young girls, known for its two hundred young girls . . . .[2] When I finished my lecture, I saw the whole room get up and run toward the stage. I said to myself, "What's going to happen to me? This is awful!" They came up, took the drawings that I had made, and tore them into a thousand pieces—well, let's say two hundred pieces; then they passed them around and asked me to autograph just about every fragment.

But the act of improvising, of waging a battle, the fact of being in a state of intensity—to jump in completely willingly and to tell oneself, "One has to fight one's way out"—is an extremely important fact in life. And I can also say that even in matters that keep me busy . . . when they are not the sordid interests that get in the way, jealous colleagues or things like that . . . well, père Corbu is always well received, because I speak naturally and spontaneously. And what is characteristic is that my ideas have ended up forming a doctrine . . . that is, perhaps even an entity: architecture and urbanism. And nowadays this concept, "architecture and urbanism," has been assimilated worldwide, professed everywhere, practiced everywhere, and today people are emulating Corbu all over the world (heartbreaking, maybe, but that's how it is). And people are very grateful to me and express it in a number of charming gestures; and here, today, with your machine recording everything, is the time to declare in public, eh, to them, that I, too, am very grateful for the kindness they have always shown me. . . . Anyway, they have maintained that I brought them something.

Desalle: What was your first building?

Le Corbusier: My first construction was on the road to Vaucresson, for a man who told me: "I read one of your articles and I liked it a lot. We would like to build a house, a little house here in Vaucresson. . . . We don't have any money, or very little." I said, "All right, I'll do it for you." It was terribly difficult to give birth to the modern architectural aesthetic, and this house was the reason for my difficulty. At the same time I was building a house for Ozenfant, and also the same year one for Raoul La Roche, who became an important collector of Cubist paintings. The La Roche house—I told La Roche: "We are going to call it the Villa della Rocca, because it's a villa in the grand style"—it's made with blocks and glass with a plaster finish, like all workers' housing; It's a house of high style, which today is still the key to all my architecture. It exists, it is there, it is visited every minute, all the time, by everyone.

Left: "Jeanneret-Gris, dit Le Corbusier": identity card. Profession: "Homme de Lettres." Courtesy FLC, Paris.

Le Corbusier's lectures in 1935 included the following: Museum of Modern Art, New York, 24 October; Yale University, 30 October; Princeton University, 4, 5, and 6 November; and Columbia University, 19 November. He used these pocket-sized cards as an aid to improvisation. Courtesy FLC, Paris.

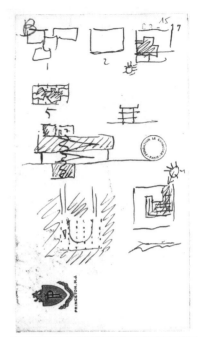

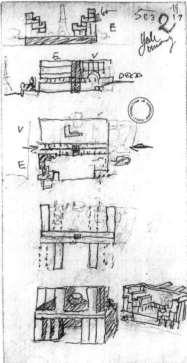

A little house in Vaucresson for George Besnus, 1923–24. Courtesy FLC, Paris.

Desalle: Where is it?

Le Corbusier: Oh, I won't tell you, because I don't want to cause my friend La Roche any trouble.

Desalle: Is it in the Paris region?

Le Corbusier: Yes, it's in the Paris region. But, you understand . . . this villa, this is where you see that at a given moment a creative idea comes forward, imposes itself . . . .

Desalle: Crystallizes?

Le Corbusier: . . . which is enclosed, which is enclosed in a mind, if this mind can conceive of it. . . . I had studied everything about art outside of schools, and outside of standard teaching, and . . . I had been nourished by a plastic aesthetic, you see—with passion, and I brought this into my work, which was, by reason, by the spirit of reason, of a crushing simplicity for most people, but rich for those who can see . . . and for those who know how to discover.

Desalle: Why, that's very beautiful, what you're saying. But this house "della Rocca," this evocative name, what year was that from?

Le Corbusier: It was in '22.

Desalle: In 1922.

Le Corbusier: That was my first house. At the same time I built those other two I told you about; it was in the same year.

Desalle: Yes.

Le Corbusier: But that's where, suddenly, I said to this fellow, who was a friend of mine, I said, "I'm going to create a fantastic thing for you, I'm going to make you . . . You're a bachelor, you might have paintings there one day, because you like painting; well, I'm going to make you one hell of an architectural promenade"—and it was done.

Desalle: And this gentleman still lives there?

Le Corbusier: Oh, yes, yes, yes!

Desalle: You haven't talked about your other works. . . . Before the war, for example, you advocated functional architecture?

Le Corbusier: It's . . . functional architecture, it's a journalist's term.

Desalle: Oh, I see.

Le Corbusier: Yes, because it's a pleonasm. Architecture is functional by definition. If it's not functional, what is it? Trash. I defined architecture as "the masterly, correct, and magnificent play of forms under light."

Desalle: Yes.

Le Corbusier: This is my first definition, the first sentence I wrote about architecture. And it's not so bad, is it? . . .

Villa della Rocca, or La Roche–Jeanneret house, Paris, 1923–25. Today it houses the Fondation Le Corbusier, which was created in 1968. Photo by author.

Desalle: No, it's very beautiful, it's very appropriate, you're right.

Le Corbusier: Yes, architecture is the masterly, correct, and magnificent play of forms under light. . . . It would unlock everything. It allowed the entire realization and permitted one to create.

Desalle: And how, M. Le Corbusier, do you place yourself, for example, in relation to Greek architecture?

Le Corbusier: Greek?

Desalle: Given the sentence you have just spoken?

Le Corbusier: Well, when I went to Athens at the age of twenty, or twenty-one, when I spent seven weeks in front of the Parthenon. . . . well! I saw that the Greeks had built a fantastic paradox. . . . There was marble carved like a sugar loaf, a fantastic modeling of wooden columns that became marble. Right, capitals in wood that became marble . . . the roofing in wood that became marble . . . triglyphs and all that. . . . Only it was done with such art that you could only raise your hat to it. Certainly one can say that architecture like that, of the Parthenon, is not functional; that's why the word "functional" is too limiting . . . is too . . . is too . . . yes, is too limiting. . . . The Parthenon is certainly one of the purest works of art that man has ever made. . . .

Desalle: So, you think, and you admit that the Parthenon is functional architecture.

Le Corbusier: No, no . . . it functions in that it moves you . . . that's it!

Desalle: It moves you. . . . Is that it?

Le Corbusier: That's it.

Desalle: Can you call it, in your mind, a decorative architecture?

Le Corbusier: Oh, absolutely not . . . .

Desalle: Then, what is it?

Le Corbusier: Architecture pure and simple!

Desalle: Pure and simple. . . . Have you been inspired by Greek architecture?

Le Corbusier: Look, I'm telling you . . . at the age of twenty-one, I received a very great shock standing before the Acropolis of Athens. And for seven weeks I remained face to face with the works that were there, and . . . the Greek scale, the Greek measure of man, the human presence in all the Greek works has stayed with me always. And when the critics . . . those who aren't hostile . . . always say that I'm the one who got close to, well, . . . who has joined with Greek culture . . . even though I have learned neither Greek nor Latin, nor anything. . . . In other words I know this very well. On one occasion, a man told me,

"You've learned neither Greek nor Latin, you'll never be able to write." . . . And it turned out later that, not being able to build certain things, I could draw them; but not being able to explain them entirely in drawing, especially when it came to urbanism, I had to explain them, so I wrote. One day Paul Valéry told me . . . I wrote like an angel. . . . He wrote it to me or he told me . . . I don't know how the situation came about, but anyway I knew Paul Valéry—he said to me, "You write wonderfully"; while everybody else was telling me, "You have no style; to have a style, you have to have a twisted style."

Desalle: Pompous?

Le Corbusier: Yes, a scholarly style.

Desalle: Is there any other architecture, other than Greek architecture, which was an important element in your life as an architect and builder-innovator?

Le Corbusier: Yes, yes! I've traveled all the countries of the world, except for two cities . . . Peking and— what is the other? . . . Peking and Mexico City. . . . I am trying to go to those countries; they have invited me often enough, but it never worked out that my planes would stop there, yet I knew they had a high opinion of me. But I knew, in addition to the palaces I saw, which were beautiful (they're often really ugly, you know? though it is maintained they are not), I admired the peasants' house, the house of men, the huts, the modest thing on a human scale. And that's where I invented a part of my Modulor, by rediscovering all the human dimensions in humble things. They are based on the cubit, the foot, the inch, etc.,— used from the very beginning of time, because there was no other way to measure.

Desalle: In fact, that's very important, because all the measures you have listed are natural.

Le Corbusier: Yes, based on man.

Top, Propylaea at top of Acropolis, sketch by Le Corbusier; *bottom,* Jeanneret–Le Corbusier at the Acropolis in Athens, 1911, as seen by his travel companion, Auguste Klipstein. Courtesy FLC, Paris.

The Modulor measuring stick and its inventor. Courtesy FLC, Paris.

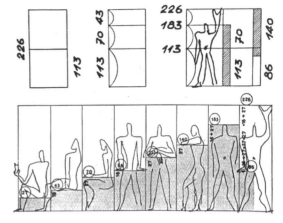

Modulor: measuring system by Le Corbusier based on human proportion, perfected between 1943 and 1947. Courtesy FLC, Paris.

Desalle: Not arithmetic, not artificial, right?

Le Corbusier: No, and what is so extraordinary about the Modulor, . . . which I invented one bright morning—I don't know how. . . . It was a series, an amazing series of surprising resources. . . . I don't know how it came to me, this thing . . . well, the highest degree of mathematics is in it. . . . And to add a little something that is an accusation made of many others. . . . I'm a mathematician at heart, although there's no evidence of this at all in my books.

Desalle: Without knowing it. You're a mathematician without knowing it.

Le Corbusier: Yes, I have an implacable sense of rigor that leads me toward proportion, you see. . . . Proportion is the appreciation of relations.

Desalle: Can one compare your Modulor to the Golden Number?

Le Corbusier: Oh, they're two different things. The Golden Number doesn't use human dimensions, standard dimensions. The Modulor is based on the human body. It's a man 1.83 meters in height, 2.26 with arm upraised: that's already a Golden Section, you see, and so on like that up and down the scale . . . .

Desalle: So it's not far away from the Golden Number?

Le Corbusier: No, it's part of it.

Desalle: It's part of it.

Le Corbusier: The Golden Number . . . I was called an idiot and incompetent. They said: "That's old fashioned, the Golden Number; these days we have pure mathematics." Well, I don't give a damn about pure mathematics! I'm as humble a person as any other, am I not? And I have a body like everyone else, and what I'm interested in is contact with my body, with my eyes, my mind . . . you see, and not with my books . . . .

Desalle: So . . . you've eluded my question as to whether any architecture other than Greek has inspired you, and continues today . . . .

Le Corbusier: No, I studied Gothic a lot. I had, for a year—I was in Paris for a whole year—I had the set of keys to Notre-Dame de Paris, given by the ministry to young people who wanted to study it. I wandered around inside, I would go to the top of the towers, into the ambulatories, into every possible corner of Notre-Dame. Notre-Dame is magnificent, it's a very beautiful thing; only my heart is turned toward Greece and not toward the Gothic, which is hard and almost aggressive next to . . . I'm talking about a Greek feeling and a Gothic feeling. They're two different feelings.

France was, according to its habit, modest and a braggart—a braggart for those who don't know anything and modest for those who do. The whole movement of an architectural renaissance was born in France during the nineteenth century, becoming more and more elevated from generation to generation. We lead with a Perret and a Freyssinet, the first an architect and the second an engineer, the two men finding each other by the same quality of synthesis—architecture as the masterly, correct, and magnificent play of forms under light. That is to say, one must be a visual artist and a poet and at the same time a completely well informed technician.

Desalle: M. Le Corbusier, have you had many struggles in your life?

Le Corbusier: Oh, yes.

Le Corbusier traveled to Princeton to show his Modulor to Albert Einstein in 1946. Said Einstein, "This is wonderful. It makes the beautiful easy, the ugly difficult." Courtesy FLC, Paris.

Desalle: Gigantic struggles?

Le Corbusier: Oh, well, as for giants, I'm 1.75 meters tall [five feet, nine inches], that's not so bad . . .

Desalle: Below the Modulor!

Le Corbusier: Yes, but . . . No, I had started the Modulor at 1.75 meters, which is the normal height of a Frenchman. Then all of a sudden I realized the Anglo-Saxon couldn't pass through Modulor doors 1.75 meters high. So I took 1.83 meters, you see, which even turns out to be a sacred number. . . . Then

I informed the person who said it was sacred that we were dealing with centimeters and that there's nothing sacred about a centimeter. . . be it 1.83 or 1.85, it's the same thing.

Desalle: And your struggles . . . because whoever says "Le Corbusier," says "struggles."

Le Corbusier: Yes, well, what can I say? . . . I acted with the greatest simplicity and in a spirit of inquiry that was studious and loyal and exact, without romanticism, precise and detailed . . . where nothing was left out. I incurred the hatred of people who saw in an artist only the pencil, the pen of d'Artagnan . . . panache, whatever! So I was attacked after the very first article that came out in *L'Esprit nouveau,* you see. There . . . what do you call it? . . . the architectural profession, the association of architects found itself, declared itself threatened, because the eventual problem of diplomas was at stake, and what diplomas were at stake, etc. It questioned the teachings in certain areas at a time when the world was changing completely in its modes of production, its forms, its aesthetic—something that was becoming evident in matters of living. . . . We are talking of modern production, mechanical things, and others that were modern in and of themselves—spontaneously. So people in the profession taught with the series . . . invented the big blocks of flats.

When I built the slab of flats in Marseilles, which has two thousand, two thousand inhabitants, I think it is sixteen hundred . . . I don't remember . . . I think it's two thousand . . . with a single entrance door, there was cause to make the future tremble, because people would say, "And what about us? What are we going to do? That makes four hundred dwellings, four hundred clients taken, stolen from us, who would have each entrusted us with a villa—work for four hundred architects." And evidently they felt that

there was a change in the profession. So, years later, much later . . . thirty or forty years later, I came to a reassuring conclusion: what has happened is not the death of architects, not at all, nor the death of engineers, nor of builders, not at all. The architect is the one who responds to the human factor in the entire process, the whole program; whereas the engineers take care of the physics of things. These are two quite different functions, which can combine admirably, even in the same man; but that's becoming difficult now, even impossible, I think, because technical calculations are very, very specialized. . . . Reinforced concrete, steel—all that requires extremely reliable calculations.

But the function of the architect, which was preeminent and dominant, felt itself followed, if not overtaken, surpassed, by engineers. And they said that I was making an architecture of engineers, because I had never allowed any ornament. But I would say: Look at the past! You will see entire cities built everywhere without ornament, with well-placed windows, good proportions. And from time to time you get palaces of kings, Louis XIV, Louis XV, even before, Francis I, which were decorated. It's not to say they were among the most beautiful! That's not what I mean. Nothing is absolute in this thing. It exposed me to violent hatred and very violent, even quite malicious attacks . . . by people who were against me. Well, I must have done something that provoked it. . . . I read an article entitled, "The Morbihan Architect Is Opposed to the Ideas of Le Corbusier." I said to myself, "So what if architects in the Morbihan don't agree with me? Let each man search in his own corner, and search as seriously as I do, as modestly, as humbly." I use the word "humility" not out of religious or any other kind of feeling, right? I mean the humility occasioned by the awareness of problems, the attitude toward problems. One cannot be anything but humble before the necessity of inquiry, and you can't be afraid. . . . Many people in architecture are bluffers. . . . That's why what I say here may elicit violent reactions. But I was not one of them, and I have contributed successive positive, and incontestable truths.

Desalle: Have you been discontented by many things?

Le Corbusier: Discontented, never. Me, I'm the kind of guy . . . who is used to getting punched in the nose and to punching back, too . . . .

Desalle: But you have also always had many causes for satisfaction; you have told me a little about them.

Le Corbusier: In life there are individuals who are weak, not expressive. . . . As for myself, I'm alert and acting. . . . So, when it comes to success, it happens that at this moment my name has become universally known, and I've been in good graces in recent years.

I stopped my subscription to *Argus* thirty-five years ago; I haven't got a single clipping at my house. I never read newspapers, but I know that they speak well of me now. There are others who say unkind things, of course—it doesn't matter. But I am told that those who praise me are the young now, and I now see in professional journals that my ideas are shared, in the execution of buildings that are being built in all the countries of the world . . . in America, as well as Germany, in Holland, as well as Sweden, in England, as well as France, etc. This adherence gives my ego a bit of a boost without my having to explode with conceit. Not at all. I tell myself, "Well, good, they're beginning to understand, and there are a few of us now instead of my being alone. This is better."

Desalle: Which of your works do you consider as essential? Which are dear to your heart?

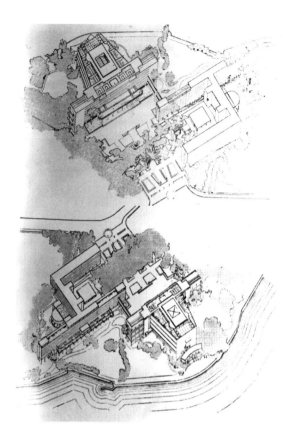

League of Nations, Competition for Geneva, 1927. Le Corbusier was awarded first prize and then disqualified. The incident triggered a worldwide controversy, and his bitterness set in.

Le Corbusier: I've told you that the La Roche house is a key, right, an open door, the beginning . . . .

Desalle: Yes, it's a starting point.

Le Corbusier: A starting point. Then there is the Garches house, which was ruined by the new owners and which used to be very beautiful. It was a palace, designed, well, with breathtaking simplicity for an

CIAM Congress working session, Barcelona, March 1932, reception at the Generalitat de Catalunya. Courtesy FLC, Paris.

Le Corbusier at CIAM meeting, Bridgwater, England, 1947. At left: Minnette de Silva, a young architect from Ceylon. She and Le Corbusier began a correspondence that continued throughout his life. After his death, de Silva wrote to his secretary: "Please give me the details. I don't understand . . . is it possible? . . . Was he alone? . . . and the secretary responded: 'Dear Miss Silva: Our Le Corbusier had a fine death. He did not suffer and he departed in full possession of his exceptional faculties. If only he could have been spared some time more for our sake and the sake of modern architecture.'" Courtesy FLC, Paris.

architect who was used to drawing cornices, capitals, and pilasters. . . . He must have sat around saying, "I thought it wasn't possible. . . ." But yes! it was possible, it was a palace, because proportion ruled absolutely there, as an absolute master.

Desalle: And your more important works?

Le Corbusier: I won first prize at the International Competition for the construction of a palace for the League of Nations in Geneva, and I received first prize, but a French delegate, not to name him . . . M. Lemaresquier, got me disqualified. . . . He said: "I demand that this project be taken out of the competition because it is drawn with printers' ink and not with India ink." And that was enough for those delegates to agree; they said, "Yes, honorable delegate from France, we agree with you to exclude Le Corbusier." That was the first time. This incident triggered a worldwide controversy. There was an incredible uproar, and as a result an international association of architects was formed called the CIAM. The CIAM became the leaders, from the point of view of technology . . . and ideas, and from a professional point of view, for ideas of the profession worldwide, for urbanism as much as for architecture. The CIAM are active everywhere: Well! that was a small victory, which gives one peace of mind at least, without remorse. I've earned the right to do without remorse.

Desalle: And this plan for Paris?

Le Corbusier: Well, my plan of Paris. I started in 1922 you see, because I adored Paris, and I saw that Paris was letting itself go. There's a bit of reaction these days and I'm partly responsible. . . . So I drew up my plan for Paris in 1922. But there were too many skyscrapers. . . so I did it over again in 1925 at the Esprit Nouveau Pavilion; where it was displayed prominently in two dioramas of a hundred square meters each. I accomplished a tour de force of juggling, you know. . . . I did a pavilion of two hundred square me-

Le Corbusier and Jawaharlal Nehru. Courtesy FLC, Paris.

Le Corbusier with the plan of Chandigarh and André Malraux, at left. Courtesy FLC, Paris.

ters in hard . . . in concrete, in 1925, at the Exposition of Decorative Arts.

Desalle: Of the Decorative Arts, yes . . . .

Le Corbusier: Well, I was shown the door; I was refused any site. In the end, there was one site left aside by the large companies. I was then in the administrative office of the exposition, they telephoned me, and told me, "M. Le Corbusier, there is a site here, take it immediately, come today." And I took some of my assistants. I told them, "Each of you bring a drawing board and a stand. All right? And we

remained on the site from nine in the morning to nightfall (it was in February). . . . What could they do to take the site from me? They weren't able to steal it. So that's where I built the Pavilion of L'Esprit Nouveau, which was an incredibly avant-garde thing for the time, fantastic! The entire cellular order of rental units was created, surprising in its appearance, without the slightest idea of luxury or anything like that.

Desalle: And I also think that, even so, that town in India that you were able to build, to create, gave you pleasure . . . .

Le Corbusier: Well, there I was given the honor and the joy of becoming the friend of Nehru, who is a great mind. He died unfortunately; however, he always supported me. I didn't have any conflicts in India. . . . They are correct in their dealings. . . . There are enemies, of course, but they're beaten from the start. I made a conclusive experiment in India and it's built now. It is a city of 150,000 people . . . which is already built, inhabited, right?. . . And it will have

500,000 when it is finished. It has been designed, and there are elements of modernism in it that are undeniable and indisputable.

Desalle: Were you able to realize your complete and integral concept?

Le Corbusier: That's it, it's contained in one city. . . . There's an administrative center where the Palace of Government is, there's the General Secretariat with four thousand employees, there's the General Assembly, there's the High Court. I built extraordinary palaces there . . . .

Desalle: Yes.

Le Corbusier: And they're there, they're up . . . and you can go to see them . . . only it's a bit far, but you can go there by bicycle. There are Frenchmen who go there by bicycle, you know.

Desalle: Yes.

Le Corbusier: I've met some who go there by bike. That's good . . . .

Desalle: So there you were able to synthesize this idea that is dear to you. You have discussed urbanism. . . . You have said, "The word is not mine." Finally this idea of construction of a whole, and not of isolated construction. . . . There you were able to carry it out, to apply it.

Le Corbusier: That is, I declared that urbanism was the science of occupying territory by human works, right?—and that there were three kinds of urbanism . . . well, there are three stages. . . . There's the radio-concentric city of exchanges; there is the city . . . there's the countryside, a unit of appropriate agrarian size; then there's the linear industrial city, where living and working conditions are coordinated, in fact ideally. It's exciting, it's wonderful, at least, for those who would kindly cast their eyes upon it and be

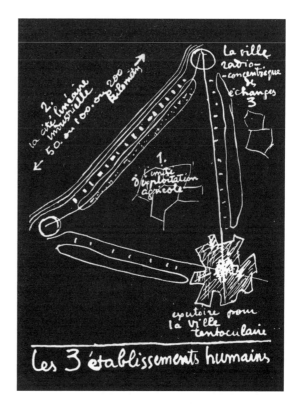

The Three Human Establishments: 1—The Agricultural Units; 2—The Linear Industrial City; 3—The Radio-concentric City of Exchanges. Courtesy FLC, Paris.

open-minded . . . instead of screaming without having seen it.

Desalle: And this hospital for Venice?

Le Corbusier: Well, the Venice hospital struck public opinion in a sensational manner, an event called "Le Corbusier in Venice," the art city par excellence that is untouchable. And to design the biggest building that city would have—it's a very big building. . . . Well, yes, I found an amazing openness there. There are

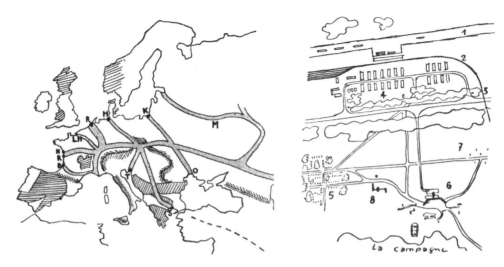

The Linear Industrial City: *left,* geographical and topological solutions to organize Europe; *right,* a fragment of the Linear Industrial City. Courtesy FLC, Paris.

minds like that, sometimes, which arise in the right places. The Venetians are very proud. There are some . . . old fossils who attack, attack it, only they remain old fogies. They are beaten from the start.

Desalle: And Le Corbusier, deep down in his heart, is he satisfied with the plan of Venice, with its construction?

Le Corbusier: Oh, yes, it's very good, of course.

Desalle: Yes?

Le Corbusier: It was very difficult, you need enormous tact, there, to say . . . Venice is a city on the lagoon. It's a city that has emerged from the water . . . .

Desalle: As a function of the water.

Le Corbusier: . . . at water level, you see, limited by the water. And to put something there, well it can't possibly be a skyscraper or anything like that. There's the

Campanile, there's Saint Mark's of Venice, there's the Ducal Palace, which are visible landmarks; well, modern Venice relates to this.

Desalle: I am going to ask you a question, M. Le Corbusier. Do you feel that you have disciples today?

Le Corbusier: Yes, well it's more than that, it's an army, see, worldwide, see. . . . As a matter of fact, in my office, I have my office boy, I have my secretary, and I have my telephone operator, who set up a screen to prevent people from reaching me. Every day I have visitors who come for "père Corbu" . . . but we don't let them in, because I want to work. Oh, no! really, the whole world wants in. They make gestures of support in the form of writings of all kinds, of studies, of books, finally. As long as I feel the need to be pleasantly tickled, I will be.

Desalle: So "père Corbu," as you say—excuse me for using your expression—is a creator. Since the begin-

Venice Hospital sketches and studies by Le Corbusier.
Courtesy FLC, Paris.

ning he has created, he has built, and then he has engendered, in other words, he has given himself a line of succession solely through his thought, through his works.

Le Corbusier: You express yourself very nicely, that's very pretty; that's nice, I have children.

Desalle: That's it, exactly.

Le Corbusier: Well, yes! there are children. And it's natural that there be a father somewhere—well, it so happens that it's me. I shall soon disappear into the celestial zones. Oh, well! I will leave them alone.

Desalle: But your work will continue . . . .

Le Corbusier: Yes, but from time to time they'll have a few kind words for me.

Desalle: So, you were telling me earlier that you love Paris very much.

Le Corbusier: Yes, all right.

Desalle: On the subject of Paris, I would like to ask you two things. First, what are the monuments, or the constructions, or the buildings, call them what you will, which move you in particular?

Le Corbusier: It is not that. What moves me about Paris is the atmosphere of Paris. And it's undefinable, you can't put your finger on it, Paris is good in itself. Partly it's because Paris is the center of France, partly because it's the center of Europe, it's a geographical situation, so to speak . . . .

Desalle: Extraordinary, yes.

Le Corbusier: . . . extremely meaningful. It is the destiny of the city, which has continued to this day . . . .

Desalle: Its destiny . . . .

Le Corbusier: Well, yes, it hasn't changed. It's because Paris has never ceased creating, and while speaking to you here for the past hour, I've had the Eiffel Tower in front of my eyes, through my window—I see the Eiffel Tower over there. . . . Well, Eiffel was abused when it was built, and now the Eiffel Tower makes a fortune, it forms a part of the Paris skyline.

Desalle: And Le Corbusier, does he find it beautiful? . . .

Le Corbusier: Oh, yes. It plays both a significant and emotional role at the same time.

Desalle: Are there other monuments in Paris that inspire the same feelings in you?

Le Corbusier: Oh, no, not the same feelings, but excellent feelings. Paris is a magnificent city. There are a lot of things. But what I like about Paris is all of it, it's the people, it's the spirit of Paris. You used to meet little Parisian types. You don't see them anymore. Before, you couldn't walk the streets without encountering them, you see. But there still exists a

Le Corbusier presenting the model of the Venice Hospital: "The Home of Man," 1965. To his right, Jullian de la Fuente, his collaborator on the hospital. Courtesy FLC, Paris.

spirit about Paris that is different from that of other cities. And when you return to Paris after a trip, you come home, you see. Whereas, when you go to another city, you say, "It's not bad," "It's very good," "It's ugly"—it depends. But Paris is Paris. What is good about Paris is that it has the straight line. Even the Beaux-Arts, which often design flourishes, kept

itself to a straight line. It's curious. It's a characteristic of Paris, the straight line, while other countries do Baroque easily, isn't that true?

Desalle: Exactly. And now, you know, they're planning to build "satellite cities," as they're called, all around Paris. What do you think of that?

Le Corbusier: I have no idea. I'm not aware of it, and haven't been informed.

Desalle: So, you don't think anything about it.

Le Corbusier: No, I'm not aware of this problem, and I don't agree, I don't agree theoretically, because I am not well informed in these matters. But I've published a book called *Les trois établissements humains,* which include a unit of agricultural exploitation, the radioconcentric city of exchanges, and the linear-industrial city. These are the three conditions of human labor. And so you see, a radioconcentric city is an eye or a sort of center. You can't make a periphery out of a center.

Desalle: That's right.

Le Corbusier: That's the great disaster of Paris, to go any old way, anywhere, and without theory.

Desalle: Without the overall plan, yes!

Le Corbusier: I am going to give you a totally picturesque detail. For the past fifty years, I've been working on these ideas, I've made a lot of plans for Paris. I was never asked about them, not a single word, not a single word by the authorities. They must consider me a terrible, a horrible person.

Desalle: You tell me Paris is unique. Paris is a geometric, an artistic place, it's a miracle, lastly, it's a determined place, which is true . . . .

Le Corbusier: Yes, yes, yes, yes . . . .

Desalle: Personally, I believe this, too.

Le Corbusier: Predetermined.

Desalle: Predetermined, that's it exactly, we don't know why, because it's there—a number of factors that intervene.

"This is Paris!" "Academism says: No!" Courtesy FLC, Paris.

Le Corbusier: Yes. There's the Seine—the heart of France—the French hexagon.

Desalle: That's right, that's right.

Le Corbusier: The three bodies of water, right, the Manche Channel, the ocean, the Mediterranean. . . . You have a country, all of France is admirably drawn by geography, by destiny . . . .

Desalle: These satellite cities they want to build around Paris, you've worked on them, you said earlier, for many years; do you think they are good or bad?

Le Corbusier: Me, I say it's a confusion. Why satellites? Why make centers next to other centers?. . . There is either competition or there is dependence, weakness. No . . . no . . . I'll tell you, I don't give a damn. That's not how you study such a serious problem; it's very difficult . . . . It should be a subject of conversation— isn't that right?—of friendly discussion among people somewhat familiar with the question, in other words, the men and their needs, their temperaments, their shortcomings, their qualities, and who know the fatalities of built-up areas, of grouping, its restrictions, and its wealth, too. . . . One must work with men and the environment.

Desalle: That is, if I understand you correctly, this decision to create satellite cities is because they're afraid of Paris becoming too big . . . .

Le Corbusier: Well, they're making it into an enormous machine now. On the contrary, the disaster of present-day cities is the little bits of suburbs and one-story houses . . . .

Desalle: That's right.

Le Corbusier: Look, I travel by plane all the time, I see it every time I approach Paris, and it's not good to see . . . .

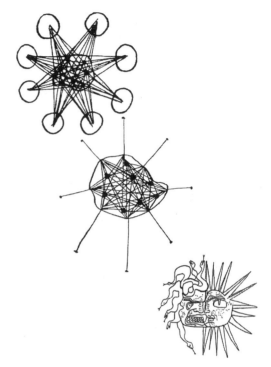

"Satellite cities: a waste and circulation hell."
"Contemporary disaster or complete spatial freedom."
Courtesy FLC, Paris.

Desalle: Exactly.

Le Corbusier: You see, one must define many other general factors of modern society. It comes down to defining modern society, to seeing what its needs are, the riches that are offered by rapid transport, etc. There are a lot of problems that come into play, only you always find yourself in front of people who say, "I beg your pardon, the styles, the schools, etc. . . . we were taught that . . . ."

Desalle: M. Le Corbusier, if today, in 1965, there were another little twenty-year-old Corbusier, an eighteen-year-old like you were when you began, what would you tell him in 1965? What architectural legacy would you bequeath him?

Le Corbusier: "Go ahead," I would tell him, "Go ahead, kid; you'll get plenty of kicks in the butt to tell you that you're doing well. Go to it, go to it, it's the fate of every man to do not what he . . . but not to succeed, that's one of the most awful words of modern times—most think that to succeed means money in your pocket, whereas to succeed really means to do something.

Desalle: Can a young architect of today be another Corbusier? That is, are the problems he will run up against very different from those you have known?

Le Corbusier: A lot will have been done. A lot will have been done. . . . We were the guys who got kicked in the butt, in the nose, in the back, in the head, wherever. Well, that's something that's done. And a lot of work has already been done. I'm sure that the two generations from now in fifty years will have arrived at something wonderful.

Desalle: So there will finally be poetry in architecture?

Le Corbusier: Oh, yes, there surely will be. If it's not there, it will be in the hearts of men or in their desires. . . . And then they'll always be chewing each other out, because there are some who make money on their ideas . . . so they always want to make money; there are others who put vanity into their ideas—they'll always put in vanity; and there are people who are socially minded, and will try to talk together. . . . Only it's difficult, it takes time: these problems require a long evolution. You know you can't flip them over like you flip a crêpe.All the tasks facing modern society call to those who want to give themselves to something and for something. They'll be called "nuts" by some of their friends; they'll be called friends of society by others. They'll be respected later . . . never . . . maybe . . . who cares? One doesn't work to be praised, one works out of duty to one's conscience. That's the key to all human actions—conscience—which is inseparable from all humans and which is there to tell them whether they act rightly or wrongly . . . .

Le Corbusier as Author, Artist, Architect

A Chronology

1887: Born Charles-Edouard Jeanneret on 6 October, 38 rue de la Serre, La Chaux-de-Fonds, in the Jura Mountains of Switzerland. His mother is Marie-Charlotte-Amélie Jeanneret-Perret, a musician and piano teacher. His father is Georges-Edouard Jeanneret, a watchmaker and clock-dial painter. He has one older brother, Albert (1885–1973), later a musician.

1900: At thirteen, apprenticed to local craftsmen in watchcase engraving. Enters local Ecole d'Art (1900–1904). Influenced by Beaux-Arts–trained Charles L'Eplattenier, who stresses study of nature.

1902: At fifteen, decorates watchcase and wins Diplôme d'Honneur, International Exhibition of Decorative Arts, Turin.

1905: Recommended by L'Eplattenier to design a house in La Chaux-de-Fonds for a school trustee: *Villa Fallet* (completed, 1907).

1907: Travels to Italy; visits for the first time Florence, Siena, Ravenna, Ferrara, Bologna, Venice, and the Carthusian monastery of Ema at Galluzzo, near Florence, among other places; then travels to Budapest and Vienna. Works for Josef Hoffmann.

1908: Travels to Munich, Strasbourg, and Nancy. Builds two houses in La Chaux-de-Fonds: *Villa Stotzer* and *Villa Jacquemet*. Visits Paris for first time; works for Perret Brothers for eighteen months. Meets Tony Garnier in Lyons.

1909: Leaves Paris residence, 3 quai Saint-Michel, and returns to La Chaux-de-Fonds.

1910: Travels to Germany (Munich, Berlin, and other cities) to study arts and crafts (thesis published, 1912). Works in office of Peter Behrens, Berlin. Retires to mountains to study technical books on reinforced concrete. Designs *School of Applied Art,* La Chaux-de-Fonds.

1911: Meets Ludwig Mies Van der Rohe in Behrens's office. Leaves Germany and travels for six months with friend Auguste Klipstein: the journey to the

Left: Family portrait, December 1889. Charles-Edouard Jeanneret is seated on the pedestal, his brother, Albert, below him, with their parents, Georges-Edouard and Marie-Charlotte-Amélie. Courtesy FLC, Paris.

East. Visits, among other places, Prague, Vienna, Budapest, Belgrade, Bucharest, Turnovo, Adrianople, Istanbul, Mount Athos, Athens, Naples, Pompeii, Rome, and Florence. Returns to Carthusian monastery of Ema to sketch it. His travel writings are serialized in the La Chaux-de-Fonds newspaper and later incorporated into his first book, *Le Voyage d'Orient* (published posthumously, 1966).

1912: Builds *Villa Jeanneret-Perret* for his parents, La Chaux-de-Fonds. Builds *Villa Favre-Jacot,* Le Locle. Teaches decorative composition as applied to architecture, La Chaux-de-Fonds. Publishes *Etude sur le mouvement d'art décoratif en Allemagne.*

1913: First exhibition in Paris at Salon d'Automne (thirteen watercolors from his journeys to Italy and the East, known as "Langage de Pierre").

1914: Studies *Les maisons dom-ino* (project), a reinforced concrete skeleton structure for mass production, with Max Dubois.

1915: Leaves La Chaux-de-Fonds for Paris to study at Bibliothèque Nationale; continues research for *La Construction des villes* (begun, 1910; published posthumously, 1992).

1916: Builds *Villa Schwob,* La Chaux-de-Fonds (completed, 1917). Redesigns Cinema *La Scala,* La Chaux-de-Fonds.

1917: Le Corbusier is thirty. Leaves Switzerland definitively and settles in Paris, 20 rue Jacob, Latin Quarter. Works as consultant to La Société d'Application de Béton Armé. Introduced by Max Dubois to Swiss society in Paris. Meets Amédée Ozenfant.

1918: Publishes *Après le cubisme* (with Ozenfant). Paints his first painting: *La Cheminée;* beginning of his Purist period. Exhibits at Galerie Thomas, Paris (two paintings). Introduced to Raoul La Roche, a Swiss banker from Basel, who later regularly buys his paintings, along with Pablo Picasso's, Georges Braque's, and Fernand Léger's. Temporarily loses sight in left eye because of a detached retina.

1919: Works as a businessman (develops a construction system known as "Maisons Monol"). Paints in Ozenfant's studio, 32 rue Godot-de-Mauroy (1919–25). Founds the journal *L'Esprit nouveau* with poet Paul Dermée and Ozenfant.

1920: First issue of *L'Esprit nouveau,* October (28 issues through 1925). Meets Léger. Plans *Maison "Citrohan,"* first study for a mass-produced house. Chooses *nom de plume* Le Corbusier (LC) to sign his first article for *L'Esprit nouveau.*

1921: Lectures in Prague, Geneva, and Lausanne. Exhibits at Galerie Druet, Paris.

1922: At age thirty-five, sets up professional practice with cousin Pierre Jeanneret, 35 rue de Sèvres, Paris. Completes second study for *Maison "Citrohan."* Builds *Besnus house,* Vaucresson. Designs *"Contemporary City for Three Million Inhabitants,"* presented at Salon d'Automne, Paris. Designs and builds *Maison and Atelier Ozenfant,* Paris.

1923: Publishes *Vers une architecture* (Towards a new architecture) from articles published in *L'Esprit nouveau.* The book reaches a wide audience and is translated into English, German, Spanish, Russian, Italian, and Japanese. Builds *Maison La Roche-Jeanneret,* Paris (1923–24). Paints simple, everyday objects (bottles, glasses). Devotes mornings to painting, afternoons to architecture. Exhibits at Léonce Rosenberg, Galerie de l'Effort Moderne, Paris.

1924: Builds *Maison Lipchitz-Miestschaninoff,* Boulogne-sur-Seine, a combination of studios and residences around a communal garden.

1925: Publishes *La Peinture moderne* (with Ozenfant); *L'Art décoratif d'aujourd' hui* (Decorative art of today); and *Urbanisme* (The city of tomorrow). Lectures in Brussels and Paris. Breaks with Ozenfant; *L'Esprit nouveau* ceases publication. Builds *Petite Villa au Bord du Lac Léman,* a minuscule house of sixty square meters for his mother. Builds *L'Esprit Nouveau Pavilion* at the *International Exhibition of Decorative Arts,* Paris. Builds *Ternisien House,* Boulogne-sur-Seine. Builds housing complex *Cité Frugès,* Pessac, near Bordeaux, for industrialist Henri Frugès using the latest techniques in reinforced concrete, prefabrication, and standardization. Proposes a "Plan for Paris" (*Plan voisin*), exhibited at *L'Esprit Nouveau Pavilion*, with suggestion to rebuild the Right Bank of Paris East-West and North of the Louvre, destroying everything but historic buildings.

1926: Publishes *Almanach d'architecture moderne.* "Architecture d'époque machiniste sur les écoles cubistes et post-cubistes" appears in the *Journal de psychologie normale et pathologique.* Builds *Maison Cook,* Boulogne-sur-Seine, for American journalist William Cook, incorporating for the first time the canonical Five Points of a New Architecture: pilotis (column or pile that lifts a building off the ground), roof garden, free plan, ribbon windows, and free facade. Builds *Maison Guiette,* Antwerp. Purist period in painting ends; LC introduces human figure into his paintings. Father, Georges-Edouard Jeanneret, dies 11 April.

1927: LC is forty. Builds *Villa Stein* (Les Terrasses), Garches, near Paris, for two families: Gertrude Stein's brother, Michael, and his wife, Sarah, both art collectors, and Gabrielle de Monzie, former wife of the minister of construction Anatole de Monzie. Builds *Maison Planeix,* Paris, for a sculptor of funerary monuments. Builds two houses at *Weissenhofsiedlung* near Stuttgart, Germany. Submits design for League of Nations Competition, Geneva; wins first prize but is disqualified for failing to use proper ink; first major professional disappointment and lifelong source of bitterness. Meets Charlotte Perriand and collaborates with her on furniture design. Lectures in Madrid, Barcelona, Frankfurt, and Brussels.

1928: Publishes *Une maison—un palais* (history of architecture and urban planning with emphasis on the failed design for the League of Nations of 1927). Builds *Nestlé Pavilion,* a steel exhibition pavilion that can be disassembled and re-erected. Creates minimum car design with Pierre Jeanneret (with maximum passenger comfort). Co-founds CIAM (Congrès Internationaux d'Architecture Moderne); prepares program for meeting, Château de la Sarraz, Switzerland (annual congresses continue in various countries until 1959). Lectures in Prague and Moscow.

1929: First volume of *Oeuvre complète* published by Willy Boesiger. Builds *Villa Savoye,* Poissy, (1929–31), his best-known building, last Purist villa, and cleanest rendition of his Five Points. Builds *Villa Baizeau,* Carthage. Restoration of *Villa Church* at *Ville d'Avray* (villa in a classic style) and adds annex (with Pierre Jeanneret, 1928–29, torn down in 1965). Renovation and adaptation of floating barge into Salvation Army shelter for the homeless. Lectures in Buenos Aires (ten), Montevideo (two), Rio de Janeiro (two), São Paolo (two), Paris, Bordeaux, and Moscow. Meets Josephine Baker while traveling to South America on the *Giulio Cesare.*

1930: Becomes a French citizen; formally adopts name Le Corbusier. Marries Yvonne Gallis, 18 December, Paris. Builds *Apartment for Charles de Beistegui,* 136 avenue des Champs-Elysées (1930–31). Publishes *Précisions sur un état présent de l'architecture et de l'urbanisme* (Precisions on the present state of architecture and city planning).

1930–33: Regular contributor to journal *Plans.* Contributes to the *Cercle et Carré* group. Designs *Maison Errazuris,* Chile (unbuilt but copied in 1933 in Japan). Visits USSR.

1931: Builds *Villa for Madame de Mandrot,* near Toulon. Designs *Palace of the Soviets Competition* (project). Plans Contemporary Art Museum, Paris (project). Begins town planning studies, Algiers (presents Plan "A"). Lectures in Algiers. Visits Spain and Morocco.

1932: Publishes *Croisade ou le crépuscule des académies.* Builds *Swiss Pavilion at Cité Universitaire,* Paris. Awarded commission by Federation of Swiss Universities, which some see as compensation for the League of Nations fiasco. Builds *Immeuble Clarté,* Geneva, apartment building, forty-five duplex units with completely glazed facade. Creates plan for Geneva's Right Bank, applying theories of the Radiant City, and master plan for Barcelona ("Macia" Plan). Exhibits plans for Paris at Deutsche Bauanstellung, Berlin. Lectures in Rotterdam, Amsterdam, Delft, and Zurich. Attends CIAM Congress, Barcelona.

1933: Contributes regularly to journal *Prélude* (1933–35). Builds apartment house, "Immeuble Molitor," with his apartment and studio at the top, Paris (moves in, 1934). Builds *Salvation Army Hostel,* Paris, his first curtain wall and air-conditioned building. Builds *Centrosoyuz* (Central Statistical Administration), Moscow. Creates town planning studies for Algiers (presents Project "B"). Designs town plans for Antwerp and Stockholm. Exhibits at John Becker Gallery, New York. Lectures in Stockholm, Oslo, and Gothenburg. Receives honorary degree, University of Zurich. Attends CIAM Congress, Athens; principles discussed are later published as *La Charte d'Athènes* (The Athens charter, 1943).

1934: Creates town planning studies for Algiers, (presents Project "C"). Lectures in Rome, Milan, Algiers, Barcelona, and Athens.

1935: Publishes *La Ville radieuse* (The radiant city) and *Aircraft.* Visits USA for exhibition at Museum of Modern Art, New York, and nationwide lecture tour; returns to France in 1936. Designs "Radiant City," calling for liberation of 88 percent of land and building surface of only 12 percent, with separation of pedestrian and automobile and construction of apartment blocks containing 2,700 inhabitants each. Builds *Maison de Week-end, La Celle-Saint-Cloud,* twelve miles from Paris. Returns to a more primitive, "cave-like shelter." Builds *Maison aux Mathes,* La Palmyre, a rural vernacular dwelling of fieldstone and timber framing.

1936: Travels (second trip) to South America by zeppelin from Frankfurt to Rio de Janeiro. Consultant for University City of Brazil and Ministry of Health and Education building, Rio de Janeiro. Lectures in Paris, Rome, Zurich, and Rio de Janeiro (six).

1937: LC is fifty. Publishes *Quand les cathédrales étaient blanches: Voyage au pays des timides* (When the cathedrals were white). Builds *Temps Nouveau Pavilion,* International Exhibition of Architecture and Urbanism, Porte Maillot, Paris. Lectures in Brussels and Lyons. Seriously ill for five months.

1938: Publishes *Des canons, des munitions? Merci! des logis . . . S.V.P.* Project: Skyscraper for Algiers, Cartesian skyscraper and cooperative village. Exhibits paintings, 1918–38 at Kunsthaus, Zurich; at exhibit entitled "Ideal Home," London (his theme is Radiant City: Sun, Space, Greenery); and at group exhibition of paintings, Galerie Balai, Paris.

1939: Begins WWII sojourn at Vézelay. Publishes *Le Lyrisme des temps nouveaux et l'urbanisme.* Plans Museum for Unlimited Growth. Submits design for monument to "Vaillant Couturier" competition. Designs museum for Philippeville. Paints murals for house of Jean Badovici and Eileen Gray, Cap-Martin. Exhibits at Galerie Louis Carré, Paris.

Nominated member of Royal Academy of Beaux-Arts, Stockholm.

1940: Germans occupy Paris in June. LC and Pierre Jeanneret close the atelier, 35 rue de Sèvres. LC leaves Paris for the Ozon, Pyrenees, where he is instructed to be ready for planning and architectural work. Earns living largely from his gouaches. Works on *School for Refugees from the War,* with Jean Prouvé (1939–40), and *Les Maisons Murondins* (temporary housing for war refugees). Commissioned by minister of armaments to build a cartridge factory, the *Moutiers-Rozeille,* near Aubusson (green factory type).

1941: Publishes *Destin de Paris* and *Sur les quatre routes.* Sojourn at Vichy. On 27 May, Marshal Pétain charges LC with a temporary mission to serve the government as part of the "Comité d'étude de l'habitation et de la construction immobilière"; the director refuses to accept LC as a collaborator. Begins studies on the *Modulor.* Visits Algiers.

1942: Publishes *La Maison des hommes* (The home of man) with François de Pierrefeu. Town planning studies for Algiers are unanimously rejected by municipal council, 12 June (representing thirteen years of experimenting).

1943: Publishes *La Charte d'Athènes* (The Athens charter) and *Entretien avec les étudiants des écoles d'architecture* (Le Corbusier talks with students). Co-founds ASCORAL (Association des Constructeurs pour une Rénovation Architecturale); presides over twenty-two committees a month for a year.

1944: Paris is liberated in August. LC returns to Paris, reopens the atelier, 35 rue de Sèvres. Period of intense activity in architecture and planning begins. Meets Claudius Petit.

1945: Publishes *Les Trois Etablissements humains* (The three human establishments). First study for *l'Unité*

d'Habitation, Marseilles. Plan for *Saint-Dié* (1946–51), city of twenty thousand destroyed by German army (unbuilt). Plan for *La Rochelle-Pallice,* town saved from destruction (unbuilt). Plan for *Saint-Gaudens.* Collaborates with Joseph Savina, carpenter from Bretagne, who makes sculptures from LC's paintings. Visits United States via cargo ship *Vernon S. Hood.* Exhibits paintings at Radio City Music Hall, New York, and Walker Art Center, Minneapolis.

1946: Publishes *Propos d'urbanisme* and *Manière de penser l'urbanisme* (Looking at city planning). Works on *United Nations Headquarters,* New York (1946–47); invited as official French representative. His controversial project, known as 23A, is later built with modifications by Wallace Harrison. Meets Albert Einstein in Princeton; travels across United States. Exhibits at Stedelijk Museum, Amsterdam, and Kunsthaus, Zurich. Nominated officer of Legion of Honor.

1947: LC is sixty. Publishes *U. N. Headquarters* and *Plan director para Buenos Aires.* Construction of *l'Unité d'Habitation* begins, Marseilles. Town planning studies for Marseilles and for Izmir, Turkey. Paints mural the atelier, 35 rue de Sèvres. Begins first wood sculptures with Joseph Savina. Exhibits in Vienna; attends CIAM Congress, Bridgwater, England. Lectures in New York, Bogota, and Paris.

1948: Publishes *New World of Space.* Designs *La Sainte Baume,* underground cathedral (rejected). Collaborates with Pierre Baudouin for tapestries at Aubusson. Paints a large mural for the Swiss Pavilion, Cité Universitaire, Paris. Exhibits at Paul Rosenberg Gallery, New York, and Boston Institute of Contemporary Art (synthesis of architecture and the "major arts"). Lectures in Paris and Milan.

1949: Publishes *Le modulor 1.* Builds *House for Dr. Currutchet,* La Plata, Argentina. Designs city plan for Bogota. Builds *"Roq" et "Rob,"* modular vacation houses, for Cap-Martin. Lectures at CIAM Congress, Bergamo.

1950: Publishes *Poésie sur Alger; L'Unité d'habitation de Marseille* in journal *Le Point*. Builds *Duval Factory,* Saint Dié (completed, 1951). Begins project, *Chapel of Ronchamp,* Vosges. Designs *House for Professor Fueter,* Lake Constance, Switzerland. Approached by government of Punjab, India, to undertake construction of new capital at *Chandigarh* (team includes Maxwell Fry, Jane Drew, and Pierre Jeanneret). Travels to United States in August. Exhibits at Porte Maillot, Paris ("Synthesis of the Major Arts" [project]), and at Paul Rosenberg Gallery, New York.

1951: Town planning study for Marseilles. Designs two Unités d'Habitation for Strasbourg. Makes master plan for Chandigarh (completed, 1985); begins plans for *Monument of the Open Hand* (completed, 1985). Appointed member, selection board for UNESCO Building, Paris. Travels to India (second visit) and United States (third visit), where he visits sculptor Costantino Nivola on Long Island and executes mural paintings and sand sculptures. Exhibits at the Museum of Modern Art, New York.

1952: Inaugurates *l'Unité d'Habitation,* Marseilles. Builds for himself and his wife *Le Petit Cabanon,* Roquebrune, Cap-Martin, a small timbered vacation cabin measuring 3.66 × 3.66 × 2.26 meters high. Commissioned to build *l'Unité d'Habitation,* Nantes-Rezé. Exhibits at Gallery Paul Rosenberg, New York; at Galerie Denise René, Paris; and in a show that tours to Belgrade, Skopje, Sarajevo, Split, Zagreb, and Ljubljana.

1953: Commissioned to build *Monastery of Sainte Marie de la Tourette*. Begins work on *l'Unité d'Habitation at Nantes-Rezé*. Awarded Royal Institute of British Architects Gold Medal. Exhibits at Musée National d'Art Moderne, Paris (thirty years of painting); Institute of Contemporary Art, London (paintings, drawings, sculptures, tapestries); and Galerie Denise René, Paris (seven tapestries). Participates in CIAM Congress, Aix-en-Provence.

1954: Publishes *Une Petite Maison*. Builds and inaugurates *Millowners' Building,* Ahmedabad, India. Exhibits at Kunsthalle, Bern (art), and Villa dell'Ormo, Como, Italy (art and architecture).

1955: Publishes *Le Modulor 2; Le Poème de l'angle droit; L'Architecture du bonheur;* and *L'Urbanisme est une clef*. Builds *Museum of Knowledge,* Chandigarh; *Maison Sarabhai,* Ahmedabad, India; and *Palace of Justice* (High Court), Chandigarh. Inaugurates and paints enameled door of Chapel of *Notre Dame du Haut,* Ronchamp. Installs wooden model, *Open Hand Monument,* Chandigarh. Receives honorary doctorate, Swiss Federal Institute of Technology. Visits Japan. Lectures in Berlin. Exhibits at Musée d'Art et Industrie, Saint-Etienne, and Takashimaya, Japan.

1956: Publishes *Les Plans de Paris, 1956–1922*. Builds *Maison Jaoul,* Paris. Completes *Villa Shodhan,* Ahmedabad. Plans Baghdad stadium to accommodate 55,000, with gymnasium for 6,000 and swimming pool for 4,000. Begins design for the National Museum of Western Art, Toyko. Refuses membership, Ecole des Beaux-Arts, offered by Institut Français. Lectures in India and Baghdad. Attends final CIAM Congress, Dubrovnik. Exhibits at Pierre Matisse Gallery, New York (paintings); Galerie La Demeure, Paris (drawings); and Musée des Beaux-Arts, Lyons (painting, sculpture, architecture, city planning).

1957: LC is seventy. Wife, Yvonne, dies on 5 October. Publishes *Chapelle Notre Dame du Haut à Ronchamp* (The chapel at Ronchamp). Completes *l'Unité d'Habitation,* Nantes-Rezé, and *Maisons Jaoul,* Neuilly-sur-Seine. Begins work on *Philips Pavilion for Brussels International Exhibition,* with Edgar Varèse and Iannis

Xenakis; prepares spectacle entitled "Poème Electronique" for pavilion. Exhibits at Dublin Building Center; Palazzo della Permanente, Milan; Haus der Kunst, Munich; Akademie der Kunste, Berlin; and Künsthaus, Zurich (retrospective exhibit). First exhibition in La Chaux-de-Fonds, at Musée des Beaux Arts (tapestries). Made honorary citizen of La Chaux-de-Fonds.

1958: Builds tomb for Yvonne and himself at Roquebrune, Cap-Martin. Publishes *Le Poème électronique*. Completes *Philips Pavilion*. Inaugurates *Secretariat Building*, Chandigarh. Plans *l'Unité d'Habitation*, Berlin-Charlottenburg (changes made; LC disowns the building). Visits United States to inspect site for *Carpenter Center for the Visual Arts*, Harvard University. Exhibits at Wilhelm Museum, Krefeld, Germany; Municipal Museum, The Hague; Moderne Museet, Stockholm; and Kunstindustrimuseet, Copenhagen.

1959: Builds *National Museum of Western Art*, Tokyo. Completes *Brazilian Pavilion*, Cité Universitaire, Paris (with Lucio Costa). Exhibits at Musée National d'Art Moderne and Galerie Denise René, Paris; Institute of Contemporary Arts, London; and Galleria Nazionale di Arte Moderna, Rome. Receives honorary degree, University of Cambridge Law School.

1960: Mother, Marie Charlotte-Amélie Jeanneret-Perret, dies at age one hundred. Publishes *L'Atelier de la recherche patiente* (Creation is a patient search), and *Un Couvent de Le Corbusier*. Builds and inaugurates Dominican monastery of *Sainte Marie de la Tourette*, near Eveux-sur-l'Arbresle. Plans *Church of Saint Pierre*, Firminy-Vert, and *Unités d'Habitations*, Meaux (unbuilt). Exhibits at Galerie La Demeure, Paris, and in show that tours to Toronto, Calgary, Vancouver, San Francisco, and Tokyo.

1961: Featured on cover of *Time*, 5 May. Awarded Gold Medal, American Institute of Architects, and

Doctor of Humane Letters, Columbia University. Builds *Assembly Building* (Parliament), Chandigarh. Builds *l'Unité d'Habitation*, Briey-en-Forêt. Plans *Carpenter Center for the Visual Arts*, Harvard University (associate architect in the United States is José-Luis Sert). Plans *Maison des Jeunes et de la Culture, l'Unité d'Habitation*, Firminy-Vert. Project *Hôtel d'Orsay*, Paris. Exhibits at Frederiksberg Radhus, Stockholm, and Galerie Mezzanin Heidi Weber, Zurich.

1962: Builds *Ecluse de Kembs-Niffer*, customs house and watchtower on branch of the Rhone-Rhine Canal. Plans *Olivetti Electronic Center*, Rho-Milan. Designs first studies for *La Maison de l'Homme*, Zurich, and *Exhibition Center*, Stockholm. Visits Rio de Janeiro to inspect site for new French embassy. Exhibits at Galerie Mezzanin Heidi Weber, Zurich, and Musée National d'Art Moderne, Paris (retrospective).

1963: Builds and inaugurates *Carpenter Center for the Visual Arts*, Harvard University. Construction begins, *l'Unité d'Habitation*, Firminy-Vert (completed, 1968). Designs *International Center*, Erlenbach-Frankfurt. Paints enamel door for Assembly Building, Chandigarh (with Jean Petit). Awarded Gold Medal, City of Florence. Promoted to Grand Officier de la Légion d'Honneur (highest honor of the French government). Exhibits at Palazzo Strozzi, Florence; Château de Rohan, Strasbourg; and Galerie Mezzanin Heidi Weber, Zurich.

1964: Builds *Museum and Gallery*, Chandigarh (completed, 1968). Builds *Yacht Club*, Chandigarh. Inaugurates *Palace of the Assembly*, Chandigarh. Designs *French Embassy*, Brasilia (1964–65), and *Palace of Congresses*, Strasbourg (both unbuilt). Receives honorary degree, University of Geneva. Exhibits at Galerie Mezzanin Heidi Weber, Zurich, and La Chaux-de-Fonds ("From Leopold Robert to Le Corbusier").

1965: Publishes *Textes et dessins pour Ronchamp*. Builds *Youth and Culture Center*, Firminy-Vert (1965–69); *College of Art and College of Architecture, Punjab University*, Chandigarh. Designs *Hospital for Venice* and *Museum of the Twentieth Century*, La Défense, Paris (both unbuilt). Dies while swimming off Cap-Martin, around 11:20 A.M. on 27 August.

1966: Publication of *Le Voyage d'Orient* (text of 1911 and 1914) and *Mise au point* (text of 1961 and 1965). Seventh of eight volumes published of *Oeuvre complète*, 1957–65 (most of text written by LC).

1967: Inauguration of *La Maison de l'Homme,* Zurich (Centre Le Corbusier, Heidi Weber).

1968: Creation of *Fondation Le Corbusier,* according to wishes of LC, located at twin houses La Roche-Jeanneret, 8–10 square du Docteur Blanche, Paris.

1985: Completion of *Open Hand Monument,* Chandigarh.

1987: Completion of *Tower of Shadow,* Chandigarh.

Appendix

The Original Text of **Mise au point**

Le texte de ce petit livre a été écrit par Le Corbusier en juillet 1965. On peut sans doute, maintenant que Le Corbusier n'est plus parmi nous, y trouver certaines résonances, y attacher certaines significations. Il ne faudrait toutefois pas se méprendre. Ce texte est un texte de lutte, une suite de constatations et de pensées dictées par l'expérience. Il convient donc de le lire, comme si Corbu était encore parmi nous, et il l'est. *[7]*

Rien n'est transmissible que la pensée. Au cours des ans, l'homme acquiert petit à petit par ses luttes, son travail, ses efforts sur lui-même, un certain capital, conquête individuelle et personnelle. Mais toute la recherche passionnée de l'individu, tout ce capital, cette expérience durement payés disparaîtront. Loi de la vie: la mort. La nature clôt toute activité par la mort. Seule la pensée, fruit du travail, est transmissible. Les jours s'écoulent, au courant des jours, au cours de la vie . . .

Tout n'est qu'accords, rapports, présences. Et aussi synthèse foudroyante, déclenchement, déclic, éclair pour la vision, l'intervention, la catalyse. Raison d'être: impassible permanent, au milieu, par de-là, au-desssus, au-dessous des événements, des éléments à travers tout.

Il y a les présences: l'éternel du permanent. Ceux de la science qui disent arriver à la connaissance! mais quelle justification, quelle explication fournir à l'existence des coquillages, des lézards, des chiens (types bien), et autres éléphants, des *[8–9]* hommes et des femmes . . . Ceux qui dissèquent mais ne voient pas; la connaissance par la raison, par l'intervention. Coexistence: le contexte, le fluide qui passe. L'Unité employée par un acte personnel, humain: compréhension. Illumination. Entre le pourquoi et le comment: l'échelonnement, la gamme des esprits.

Observez! Où sont les observateurs? Savoir que les fourmis ont un radar, d'accord. Mais savoir pourquoi elles existent et pourquoi elles ont de tels lots. La vie tisse sa trame, ne revient jamais en arrière . . .

Dès ma jeunesse j'ai eu le sec contact avec le poids des choses. La lourdeur des matériaux et la résistance des matériaux. Puis les hommes: les qualités diverses des hommes et la résistance des hommes et la résistance aux hommes. Ma vie fut de vivre en leur compagnie. Et de proposer au poids des matériaux des solutions téméraires . . . mais ça a tenu! Et de savoir que les hommes sont tels ou tels. De m'en étonner parfois et encore aujourd'hui d'en être stupéfié parfois. Mais de le *[10]* reconnaitre, de l'admettre, l'ayant vu, le voyant . . . Et de jouer mon humble partie à travers les vents et les soleils. Et de n'avoir jamais été amer, si ce n'est de l'avoir paru tel parfois devant . . . les journalistes et surtout devant leurs photographes qui, par leur à peu près, leur moyen esprit, exigent de vous (et y arrivent) votre propre mascarade, par leurs erreurs multipliées, étourderies, légèretés, conformisme, etc . . . . Et ça rime avec journalisme cette forme d'activité basée sur le jour le jour (son nom l'indique) et cette notion: tout ça n'est que pour un jour.

"Il faut de nouveau creuser dans la vie afin de refaire de la chair."

Ce n'est pas moi qui prononce ces propos éternels, mais Henri Miller, et cependant, il me semble les avoir déjà pensés. A nouveau creuser dans la vie . . . refuser la guerre, abondance sur toute la terre . . . métamorphose par équipement: machines et esprits pour les jaunes, les noirs et les blancs. Alors ce sera le réveil général des civilisations. Alors mort de Wall Street, et nourritures terrestres *[11]* conquises. Il reste à plonger dans l'humain-divin: assez pour retrouver le grand fait des grandes significations.

Drôle d'aventure que la vie. On est une boule, une sphère. Et cette molécule, cet astre glisse, heurte, fracasse, on fait plaisir à X ou à Y. On est dedans sa propre sphère et celle-ci commande à son destin.

J'ai 77 ans et ma morale peut se résumer à ceci: dans la vie il faut faire. C'est-à-dire agir dans la modestie, l'exactitude, la précision. La seule atmosphère pour une création artistique c'est la régularité, la modestie, la continuité, la persévérance.

J'ai déjà écrit quelque part que la constance est définition de la vie, car la constance est naturelle et productive. Pour être constant il faut être modeste, il faut être persévérant. C'est un témoignage de

courage, de force intérieure, une qualification de la nature de l'existence.

La vie vient au travers des hommes, ou bien les hommes viennent au travers de la vie. Ainsi naissent toutes sortes d'incidences. Regardez donc la sur-*[12]*face des eaux . . . Regardez aussi tout l'azur tout rempli du bien que les hommes auront fait . . . , car pour finir, tout retourne à la mer . . . En fin de compte, le débat se pose ainsi: l'homme seul face à lui-même, lutte de Jacob et de l'Ange à l'intérieur d'un homme. Il n'y a qu'un seul juge. Sa propre conscience, c'est-à-dire vous-même. Ainsi tout petit ou tout grand mais pouvant aller (petit ou grand) du dégueulasse au sublime. Cela dépend de chacun, dès le début. On peut choisir le côté digne, pour soi, pour sa conscience, mais on peut aussi choisir l'autre possibilité: l'intérêt, l'argent.

Toute ma vie a été occupée à des découvertes. C'est un choix. On peut conduire de magnifiques Cadillac ou Jaguar, on peut aussi se passionner pour le travail que l'on fait. La recherche de la vérité n'est pas facile. Car il n'y a pas de vérité aux extrêmes. La vérité coule entre deux rives, mince filet d'eau ou masse croulante du fleuve . . . Et à chaque jour différente . . .

Et nous sommes dans un monde de fonctionnaires fermés sur eux-mêmes, incapables de déci-*[13]*sions. Voilà les assemblées . . . les conseils . . . Il est bon que les cons y prennent la parole, car nous autres nous pourrions oublier le poids des pierres et la sueur qu'il faut pour les remuer.

A 17 ans et demi, je construisis ma première maison. Déjà j'avais risqué contre l'avis des sages. Une témérité: deux fenêtres d'angle. Sur le chantier, au début, je saisis une brique et la soupèse. Son poids m'effraie. Je reste pétrifié. Alors une brique . . . alors des millions de briques maçonnées l'une sur l'autre.

L'avis des sages, de nos fonctionnaires? Il importe peu. Je me souviens d'une conversation avec Maurice Jardot vers 1953. Il était question de Picasso. Picasso avait demandé à Jardot: «Cela faisait bien mon exposition de Rome, etc.?» Je répliquai à l'ami Jardot: «Si vous aviez répondu "Non, l'exposition faisait plutôt mauvais effet", Picasso vous aurait dit: "Je m'en fous, j'ai raison, l'opinion m'est indifférente".»

J'avais 60 ans lorsque me fut passée ma première et seule commande d'Etat, et ceci, sans doute, *[14]* pour rire un peu! Le monde fut alerté partout. L'Esprit: un moyen âge. Après la guerre: reconstruction, pour Corbu: zéro. Toutes mes constructions sont dues à des initiatives privées. Grand nombre de projets épatants, ayons la modestie de le dire, furent torpillés par les fonctionnaires. Une fois, alors qu'on me remettait un illustre hommage, pour mieux m'écarter, j'ai dit que j'avais tout raté. C'est vrai dans la mesure où mes projets n'ont pu se concrétiser, c'est vrai dans la mesure où lorsque plus tard, lorsque j'aurai rejoint quelques zones célestes, les années de cheval de fiacre continueront. Messieurs les Non, vous serez toujours à l'affût, toujours contre. Les médiocrités continueront, les idioties seront toujours écrites, dites ou proclamées . . . les barrages toujours installés . . . les chers confrères . . . les autorités, les ordres, les conseils supérieurs . . . Souvenez-vous des coups bas, pour l'Unité d'habitation de Marseille, par exemple: «Des taudis à se taper la tête contre les murs . . .» Et ce médecin psychiatre, président de l'ordre: «Eclosion de maladies mentales . . .» *[15]* Et aussi: «Contre les lois de l'hygiène . . .» (du Conseil supérieur de l'Hygiène et de la Santé publique).

Je pourrais donner le vrai fond du sac: où sont les déchets? Trop facile et trop puant . . . Un boxeur sait qu'il doit saigner du nez et un joueur de rugby qu'il doit se démettre l'épaule ou se luxer le genou . . . Je dis ici, le problème n'est pas de gagner de l'argent, le problème est de faire quelque chose (produire, créer, administrer, organiser, etc.). Là seulement il y a du bonheur. Le bonheur se porte à l'intérieur et me dispense des corvées du Palm Beach ou des demoiselles et des fastes des Petits Lits Blancs. Il faut savoir, tout voir, prévoir, etc., et ensuite, et par dessus tout, faire la part de l'imprévisible: ça c'est sentir, flairer le fruit d'un don, d'une expérience, d'une vie quotidiennement ajoutée.

A 32 ans j'étais à l'«Esprit Nouveau», par ferveur, loyauté, témérité, mais aussi courage, risque accepté. A 32 ans est écrit «vers une architecture» apparition claire et affirmation d'une vision des *[16]* choses (risques compris) quand les racines étaient faites, les racines étant faites. La jeunesse, c'est la dureté, l'intransigeance, la pureté. Le ressort se détend, s'est détendu. C'était inscrit dans l'homme, dans une destinée. De l'enfance à 30 ans, quelle rumeur intense, quel brassage, quelles acquisitions! Il ne l'a jamais su le petit. Il allait sa route. De même, on voit dans les files de gosses (cheveux en brosse) qui vont à la piscine, à Paris, le matin avec leur classe, ou à la mer, en vacances, une intensité dans les gestes, dans les propos, les regards, la marche, le geste amical vers les copains. Combien en restera-t-il de tant de possibilités, de tant de propreté? . . .

La ligne de conduite pour les jeunes qui prennent aujourd'hui le relais des aînés ne me semble pas devoir être la découverte d'un esthétisme passager, mais la recherche profonde, passionnée, intime, de tous les secrets des métiers qui permettront de constituer des objets précis et exactement faits, aptes à réaliser un outillage pour la nouvelle société qui se forme sous nos yeux dans le monde *[17]* entier. Tout est dans la manière de faire (travail intérieur) et non pas dans la manière d'être qui n'intéresse personne.

A Bogota, en 1950, j'avais eu le sentiment d'une page à tourner: fin d'un monde, immanente, imminente. Il ne reste plus à connaître que la durée en heures humaines, des secondes ou des minutes de cette . . . catastrophe? Non, amis, de cette délivrance. Une circonstance sans emphase et nullement solennelle: un voyage d'affaire à Bogota me remplit les mains en cinq jours seulement d'une récolte de faits et de preuves d'ordre général et d'ordre personnel capables d'affirmer sans angoisse, mais bien dans la joie de demain, que la page va tourner, une grande page de l'histoire humaine, l'histoire de la vie des hommes avant la machine et que celle-ci a brisée, broyée, mise en miettes. Exemple aux U.S.A. A New York 15 millions d'habitants, l'horreur d'une Société d'abondance sans but ni raison. A Long Island, mon ami Nivola, fils d'un maçon, cultive des légumes entre les murs détermineurs d'espaces. U.S.A.: les femmes, la psychanalyse [18] partout, l'acte sans écho, sans but. Des journées sans suite, autre que d'arriver au bout. On travaille pour vingt-quatre heures, sans prévisions, sans sagesse, sans plans, sans étapes. New York! Cette ville est atroce sur le ciel, hirsute, sans politesse, chacun pour soi. Le terrain est vendu sur plan, par bloc au mètre de superficie. Tu as le droit de faire ce qu'il te plaira! Ville de «trade», fabriquer et vendre, sortir sa journée! On fonce dans tous les sens . . . sans pitié, sans jeu . . .

A Chandigarh, un soir, j'ai dit à Pierre Jeanneret: «Il n'y a que ceux qui jouent qui soient des types sérieux!» Pierre ayant protesté, j'ai repris: «Les alpinistes, les rugbymen et les joueurs de cartes, et les joueurs de roulette sont des fumistes, car ils ne jouent pas . . .» Ils ne jouent pas . . . Conformisme et non-conformisme. Tout ce que l'on apprend dans les écoles, dans les clubs politiques, dans les cours de danses arrive à constituer pour chaque individu et selon son caractère une constellation de points fixes formant un dessin indéformable, forteresse entre le libre jugement et le libre et juste usage des [19] choses que donne le bon Dieu, ou les arrangements

qu'en offrent les hommes. Montaigne ici alors est le bienvenu: «Au plus élevé trône du monde n'est-on encore assis que sur son cul.» Oui, la règle c'est le jeu. Il y a eu l'argent pour servir, puis il asservit et les hommes ont oublié de jouer. Quand mon client me remplit la tête de tels de ses petits besoins, j'accepte, j'accepte jusqu'à un certain point où je dis non, impossible! Car c'est alors hors de la règle de mon jeu, du jeu en question: le jeu de cette maison, de cette combinaison dont la règle a surgi à l'heure de la création, s'est développée, affirmée, devenue maîtresse. Tout à l'intérieur de la règle! Rien hors de la règle! Sinon je n'ai plus de raison d'exister. Là est la clef. Raison d'exister: jouer le jeu. Participer, mais humainement, c'est-à-dire dans l'ordre, dans un ordre pur. Mais il faut d'abord avoir regardé, vu, observé. Alors on peut dégager des sensations, des perceptions et des idées. La métaphysique n'est que l'écume d'une conquête, le versant qui redescend, un fait où les muscles de l'action ont cessé de fonctionner. Ce n'est pas un [20] acte, pas un fait, c'est un écho, un reflet. Et ça touche et affecte des types humains particuliers: les parleurs de discussions. On me prête des capacités occultes, mathématiques, nombres, etc.

Je suis un âne mais qui a l'œil. Il s'agit de l'œil d'un âne qui a des capacités de sensations. Je suis un âne ayant l'instinct de la proportion. Je suis et demeure un visuel impénitent. C'est beau quand c'est beau . . . Mais c'est au Modulor! Je m'en fous du modulor, qu'est-ce que vous voulez que ça me fasse le modulor? Et puis, non! le modulor a fatalement raison, mais c'est vous qui ne sentez rien. Le modulor rallonge l'oreille aux ânes. (Ici, il s'agit d'un autre âne que l'âne moi-même cité plus haut.)

Mon carnet de voyage à Bogota, 50 ou 51, comprenait quelques notes remises ensuite à Jardot, le 31 janvier 53. Les voici bienvenues à ce point de nos propos:

«Réapparition de la proportion dans l'œuvre d'art», «L'apport de L.C.». [21]

1919: les tracés régulateurs-(la preuve: Choisy). Désormais, recherche exclusivement personnelle. J'ignore tous les traités. Mais je déclare la guerre, la guerre à Vignole (et Compagnie) dont je renifle partout les émanations cadavériques.

Corbu devant: 1922. La ville contemporaine de 3 millions d'habitants. L'immeuble-villas (découvert en 1910 à la Chartreuse d'Ema).

1919: la volonté de la tâche est apparue, dans la peinture, dans le dessin. Et l'esprit d'architecte s'est intégré, manifesté. Dès lors, uniformité de la recherche: architecture, peinture (en fait, sculpture, car espace, lumière sur forme d'une nouvelle éthique).

Jusqu'en 1928, non pas objets, verres et bouteilles, mais supports de géométrie, fauteurs de proportionnement. Après 28, alors, figure humaine et objets à réaction poétique . . .

Au bout de la course 1951, à Chandigarh ; contact possible avec les joies essentielles du principe hindou: la fraternité des rapports entre cosmos et êtres vivants: étoiles, nature, animaux [22] sacrés, oiseaux, singes et vaches, et dans le village, les enfants, les adultes et les vieillards actifs, l'étang et les manguiers, tout est présent et sourit, pauvre mais proportionné.

Depuis ma première maison construite à 17 ans et demi, j'ai poursuivi mes travaux parmi les aventures, les difficultés, les catastrophes et de temps à autre le succès. Maintenant, à 77 ans, mon nom est connu dans le monde entier. Mes recherches, mes idées semblent être partagées quelquefois, mais les obstacles sont toujours présents comme les obstructeurs. Ma réponse? J'ai toujours été actif et agissant et je le demeure. Ma recherche a toujours été dirigée vers la poésie qui est dans le cœur de l'homme. Homme

visuel, travaillant avec ses yeux et ses mains, je suis animé par des manifestations tout d'abord plastiques. Tout est dans tout: cohésion, cohérence, unité, Architecture et urbanisme conjugués: un seul problème, réclamant une seule profession.

Je ne suis pas un révolutionnaire, je suis un type timide, qui ne se mêle pas de ce qui ne le regarde [23] pas, mais les éléments sont révolutionnaires, les événements le sont, et il faut considérer ces choses avec sang froid, avec la vue à distance. Dans mes voyages, je vois des choses caractéristiques. Les ambassadeurs étaient autrefois indispensables, ils avaient des missions pour quelques années, deux ou trois, qu'ils faisaient en calèche avec, non pas des mots croisés, mais des mots secrets. Ils agissaient au mieux des intérêts du patron qui était le roi ou le prince ou la république, peu importe. Maintenant, lorsqu'une question se pose, immédiatement vous prenez l'avion, en dix heures, en vingt heures vous êtes à pied-d'œuvre chez votre adversaire, vous posez le dossier sur la table, vous liquidez le problème, vous rentrez deux ou trois jours après. Ce changement se passe dans toute la gestion des affaires du monde, cela a des conséquences extraordinaires. J'ai été conduit à Bogota pour y faire les plans de la ville. J'y suis allé en avion et, en arrivant, j'ai appris une chose extraordinaire. C'est une ville de quatre siècles, faite par le conquistador du Mexique qui, avec cinquante [24] chevaux, a battu les Indiens qui, eux, n'avaient pas de chevaux. Pour aller de Bogota à Barranquilla, le port, il fallait vingt-cinq jours, maintenant il faut deux heures et quart. Dans cette ville hispanique il y avait depuis vingt années des écoles, des livres qui arrivaient; tout à coup, les types ont dit: «Mais on peut sortir!» et ils sont allés voir le monde, ils ont dit à d'autres gens qu'ils ont rencontrés: «Vous pouvez venir chez nous, venez voir, il y a à faire.» Les gens sont allés, ils ont trouvé le sous-sol, le sol; ils ont dit: «On va faire une ville d'un million d'habitants . . .»

Vous êtes devant des faits, sous nos pieds la terre bouge, mais en vérité ce n'est pas la terre qui bouge. Nous sommes sur un tapis roulant qui est l'évolution de l'époque. Nous sommes une civilisation machiniste, nous devons prendre une tournure d'esprit. La sociabilité est un phénomène humain naturel: Adam et Eve pour commencer et cela a continué. La conséquence extrême est l'occupation du territoire. Au Ministère de la Reconstruction il y a eu des gens gentils (d'autres beau-[25]coup moins). Ils ont pris mon «petit bobard» et ils ont appelé cela l'«aménagement du territoire». A la télévision, on peut même voir des gens très sérieux parler de cela le dimanche soir, pour enfoncer des portes ouvertes par moi depuis quarante années au moins. Passons, c'est le prix de l'amitié . . . J'ai donc dit: «Messieurs, attention! avant l'aménagement il faut occuper le territoire, et où est le territoire?» Voilà le problème d'aujourd'hui. Il faut tracer les routes du monde actuel conduites par les cités linéaires des transformations. Ce sont des routes fatidiques, anciennes routes de tous les temps. Au long de ces routes, les cités linéaires industrielles pourront venir étaler leurs conjugaisons de routes de terre, de fer, d'eau, par dessus les frontières administratives. Si les routes topographiques traversent les frontières et avec, les produits fabriqués, les méthodes de fabrication, il n'en demeure pas moins vrai que toute Société humaine nécessite d'être administrée, et qu'on ne peut pas administrer tout. Le mondialisme est une des grandes choses des temps modernes, mais [26] il y aura toujours une limitation administrative pour qu'on puisse donner des ordres à des groupes déterminés, pour que d'un autre côté arrive un autre ordre. Au lieu d'ordres à coups de canons, ce seront des ordres d'aménagement de necessité mondiale.

L'administration maintient des limites, alors que celles-ci sont déterminées par l'évolution. Il y avait autrefois les fortifications, limites de Paris. Depuis que Paris a évolué, il y en a eu cinq ou six. Puis, après la guerre de 1914, on a enlevé les dernières limites parce que l'avion était intervenu. Les routes traversent et animent. La terre est ronde et continue, tout se touche; elle est mal occupée, inoccupée, il reste beaucoup à faire pour occuper la terre au lieu d'aller dans la lune. C'est comme l'affaire Stavisky, c'est pour occuper l'opinion. La construction de routes, l'adduction d'eau seraient le grand travail civilisateur de notre société moderne. Cela peut se faire avec une facilité fantastique. Si vous survolez la terre, vous verrez où il y a des habitants et vous verrez qu'il reste une place immense; mais sans eau. Pas d'eau? Il faut l'amener. Pas de [27] routes? Il faut les faire . . .

En 1961, profitant de quelques jour de grippe, j'avais écrit un petit texte que j'adressais à mon ami Jean-Jacques Duval, de Saint-Dié. Je lui écrivais alors: «Je vous envoie copie de la première frappe de mon texte Le Graphique "irrécusable". C'est véritablement pour vous un "job". Dans votre bonneterie, votre père faisait des chaussettes pour la campagne et des sous-vêtements pour sexagénaires. En 1961, vous êtes l'élégance même de la bonneterie pour zazous! Vous faites des chaussettes qui sont des poèmes, des chandails, etc. Vous avez conservé vos machines, vous avez conservé vos ouvriers, votre administration, votre comptabilité. Vous n'avez rien changé, sauf votre programme. Là, vous avez imaginé, vous avez créé. Vous avez donc fait une reconversion de vos établissements en faveur d'une évolution sociale complètement indépendante de votre volonté. Mon pro-[28]blème est le même. On fait des canons, de l'atomisme, de l'anti-chômage, des atmosphères d'avant-guerre, des successions d'armements préventifs. Alors, aujourd'hui, je propose: on tire la ligne verticale! A gauche, on met une croix en travers. A droite, on fait le nouveau bilan: ouvriers, patrons, problèmes sociaux, organisation du travail, programme industriel, préparation de la mise aux machines, propagande par personnel nouveau en faveur d'une nouvelle Société qui est maintenant debout à l'horizon . . .»

Ce texte où se trouve être fait le point en matière d'urbanisme me semble devoir trouver sa place ici. Le voici.

«LE GRAPHIQUE IRRECUSABLE», «LA LIGNE IRREVOCABLE'' OU «LA FIN DU POTARD»

Une délicieuse petite révolution dans la pharmacie, révolution fraternelle, maternelle, a refermé [29] la porte sur le nez de M. Potard; elle a installé dans chaque foyer une réforme décisive. Fait nouveau, mieux que cela: miracle accompli jusque dans ses conséquences; la longévité, en France, a fait un saut stupéfiant: en moins d'un siècle, la durée de l'existence a été porté de 28 à 40 ans et, aujourd'hui, à 68 ans. Au sein des familles, la maladie est combattue par des moyens «civilisés»; la pharmacie du XXe siècle est née! Dans le foyer, la page est tournée sur les atmosphères balzaciennes. J'ai précisé ici les qualificatifs de «fraternel», de «maternel», d'«amical» . . .

Parlons du «foyer» maintenant (thème de l'actualité bavarde), du logis: la famille, le travail, le repos. Mieux encore, parlons des «trois établissements humains» qui conduisent à l'occupation harmonieuse du territoire par les travaux de la civilisation machiniste.

Tout n'est encore que confusion, obscurité, hostilité, jalousie, férocité, spéculation, voracité d'argent, étalage de la sottise, soif de vanités; à vrai dire, ignorance pure et simple du phénomène [30] essentiel, immanent: la réalisation des travaux de paix . . . La discussion est dans le vide, face aux bombes. Tout est Khroutchev, Mao Tsé Tung, de Gaulle ou Reine Elizabeth, Kennedy! Autant d'«hommes de confiance», de mandatés authentiques, honnêtes, intelligents, capa-

bles, passionnés. Mais aussi autant de personnages adversatifs occupant des forteresses, adversativement affrontées. Autant de prétextes à devoir se tuer plutôt que de s'entendre! Chacun sur son socle, celui d'une civilisation machiniste, est particulièrement chargé de sauver notre esprit, notre volonté, nos buts, notre idéal . . . Tenant tous les mêmes propos, ils ont tous le cœur gentil et dévoué; mais ils sont tous à fourbir des armes, des bombes, des canons. Le monde va s'écrouler! Ils vont le faire sauter! Ça ne va pas rater! Et au bout de la course, pourquoi pas! [31]

En moi, je porte un réconfort, j'apporte un réconfort, comme un honnête âne, qui a fait son travail accompli sa tâche! Je sais que l'horizon est libre et que le soleil va s'y lever . . . Méditez cette historiette: une fois, il y a un siècle, on installa le gaz dans toutes les cuisines de Paris . . . Le lendemain matin, la population s'est «réveillée vivante». Il n'y avait pas de morts à tous les étages; il n'y avait pas d'ambulances dans la rue pour enlever les cadavres. Les pompiers étaient restés chez eux. Que s'était-il passé. Pour chauffer la soupe du soir on avait ouvert le robinet du gaz et on l'avait refermé jusqu'à l'heure du café au lait du matin . . . Et depuis, on apprend ceci aux enfants: «Touche pas au robinet du gaz!»

Hors des bruits et des foules, dans ma tanière (car je suis un méditatif, je me suis même comparé à un âne, par conviction), depuis cinquante années j'étudie le «bonhomme Homme» et sa femme et ses gosses. Une préoccupation m'a agité, impérativement: introduire dans le foyer le sens du sacré; faire du foyer le temple de la famille. Dès ce [32] moment, tout devenait autre. Un centimètre cube de logis valait de l'or, représentait du bonheur possible. Avec une telle notion de la dimension et de la destination, vous pouvez faire aujourd'hui un temple à la mesure de la famille, en dehors des cathédrales elles-mêmes qui furent bâties . . . autrefois; vous pouvez le faire par ce que vous y mettrez de vous-même. Or, le XIXe et le XXe siècle instituaient les diplômes d'architecture, définissaient la notion d'architecture, en remettaient le contrôle à l'Institut des Beaux-Arts, le chargeant de veiller sur la chose . . . Jusqu'à la défaite de 1940, la France était le seul pays n'imposant pas de diplôme officiel à ses constructeurs, laissant aux esprits neufs et libres la possibilité d'inventer et de bâtir. La France eut des pionniers, la France, pays des inventeurs . . . La première loi de Vichy fut celle du diplôme obligatoire, que le Parlement avait jusque-là toujours rejeté. On apprenait dans les écoles à faire des palais à toutes fins utiles et non pas des «contenants de famille», des «contenants de travail», des «contenants de loisirs», etc., c'est-à-dire des [33] locaux. On a bâti les «maireries» de France, des églises en styles divers, des gares comme celle d'Orsay où des trains pour un quart de la France y aboutissent dans un sous-sol, sous un plafond haut de 3,50 m; au-dessus, une nef titanesque dépassant en dimensions les thermes de Caracalla de Rome sert aux moineaux. On bâtissait encore le «Grand Palais», proche de là, titanique aussi, pour les expositions. Qu'exposait-on? Des objets d'hommes et de femmes. Les hommes mesurant une moyenne de 1,70 m de haut, la nef du «Grand Palais» eut aussi 50 m de haut!

Depuis soixante et un ans, les bâtons de rouge à lèvres, les sièges de 43 cm de haut, les tables de 0,70 m de haut s'y perdent sous des voûtes augustes! Ce palais fut l'ennemi mortel de toutes les expositions: les tableaux y étaient sans échelle, les statues idem. Depuis soixante et une années, il fallut à chaque fois (et plusieurs fois par année) consentir des aménagements coûteux pour mettre à l'aise les objets exposés. Des fortunes y passèrent, — des milliards et des milliards! Des [34] concessions à vie furent accordées pour ces équipements annuellement répétés. Malgré cet échec inconcevable, malgré cette leçon admin-

istrée pendant soixante années, on n'hésita pas à répéter l'erreur, on n'hésita pas à la faire, à la Défense, la plus grande voûte du monde «qui peut recouvrir la place de la Concorde d'un seul coup». Mais la place de la Concorde reste à Paris! La Défense est à vingt kilomètres. Il y aura sous la coupole de la Défense des bâtons de rouge à lèvres, des chaises de 43 cm de haut et des tables de 0,70 m de haut. «The greatest in the world», telle fut qualifiée cette voûte. Mot magique! Mais les autos et les piétons n'y parviennent pas et n'en reviennent pas. On en est à faire des métros, à élargir le pont de Neuilly, à aménager l'«Avenue Triomphale» baptisée telle par les marchands de terrains.

Elle aboutira (l'Avenue) sur l'Arc de Triomphe, aujourd'hui déjà démesurément embouteillé, à l'Obélisque de la Concorde; elle butera aux Murs des Tuileries . . . On parle déjà de passer sous le Louvre, sous Saint-Germain-l'Auxerrois; on tom-[35]bera sur l'Hôtel de Ville et on lui passera dessous. Jamais le mot «grrrrand» ne fut employé si tragiquement.

Ainsi donc fut faite l'architecture des «temps modernes» de Paris.

La tâche est de s'occuper de lieux et de locaux. C'est la tâche des «constructeurs». Et les «constructeurs» sont précisément la nouvelle profession qui doit lier en un dialogue inlassable et fraternel l'Ingénieur et l'Architecte, cette main gauche et cette main droite de l'art de bâtir.

Le logis dans cette conjoncture n'avait eu aucune chance de devenir le temple de la famille. On fit la boîte à loyers et on gagna sa vie avec la boîte à loyers. La notion d'architecture fut bancale, car elle n'obéit pas à une définition juste, c'est-à-dire créer les lieux et les locaux pour l'habitation, le travail et les loisirs en plaçant ceux-ci dans les «conditions de nature», c'est-à-dire sous [36] l'injonction péremptoire du soleil qui est notre maître irrécusable, puisque le jour et la nuit sont l'alternance qui dictera à jamais l'enchaînement valable de nos actes. Le soleil (notre maître, ami ou ennemi) ne fut pas pris en considération. Les Américains s'étant réveillés tardivement à l'occasion du Palais de l'O.N.U., décidèrent de l'entourer d'un vitrage continu; mais sans l'accompagner d'un «contrôle du soleil». New York, latitude de Naples, reçut le soleil de plein fouet à travers des vitrages fixes. On ne fait pas mieux pour cultiver des orchidées . . . On installa l' «air conditionné»; les frigories coûtent très cher. La chaleur n'en fut pas diminuée suffisamment? L'enthousiasme aidant et l'esprit soufflant, on baptisa ces façades de verre: «murs-rideaux». La mode séduisit Paris . . . des aventures cruelles frappèrent les usagers des murs-rideaux. On s'obstine! Cher soleil! . . . cher soleil devenu l'ennemi de l'habitant.

Tout était devenu d'une telle confusion après les guerres de 18 et de 40 qu'on perdit la tête! Le laissez-aller déborda, la négligence coupable, [37] l'inconscience. Les villes tentaculaires naquirent, se développèrent, atteignirent leur apogée: le scandale, le désastre. C'est New York, douze millions d'habitants; c'est Londres, dix millions; c'est Moscou qui en est déjà à cinq millions . . . Paris en arrive glorieusement cette année, 1961, à huit millions d'habitants! C'est fait, on l'a laissé faire. Quelqu'un avait à sonner le tocsin, à temps . . . Il ne l'a pas fait!

Cent ans que l'industrie est née, que la civilisation machiniste apparut. On ne sut pas que c'était l'apparition d'une civilisation, la naissance d'une nouvelle société. On pensa plutôt que c'était une malédiction, un peste, un pis-aller . . . une machine à faire de l'argent. Un siècle s'est occupé à installer les gens dans cette machine infernale: patrons et ouvriers, exploitation et statut; révolte! Un siècle de violences, de tentatives d'aménagement, de solutions proposées pour l'harmonisation des conditions du travail, de postulats pour motiver la raison d'être du travail! Un jour, rendre le travail amical.

Sur la Terre Ronde, deux établissements humains [38] existaient depuis les origines: l'«Unité d'Exploitation Agricole» déterminée par le pas du cheval ou du bœuf (quatre kilomètres à l'heure) et la force de leurs jarrets; la «Ville Radio-concentrique des Echanges» apparue au croisement de deux chemins, de trois chemins, de quatre chemins, provoquant automatiquement le rassemblement et la dispersion d'objets de consommation (marchandises), d'idées (écoles et universités), de forces de commandement et d'administration (gouvernement). Lieu des échanges.

Par impéritie, le travail moderne s'installa au petit bonheur la chance autour des agglomérations et dans les agglomérations. L'événement est à maturité: la journée de vingt-quatre heures complètement dénaturée par les distances non conjuguées, totalement arbitraires, entre les lieux d'habitation et les lieux de travail.

Les hommes se mirent à vivre sur roues: trains de banlieue, autobus de banlieue, bicyclettes, motocyclettes, automobiles personnelles. Le soleil tournait impassiblement en vingt-quatre heures, parta-[39]geant en deux la journée solaire: le jour et la nuit. Et ce fut une dépense insensée: le gaspillage des temps modernes (1).

On s'écria: le désastre est total. Il faut disperser désormais l'industrie. Ce n'etait pas une réponse valable.

_____

(1) Exemple: U.S.A., «Quand les cathédrales étaient blanches», 1936 [1937], chez Plon.

Il fallait dire: «Il faut localiser l'industrie!» et découvrir le sens de ce terme: localiser.

A force d'étudier en tous pays, sous tous climats, ce même et unique problème de l'équipement d'une civilisation machiniste, il m'est arrivé de découvrir (comme on apercevrait subitement une soucoupe volante ou un Spoutnik, c'est-à-dire avec stupeur) que la société machiniste ne possédait pas d'établissement humain industriel, ne disposait pas de Cités Industrielles. Et de découvrir que la nature de ce nouvel établissement humain, le troisième, la «Cité Linéaire Industrielle», était d'une forme impérative salvatrice apportant solution aux problèmes qui préoccupent les réformateurs de vraie [40] et bonne volonté, dans tous les camps, même les plus opposés.

La «Cité Industrielle» est «linéaire», formée des trois routes d'eau, de terre et de fer par lesquelles arrivent les matières premières et s'en vont les produits fabriqués. Les routes d'eau, de terre et de fer ont un destin commun dicté par la topographie: la pente du thalweg, la où descendent les eaux qui, des montagnes, vont à la mer,—vallées étroites ou élargies ou plaines étalées. Ces trois routes sont conjuguées par le relief du sol, ou conjugables.

Une innovation capitale intervient: le «transbordement», invention des temps modernes. Les moyens de distribution de ces routes d'eau, terre et fer étaient, jusqu'ici, des «embranchements» sur eau, sur route ou sur fer. Ces embranchements (surtout pour le chemin de fer) exigent des étalements au sol, des superficies de terrain parfois immenses, provoquant des encombrements titanesques (les gares de triage des grandes villes en sont une manifestation). L'innovation, c'est le [41] «transbordement», remplaçant les «embranchements». Désormais on saisira, on transbordera et on distribuera les marchandises par «ponts roulants» installés perpendiculairement aux trois voies de terre, de fer et d'eau et au-dessus, dans

l'espace libre. Ceci est d'importance capitale: c'est l'articulation de la solution.

«LA LIGNE IRRÉCUSABLE

LE GRAPHIQUE IRRÉVOCABLE»

Je puis donc tracer cette figure:

Une ligne verticale. A gauche de cette ligne verticale, une zone noire, une flèche descendante, trajectoire d'une catastrophe, la guerre atomique (tout sera détruit, y compris les enrichis de l'aventure).

A droite de la verticale s'élance une flèche dans la lumière, entraînant le destin des «Trois Etablissements Humains». [42–44]

DERRIÈRE NOUS...

LA LIGNE IRRÉCUSABLE

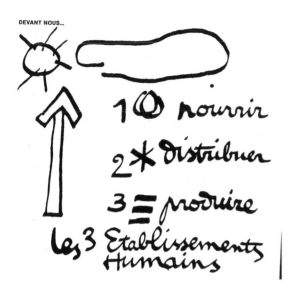

DEVANT NOUS...

1 ◎ nourrir
2 ✳ distribuer
3 ☰ produire
les 3 Etablissements Humains

Deux livres sont parus. L'un (1) à la Libération, sous le signe de l'ASCORAL (Association des Constructeurs pour une Rénovation Architecturale, créée pendant la guerre et comportant onze sections d'études), livre intitulé: «Les trois établissements humains». Petit format n'exigeant qu'une tonne et demie de papier pour six mille exemplaires, papier qui fut refusé pendant trois années. L'édition fut vendue totalement sans que personne s'en occupât particulièrement. En octobre 1959, douze années plus tard, les Editions «Forces vives», de Jean Petit, ont réimprimé sous un autre aspect cet ouvrage auquel furent ajoutés quantité de graphiques explicites (2).

———————————

(1) Urbanisme des CIAM-ASCORAL, sections 5 a et 5 b, «Une civilisation du travail: les trois établissements humains» (Denoël).

(2) 1959: l'urbanisme des trois établissements humains (Cahiers «Forces vives», aux Ed. de Minuit).

Tout se construit alors. Tout s'installe. Le programme s'établit ponctuellement et la «reconversion du travail» apparaît possible, tournant désormais le dos aux préparations atomiques, [45] aux chômages. Reconversion du travail voué au bien des hommes. Pour les hommes: un programme pour une civilisation machiniste.

J'ai commencé cette rédaction par une incidence tout à fait accidentelle: la petite révolution de la pharmacie, fraternelle et maternelle, et l'effacement de M. Potard. Une modeste invention était intervenue, la création des matières plastiques dont les débuts furent l'invasion puérile de jouets d'enfants, poupées boursouflées et toutes nues et dont l'un des aboutissements, dans la pharmacie moderne, a autorisé le prolongement inouï de la vie des hommes sur terre, la mortalité reportée à la soixantaine. Une loi sur les Assurances avait déclenché l'événement, une loi généreuse qui dit: penchons nous sur chacun de nos frères, hors de toutes classes. Le statut des médecins s'en trouva bouleversé et désormais fixé: la médecine mise pratiquement au service de l'homme . . . La pharmacie [46] devint aussi naturelle qu'une nourriture; pour chacun: l'exactitude, la propreté, l'efficacité, etc. Une nouvelle industrie en naissait; c'est désormais un état de choses acquis. L'auteur de ces lignes se permet modestement d'attirer l'attention du lecteur sur cet événement à l'actif de la société moderne . . .

Passons au grand fait présent: «Les Trois Etablissements Humains». Frontières à canons, haines sociales, haines des classes, frénésie de la concurrence; brutalité honteuse des affaires: «Struggle for Life», «Time is money» . . . Fermons la porte à la guerre atomique. Installons sur la topographie de la Terre Ronde, les Trois Etablissements Humains dont le premier, l'Unité d'Exploitation Agricole, va être réglé par le tracteur et non plus par le pas du bœuf ou du cheval. C'est ici, l'innovation imminente et immanente. Le second établissement, «La Cité Radio-concentrique des Echanges», sera la mise au point qui va éclairer d'une lumière foudroyante le drame des villes tentaculaires contemporaines et trouver immédiatement le salut dans l'exode au long de la «Cité Linéaire Industrielle». [47] Ce troisième établissement, la «Cité Linéaire»; fait face aux conflits, riposte aux haines et aux égoïsmes. Devant une source si prodigieuse de travaux féconds offerte à la société moderne, le choix est entre la nuit sans espoir (installée à gauche de la verticale irrécusable tracée plus haut) et la liberté complète d'action, l'immensité des programmes, l'illimité des solutions confiées aux sociétés modernes (à droite de la verticale): construction des logis radieux (habiter), des usines vertes (travailler), aménagement des loisirs (cultiver le corps et l'esprit), circuler!

Ceci n'est pas de la folie. Non! C'est, depuis 1933, la prophétie de la «Charte d'Athènes» des CIAM. C'est la conclusion des CIAM, «Congrès Internationaux d'Architecture Moderne», qui, au cours des trentes années (1928–1959) ont installé dans le monde moderne les bases d'un urbanisme urbain, recherche loyale, désintéressée, persévérante, minutieuse et créatrice: sa valeur c'est la loyauté! [48]

Urbanisme, humaine recherche loyale et créatrice. Oui . . . il faut secouer les paresses du statu quo. Nous devons nous tourner au-delà des petits égoïsmes, de toutes les petites choses. Il faut essayer de découvrir la vie, de suivre la vie. Seulement, il faut au moins vingt années pour qu'une idée soit connue, trente pour qu'elle soit appréciée et cinquante pour qu'elle soit appliquée, lorsqu'elle devrait alors évoluer. C'est à ce moment-là que pleuvent les discours sur les tombes et les plaques commémoratives. Il est trop tard, tout est à refaire. Pourquoi attendre le malheur ou la catastrophe pour prendre les décisions utiles?

Pour ma part j'ai voué cinquante années de ma vie à l'étude du logis. J'ai ramené le temple dans la famille, au foyer. J'ai rétabli les conditions de nature dans la vie des hommes. Toute cette entreprise, je n'ai pu la mener à bonne fin qu'avec l'aide admirable des jeunes de mon atelier, 35, rue de Sèvres: passion, foi, probité. Je leur dis merci à tous. Il restera là, sans doute, avec tous ceux passés rue de Sèvres, une semence utile. Peut-être [49] plus tard, quelques fois, penseront-ils un peu au père Corbu qui leur dit aujourd'hui: «On travaille en fonction de sa propre conscience . . . C'est dans ce cercle que le drame humain se poursuit . . .»

Soltan, de Varsovie, un ancien de l'atelier, m'écrivait vers 1954 (sans dater sa lettre) les bonnes paroles que voici et qui sont pour moi un petit réconfort: «Les dernières nouvelles de vous: c'est le dernier Girsberger. J'ai réussi à avoir dans mes mains, pendant quelques heures, l'unique exemplaire de ce livre qui se trouve à Varsovie actuellement. Vous savez certainement bien qu'on vous reproche, dans l'Est de l'Europe, "le formalisme et le constructivisme". Evidemment, ces reproches-là sont des bêtises, mais ce qui est frappant quand on regarde vos oeuvres récentes, c'est la grande croissance de l'importance du contenu et du sujet. "La main ouverte" de Chandigarh, par exemple.

«Cette importance de la poétique du sujet commence à donner à votre oeuvre des valeurs extra-plastiques toutes pharaoniques, quoiqu'elles [50] explorent la sensibilité et la subconscience bien modernes (c'est d'ailleurs le grand apport de ces œuvres). Alors vous reprocher le formalisme devient purement comique, si ce n'était pas tragique! Tragique, car les auteurs de ces reproches construisent beaucoup, mais alors comment? C'est bien là le tragique! Personnellement, je suis absolument certain que, même indépendamment de l'avenir social et politique qui vous attend, vos idées vont triompher dans le monde entier. N'ont-elles pas d'ailleurs une solide base sociale?

«Le triomphe futur des idées Corbu dans tout le monde viendra un jour, mais quand viendra-t-il? Est-ce à l'échelle d'une vie humaine? La mienne, par exemple.

«Pourrai-je un jour vous voir et vous parler des choses que je n'arrive pas à résoudre, des problèmes très "Europe de l'Est": la facilité de l'œuvre d'art au point de vue du consommateur (par exemple)? La question d'être toujours à la portée des masses, etc. Vous connaissez certainement bien ces chansons-là . . . Mais il y en a telle-[51]ment d'autres aussi . . . Cher Monsieur Le Corbusier, les amis qui me connaissent bien rigolent en disant que je pense toujours à vous quand je travaille; je crois que c'est quand même bien vrai . . .»

De tels propos permettent d'espérer que tous les efforts du père Corbu n'auront pas été complètement inutiles . . .

A Soltan, à tous les autres je puis dire: la solidarité est un édifice où tout est cohérent, où se trouve toute la gamme des intérêts indispensablement présents, les uns porteurs d'ombre, les autres de lumière. La lumière exprime les intérêts supérieurs de l'amour, de l'amitié, de la fraternité. L'ombre, les intérêts matériels et les égoïsmes. Et, selon que la source éclairante est à bout portant ou reculée, varient en voyance et en quantité l'égoïsme ou l'altruisme.

Le monument de la Main ouverte, par exemple, dont parle Soltan, n'est pas un signe politique, une création de politicien. C'est une création d'architecte, c'est un fruit d'architecture. Il y a dans cette création un cas spécifique de neutralité [52] humaine: celui qui crée est en vertu des lois de la physique, de la chimie, de la biologie, de l'éthique, de l'esthétique, toutes ensembles réunies en une seule gerbe: une maison, une ville. La différence avec la politique, c'est

que son équation comporte physique, chimie, résistance des matériaux, loi de la pesanteur, biologie, faute de quoi tout crève, tout casse, tout s'écroule. C'est comme l'avion: ça vole ou ça ne vole pas et la sanction est vite là. Alors, dans le complexe homme et matière (complexité des programmes) on s'aperçoit que tout est possible et tous les conflits réductibles. Il n'y a qu'à en être persuadé et à étudier le problème, ouvrir les mains à toutes matières, techniques et idées, trouver la solution. Etre content, être heureux. Et ne pas passer à la caisse. Qui me suit?

Cette main ouverte, signe de paix et de réconciliation, doit se dresser à Chandigarh. Ce signe qui me préoccupe depuis de nombreuses années en mon subconscient doit exister pour porter un témoignage d'harmonie. Il faut annuler les travaux de guerre, la guerre froide doit cesser de faire vivre [53] les hommes. Il faut inventer, décréter les travaux de paix. L'argent n'est qu'un moyen. Il y a Dieu et le Diable—les forces en présence. Le Diable est de trop: le monde de 1965 peut se mettre en paix. Il est encore temps de choisir, équipons plutôt que d'armer. Ce signe de la main ouverte pour recevoir les richesses créées, pour distribuer aux peuples du monde, doit être le signe de notre époque. Avant de me retrouver un jour (plus tard) dans les zones célestes parmi les étoiles du Bon Dieu, je serai heureux de voir à Chandigarh, devant l'Himalaya qui s'élève droit sur l'horizon, cette main ouverte qui marque pour le père Corbu un fait, une étape parcourue. A vous, André Malraux, à vous mes collaborateurs, à vous mes amis, je demande de m'aider à réaliser ce signe de la Main ouverte dans le ciel de Chandigarh, cité voulue par Nehru, disciple de Gandhi.

En me demandant ces propos, pour ses petits [54] carnets Corbu, Jean Petit souhaitait un tour d'horizon . . . Moi je n'aime pas parler de ma petite personne. Il faut laisser cela aux journalistes lorsque l'on aura passé les pieds devant. Mais il est bon toutefois de tenir certains propos qui peuvent être utiles. L'autre jour, un gros monsieur, de taille et rebondi, est venu me voir: «Monsieur Le Corbusier, pour un nouveau disque!—Il y en avait déjà donc un? —Oui, il y a déjà quelques années . . . —Hein, quoi! vous vous foutez de moi? —Non, c'est vrai. Alors, c'est oui? —Ben oui, mais je vous défends de prononcer un mot, de prononcer une question. —Mais, pour rompre un peu . . . —Non, ça sera du cousu Corbu . . .»

On m'a apporté, ces jours-ci, des plaques de cuivre épaisses de 2 millimètres et que je grave au burin. Le burin est un outil féroce. A 14 ans, j'ai un peu tenu le burin. Toute la force du bras et l'élasticité du poignet ouvrent une piste aiguë. Il faut aller devant, ni à droite ni à gauche. Un type qui sait et peut faire du burin est conduit sur le chemin de clairvoyance, de loyauté et d'honnêteté. *[55]* Etre vus ou regarder, tout est là. Qualification d'hommes. Ceux qui se montrent, qui exhibent, n'agissent qu'en fonction de la réaction sur autrui, se font «poètes» supérieurs d'une humanité autrement ressentie, autrement supérieure. On coupe les ponts, sans répit. D'autres, les architectes, dignes de la vocation, qui sont assimilés à une œuvre. Simple véritable force motrice de l'œuvre. Celle-ci doit surgir de la physique, de l'imagination, de l'invention, du courage et du risque. Elle n'est intense que si elle est risquée. Lui est dans le risque: toute sa personne, tout son esprit, et sa bourse et sa famille et sa situation. Il ne maudit personne autre que les entraves-mêmes, les réglementations, les astuces des ambitieux, les coups de cochons de gens d'affaires. Il est en plein combat toujours découvert. Il ne pense pas à lui, ni à son attitude, ni à l'effet qu'il produit, mais à ce qui est devant: l'œuvre. Ce n'est pas liquidé en un bref sonnet ou en une pièce de mots en liberté, en un bouquin d'invectives, en débats au Flore ou à la Rotonde. C'est le temps d'une année, de deux années, le *[56]* temps de cinq

années pour que l'œuvre soit accouchée et se présente non entre des feuillets largement imagés de blanc, mais dans le domaine public. Ici, tout est responsabilité, vigilance, état d'alerte permanent. Lente, lente, très lente patience de l'expression et fuite de l'élan butant inlassablement contre les lois physiques et intellectuelles. Résistances, usages, et le grand non! inlassable.

Il y a une attitude, s'avancer comme un dieu vainqueur auréolé de cheveux blonds, surpassant tout ce qui s'est vu jusqu'ici et ne pas hésiter à dire «merde» à tout et à toutes choses. L'autre attitude: vaincre et peut-être aussi bien être vaincu, sans cheveux blonds, mais en cheveux blanchis pour avoir persisté chaque matin à réaliser la tâche, sans prédestination, sans signes apparus dans le ciel, mais parce qu'il avait voulu tenter l'aventure, parce qu'il s'était embarqué sur le bateau, sur l'avion, sur la chimère . . . Moralité: honneur au commerce et merde pour l'industrie. Messieurs les Créateurs, vous êtes priés de vous acheter un cure-dent et de le sucer publiquement pour faire riche. Il faut, *[57]* sinon on vous foutra des cailloux sur la gueule.

Ici, à ce point, je dois dire merci à deux hommes: Cervantès et Rabelais. La plus belle lecture pour un homme engagé dans la bataille, c'est l'admirable Don Quichotte de la Manche. Et la vie en trois compagnons, entre Don Quichotte et Sancho Pança, trouve son explication, sinon ses justifications. Béats, les gens, les autres restent bouche-bée et ne lisent pas l'admirable Don Quichotte de la Manche. Don Quichotte et Pança montrent l'homme dans le martèlement du sac, du ressac, dans les plus optimismes déchaînements: confiance, foi, amour, don, épanouissement, floraison et extase, et les chutes les plus verticales nettes et sans conteste: tapes sur le nez préparées par des fessées. Pança passe, surnage toujours et pense à manger. Il a toujours raison. Il sait accepter (proposer ou discuter les compromis). Il s'en sort. C'est extraordinairement vrai. A un autre bout, Panurge et Jean ont trouvé *[58]* la discussion des commentaires, au-delà des limites du poli et s'élèvent au-dessus de tout, au nom des plus sages points de vue, par l'hilarante grossièreté gagnant ici ses lettres de plus haute noblesse. Merde, merde! . . . braguette et balletron, vieilles putains belles comme déesses, dypsode et loup-garou, Homère et Pline. Homérique, au-dessus, par dessous, hors les petites choses, les grands mots, les cliquetis des batailles, les braquemards. On se met à l'abri de l'abrutissement, on rit! Merci à Rabelais et Cervantès.

Il y a des rencontres, la permanence de faits existants, des contacts . . . Ainsi Mallarmé:

«Au-dessus du bétail ahuri des humains
Bondissaient en clarté les sauvages crinières
Des mendieurs d'azur, le pied dans nos chemins.»

J'avais à corriger, ces jours-ci, le manuscrit d'un livre écrit en 1911: «Le voyage d'Orient». Tobito, un ancien de l'atelier 35, rue de Sèvres, était venu *[59]*me rendre visite depuis le Venezuela à mon domicile rue Nungesser. Jean Petit est ensuite arrivé avec le texte du «Voyage d'Orient». Ensemble, nous avons bu le pastis et avons beaucoup parlé. Je me souviens leur avoir dit à tous deux que la ligne de conduite du petit Charles-Edouard Jeanneret à l'époque du voyage d'Orient était la même que celle du père Corbu. Tout est question de persévérance, de travail, de courage. Il n'y a pas de signes glorieux dans le ciel. Mais le courage est une force intérieure, qui seule peut ou non qualifier l'existence. J'étais heureux de revoir Tobito, de voir qu'il poursuivait, qu'il était parmi les fidèles. Lorsque nous nous sommes quittés tous trois, j'ai dit à Tobito qui pensait revenir me voir l'an prochain: «Oui à Paris ou dans une autre planète . . .», et je me suis dit en moi-même: «Alors, sans doute, auront-ils de temps en temps une gentille pensée pour le père Corbu.»

Me retrouvant seul, j'ai pensé à cette phrase admirable de l'Apocalypse: «Il y eut dans le ciel un silence d'environ une demi-heure . . .»*[60]*

. . . .

Oui, rien n'est transmissible que la pensée, noblesse du fruit du travail. Cette pensée peut ou non devenir une victoire sur le destin au-delà de la mort et peut-être prendre une autre dimension imprévisible.

Certes, les politiques font flèche de tout bois et tirent parti des faiblesses pour faire du recrutement: on tient à rassurer les faibles et les indécis, les apeurés. Mais la vie peut renaître avec les plans, vie en potentiel dans les herbages et dans les troupeaux, en ces terres abandonnées, en ces villes tentaculaires qu'il faudra démanteler, dans les lieux de travail, les usines qu'il faut rendre belles comme l'enthousiasme . . . hors des routines et des fonctionnaires blasés.

Il faut retrouver l'homme. Il faut retrouver la ligne droite épousant l'axe des lois fondamentales: biologie, nature, cosmos. Ligne droite infléchissable comme l'horizon de la mer.

L'homme de métier, aussi, infléchissable comme l'horizon de la mer, doit être un outil de mesure *[61]* pouvant servir de niveau, de repère au sein du fluctuant et de la mobilité. Son rôle social est là. Ce rôle le désigne pour être clairvoyant. Ses disciples ont installé l'orthogonal dans son esprit. Moralité: se foutre des honneurs, compter sur soi, agir pour sa conscience. Ce n'est pas par des traits de héros qu'on peut agir, entreprendre et réaliser.

Tout cela se passe dedans la tête, se formule et s'embryonne petit à petit au cours d'une vie fuyante comme un vertige, dont on arrivera au terme sans même s'en rendre compte.

Paris, Juillet 1965

Notes

Le Corbusier is referred to throughout as LC.

Introduction

Note to epigraph: Eugène Claudius-Petit, "L.C.: Dernier projet pour Paris," *Architecture d'aujourd'hui* 249 (February 1987), liv.

1   See, in Italian, an "expanded" edition with photographs in addition to LC's sketches: Giuliano Gresleri, *Viaggio in Oriente* (Venice: Cataloghi Marsilio, Fondation Le Corbusier, 1984); and in English an edition that attempts to reproduce more closely the 1966 French original, supplemented by selected original drawings by Charles-Edouard Jeanneret: LC, *Journey to the East,* ed. and trans. Ivan Žaknić (Cambridge, Mass.: MIT Press, 1987).

2   "Le Corbusier: Nothing Is Transmissible But Thought," in LC, *Oeuvres complètes,* vol. 8: *The Last Works,* ed. Willy Boesiger (Zurich: Editions d'Architecture, 1970), 173–77. The entry is prefaced by an explanatory epigram: "The following was written by Le Corbusier one month before his death. It is the last thing he ever wrote. It reads like an autobiographical monograph, like an intellectual testament, or like the dialogue of a man with himself in the act of summing up his life's work. The following text is an excerpt." The "excerpt"—it is not said from what larger whole—is followed by the notation "Paris, July 1965."

3   Eduard Sekler and William Curtis, writing in *Le Corbusier at Work: The Genesis of the Carpenter Center for the Visual Arts* (Cambridge: Harvard University Press, 1978), cite a passage in translation from *Oeuvres complètes,* vol. 8, and refer to the source text simply as "the last essay Le Corbusier wrote a month before his death" (73), citing the passage as LC's excerpt "Nothing Is Transmissible But Thought" but with no reference to *Mise au point*.

4   Jacques Guiton, *The Ideas of Le Corbusier on Architecture and Planning* (New York: George Braziller, 1981), 112, 116.

5   Jean Petit, an independent consultant, author, and friend who collaborated with LC on various projects and played multiple roles in the architect's life—including that of editor of several books and pamphlets, and as go-between for the unrealized project Olivetti-General Electric, Milan. LC said of Petit: "Jean Petit est absolument remarquable comme sérieux, comme enthousiasme, comme dévouement total et comme capacité technique: imprimeriè,

polycopie, secrétariat, etc." LC to J. L. Sert, 22 Mar. 1957, Fondation Le Corbusier, Paris (abbreviated hereafter as FLC), doc. R3 03, 305).

6   One of the greatest contributions to the reconstruction of France and the New Urbanism was LC's l'Unité d'Habitation at Marseilles, nicknamed for a time "Maison du Fada" (looney bin). According to Claudius-Petit, at the time minister of Reconstruction, LC often spoke disdainfully of the public's failure to understand his ideas. "They can spend billions for a new prototype of a plane, submarine or guns, and more recently the atomic bomb; but the prototype of new housing for a man and his family: it's always too expensive." Claudius-Petit, *La Feuille d'avis* (Neuchâtel), 24 Sept. 1963.

7   In 1961, LC concluded a book of five lithographs entitled *Série Panurge* with the following words: "This book . . . a book in the most concrete language, is always within reach of my hand, somewhere with its companions Don Quixote and Ulysses, between three continents united by the sea. This book is the quintessence of complete human contact, mind, body, health. . . . That's why, during these days of August '61, Panurge was 'UBU' and played the puppet!" (author's translation).

8   For more on this book, see Paul Venable Turner, *The Education of Le Corbusier* (New York: Garland, 1977), 24–29. Turner is mistaken, however, in his assumption that Jeanneret did not read the book until he was settled in Paris (24); according to letters written from Florence to his parents dated 8 Oct. 1907 and 31 Jan. 1908 from Vienna, located at the Bibliothèque de la Ville, La Chaux-de-Fonds, Jeanneret had read the book on the road. As he wrote: "Un beau livre, *Les Grands Initiés,* qui paraît au premier juger être bien noble et bien édifiant, philosophique et peu facile" (8 Oct. 1907); "J'ai fini la lecture, il y a 15 jours des *Grands Initiés. . . .* Ce bouquin-là est superbe!" (31 Jan. 1908).

9   From a letter of Jeanneret's to his parents written from Vienna, 11 Feb. 1908, transcribed typescript,

Bibliothèque de la Ville, La Chaux-de-Fonds, doc. no. LC ms. 36, 1.

10   "Paris, Dimanche 22 Novembre 1908: Lettre à M. Charles L'Eplattenier," in Jean Petit, *Le Corbusier lui-même* (Geneva: Editions Rousseau, 1970), 34.

11   Sekler and Curtis, *Le Corbusier at Work,* 47, 311. Another scholar to develop this claim is Charles Jencks, in his *Le Corbusier and the Tragic View of Architecture* (Cambridge: Harvard University Press, 1973).

12   M. Nussbaum, "'J'envie, monsieur, l'efficacité de votre style,' lui écrivit un jour Paul Valéry," in *La Feuille d'avis* (Neuchâtel), 24 Sept. 1965. LC quoted this sentiment in his interview of May 1965 : "Un jour, Paul Valéry m'a dit que j'écrivais comme un ange" (see translation in this volume, 117).

13   This international journal on contemporary issues was published in Paris between 15 Oct. 1920 and 1925. Twenty-eight issues were published under the editorship of Charles-Edouard Jeanneret (LC) and Amédée Ozenfant. Jeanneret was also a major contributor on the subjects of architecture and urbanism. He wrote under the various pseudonyms Le Corbusier, Le Corbusier-Saugner, Paul Boulard, and Vauvrecy or Fayet when in collaboration with Ozenfant. See also LC's interview in this volume.

14   From a letter to LC of 4 Feb. 1957 from a friend, Paul Baudry, of Lausanne, who worked for LC at *L'Esprit nouveau* around 1922 and who briefly considered writing a book on Corbusier in 1928. FLC, doc. U3 07, 171.

15   "En août 1965, j'avais envoyé à Le Corbusier à Cap-Martin un exemplaire du manuscrit définitif. Il devrait donc logiquement se trouver dans les archives de la Fondation." Jean Petit to author, 28 July 1992.

16   The architect Robert Rebutato, who worked for LC during his last years, told me: "Le Corbusier gave me the manuscript to take to Paris, which I did in my car at the end of August and gave it to Mr. Besset" (Besset was one of three trustees LC chose to set up the FLC, the other two being Michel

Pomey and Jean-Pierre de Montmollin). Interview with author, 13 Oct. 1984.

17 "Page qui tourne . . ." begins as does "'Le graphique irrécusable . . .'" but is somewhat shorter overall. The targeted audience for this essay is unclear (see FLC, doc. U3 9, 93–99).

18 The text was sent from LC to Jean Petit, 10 Nov. 1961. FLC, doc. G1 20, 308.

19 LC, *Journey to the East,* 266.

20 In the chapter "Danube" Jeanneret admits in several places to his own inability to write and yet criticizes the editor of *La Feuille d'avis* for taking liberties with his prose: "Do you know, readers, that my beautiful Danube was mutilated by an editor and a pair of scissors? . . . I recognize that the scissors were acting benevolently, aiming only to purify an uncertain style. I acknowledge their charitable intentions but decline their offer of help. For— allow me just one further word, weary reader—I do not offer you literature, since I have never learned to write. Having educated my eyes to the spectacle of things, I am trying to tell you of the beauty I encountered with sincere words." *Journey to the East,* 40–41.

21 "Voyez-vous, le créateur est toujours là pour rappeler aux gigolos dans mon genre, qu'ils sont peu de chose, et c'est justement là qu'il faut réagir, qu'il faut se battre." Jean Petit, *Le Corbusier parle* (Geneva: Editions Forces Vives, 1967), 10.

22 LC, speech at the closing session of the Permanent Headquarters Committee, Lake Success, 13 Dec. 1946, in LC, *U.N. Headquarters* (New York: Reinhold, 1947), 74.

23 For an intimate portrait with this focus, see *Les Mains de Le Corbusier* by his longtime collaborator André Wogenscky (Paris: Editions de Grenelle, 1987).

24 LC, "A Letter to Friends," *Journey to the East,* 18–19.

25 Ibid., 14.

26 Petit, *Le Corbusier lui-même,* 105.

27 LC was given up to a thousand words by the Jawaharlal Nehru Souvenir Volumes Committee for his entry to the volume *The Changing World.* For the letter, see Shrimen Narayan to LC, 30 Mar. 1964, FLC, doc. T1 11, 244.

28 From an essay entitled "Tout arrive enfin à la mer," written by LC for Pierre Richard of the Institut de l'Avenir Humain, dated 22 Dec. 1954, author's translation. FLC, doc. A3 2, 659–64.

29 LC to Jean Petit, 5 Apr. 1965, FLC, doc. G3 07, 121.

30 LC, *Oeuvre complète, 1957–65,* ed. W. Boesiger (Zurich: Editions Girsberger, 1965), 203. See also *Le Corbusier Sketchbooks,* vol. 4: *1957–1964* (Cambridge, Mass.: MIT Press, 1982), S-67, sketches 916, 920; and the note dated 17 July 1962: "Ecrire un livre. La fin d'un monde . . . délivrance."

31 LC to Malraux, 21 July 1958.

32 P. Prabhawalkar and S. J. Malhotra were senior architects, Office of the Chief Architect, Punjab, and town planning advisers to the Capital Project, Chandigarh. LC to Pierre Jeanneret, 17 Mar. 1965, FLC, doc. G3 07, 63. See also two other letters containing specific instructions to Pierre about major projects LC built in Chandigarh (letter from Paris, 15 Feb. 1965, FLC, doc. G3 07, 63, and letter to Jeet Malhotra concerning the model of the Open Hand, from Paris, 28 Jan. 1965, FLC, doc. G3 07, 25).

33 "Chandigarh Forty Years after Le Corbusier," *Architectura and Natura Quarterly* (Amsterdam), 25.

34 LC to Claudius-Petit, 14 Sept. 1962, FLC, doc. E 1(16), 301.

35 Mary Patricia May Sekler, "Le Corbusier, Ruskin, the Tree and the Open Hand," in Russell Walden, ed., *The Open Hand: Essays on Le Corbusier* (Cambridge, Mass.: MIT Press, 1977), 42–95.

36 Wogenscky told me that the "hand to give and receive," long a symbolic ideal for LC, tended toward the horizontal, whereas the Open Hand monument is a stiff vertical gesture ascending toward the sky—not necessarily toward a fellow

human for giving and receiving. An approximate right angle is realized between the two extreme fingers and the three middle ones, a vertical axis toward the heavens. LC was an agnostic and thus this symbol should not be interpreted as gesturing toward God, but rather toward the infinite, toward forces that are stronger than us and deserve our respect. In short: in its final form, the Open Hand Monument might be a gesture neither to receive nor give, Wogenscky noted. Interview with author, 21 Nov. 1994.

37 See Sekler, "Le Corbusier, Ruskin, the Tree and the Open Hand," 83, and André Malraux, "In Memory of Le Corbusier," in *Oeuvres complètes,* 8:186–90 (homage to LC on behalf of the French government, pronounced at the Louvre [Cour carrée], 1 Sept. 1965).

38 For more information on Pierre Jeanneret, see Hélène Cauquil, "Vous avez dit Jeanneret?" in *Le Corbusier vu par* (Liège: Pierre Mardaga, 1987), 75–77, and Cauquil, "Pierre l'autre Jeanneret," in "Le Corbusier l'atelier 35 rue de Sèvres," *Bulletin d'informations architecturales* 114, suppl. (Summer 1987), 4–8. Charles Jencks has also suggested this association between the two Jeannerets and Cervantes's pair: "No doubt he [LC] often saw himself and Pierre Jeanneret as this knight errant and Sancho Panza." See Jencks, *Le Corbusier and the Tragic View of Architecture,* 178.

39 From an interview with Alfred Roth, who worked with the two Jeanneret cousins from 1927 to 1929, quoted in Hélène Cauquil, "Pierre Jeanneret: La passion de construire" (Diploma thesis, University of Paris, Unité Pedagogique 8, 1983), FLC, doc. B 413.

40 Petit, *Le Corbusier parle,* 17.

41 Cited in ibid.

42 LC to Eulie Chowdhury, June 1965, FLC, doc. G3 07, 215.

43 "Le Corbusier l'atelier 35 rue de Sèvres," 3.

44 Max Daireaux, *Cervantès* (Paris: Desclée de Brouwer, n.d.). LC scribbled in the margin of page 42, "Cer-

vantes, like Rabelais, traveled and saw. And it was done on foot: eyes, walking on and on!" In the same margin, concerning the artistic images and quick sketches that would one day be used for great compositions, he also wrote, "Bien dit M. Daireaux" (Well said, Mr. Daireaux). Quotations on 42, author's translation.

45 Albert Jeanneret to Maurice Besset, Vevey, 7 June 1966, FLC, doc. E2 5, 217.

46 From "Biographical Notes," in LC, *New World of Space* (New York: Reynal and Hitchcock / Boston: Institute of Contemporary Art, 1948), 13.

47 Hughes Desalle interviewed LC on 15 May 1965 and recorded the interview on two 33-RPM records; see the complete translation in this volume.

48 LC to Abel Sorensen, 23 Feb. 1965, FLC, doc. T1 5, 461.

49 George A. Dudley, *A Workshop for Peace: Designing the United Nations Headquarters* (Cambridge, Mass.: MIT Press and Architectural History Foundation, 1994), 371–76.

50 *Niemeyer par lui-même, l'architecte de Brasilia parle à Edouard Bailby* (Paris: Editions Balland, 1993), 66–71.

51 David Underwood, *Oscar Niemeyer and the Architecture of Brazil* (New York: Rizzoli, 1994), 155.

52 "The Secretariat: A Campanile, a Cliff of Glass, a Great Debate," *Architectural Forum* (November 1950), 97, marked copy, FLC.

53 Abel Sorensen to LC on official U.N. letterhead, 7 Jan. 1947, FLC, doc. D1 20, 302.

54 Wallace K. Harrison, "The United Nations Building in New York," *Journal of the Royal Institute of British Architects* (March 1951), 171–75.

55 See, for example, LC to Wallace Harrison, inviting him and his wife to lunch or dinner and a friendly exchange of ideas (21 Apr. 1947, FLC, doc. D1 18, 148) and the letter of 16 July 1947, offering Harrison the services of ATBAT [Atelier des Bâtisseurs], which LC directed. It also called Harrison's atten-

56 LC to Jean-Pierre de Montmollin, 14 Jan. 1962, sent 19 Jan., FLC, doc. E2 16, 155, author's translation.

57 This slip of paper is FLC, doc. B3 9, inside doc. 150, 29.

58 The biographer is Maurice Jardot, "Sketch for a Portrait," in LC, *Creation Is a Patient Search* (New York: Praeger, 1960), 9–14; LC to Philip Will, Grayson Kirk, and Wolf von Eckardt, 2 Mar. 1961, FLC, doc. T1 18, 548–49.

59 Telegram from Charles Colbert, dean of the School of Architecture, Columbia University, 3 Mar. 1961, FLC, doc. T1 18, 551–52.

60 Sekler and Curtis, *Le Corbusier at Work,* 45.

61 Ibid., 310.

62 *Architectural Forum,* December 1959.

63 *The City of Tomorrow* (Cambridge, Mass.: MIT Press, 1971), 1.

64 *The Radiant City* (New York: Orion Press, 1964 [orig. publ., *La Ville radieuse,* Paris, 1933]), 260.

65 LC, "Sort de Paris," 22 July 1958, FLC, doc. E2 14, 96–97.

66 "Le Corbusier and Media: A Dialogue with Jean-Louis Cohen," *Design Book Review* 14 (Spring 1988), 15–18, esp. 18.

67 Paul Delouvrier to LC, 7 Apr. 1962, FLC, doc. E1 18, 153. *The Athens Charter,* a document dealing with "the functional city," was a result of the Fourth CIAM Congress, held in Athens in 1933.

68 "Où en est-on 26 ans après *la Charte d'Athènes?*" 27 pp., 2 May 1962, FLC, doc. U3 2, 310–59. LC finished this document in Chandigarh on 2 May and sent it to Delouvrier from Paris on 2 June for inclusion in the "District de Paris," published later as *Paris en question* (Paris: Presses Universitaires de France, 1965).

69 Paul Delouvrier to LC, 28 Sept. 1962, FLC, doc. E1 18, 192.

70 LC to Delouvrier, 6 Oct. 1962, FLC, doc. E1 18, 193.

71 "Quel sera le nouveau visage de Paris?" *Le Figaro littéraire,* 18–24 June 1964, 8–9. A copy of this newspaper preserved at FLC shows that LC read this report and marked it in pencil, circling Wogenscky's "Corbusian" answer to the editor-in-chief's question. When, in 1994, I contacted the seventy-eight-year-old Wogenscky to comment further on this event now thirty years distant, he declined tactfully. "I would prefer to look forward," he wrote. "To reread these articles would take me backward." André Wogenscky to author, 28 Nov. 1994.

72 Siegfried Giedion, "Le Corbusier and the Contemporary Means of Architectural Expression," English text in catalogue for *The North American Tour, 1959–60, of Le Corbusier Exhibition* (Zurich: Verlag Girsberger, 1957), 12.

73 Among LC's private correspondence, for example, is a letter to Claudius-Petit with photocopies of the A.I.A. gold medal, the Columbia honorary degree, a medal cast by La Monnaie, Paris, and his entries in *Famous Architects* and *Who's Who in Art.* LC wrote: "Une cabale très forte est montée contre moi par les Prix de Rome et une cabale très active est montée contre moi par Zehrfuss (vous me dites que je me trompe totalement)." LC to Claudius-Petit, Paris, 29 Sept. 1961, FLC, doc. 13 14, 42.

74 *Le Corbusier Sketchbooks,* vol. 4, T-69, sketch 965.

75 The Museum of the Twentieth Century idea was abandoned until 1969. It was eventually incorporated into the futuristic Pompidou Grand Project for the Beaubourg, which became Centre National d'Art et de Culture, built between 1972 and 1977, the year it opened to the public, and known today simply as Centre Georges Pompidou.

76 Dr. Plichet, president of the Medical Association of the Seine-et-Oise, published the following: "M. Le Corbusier va multiplier le nombre de fous en France, dans la promiscuité et le vacarme," FLC, doc. U3 07, 489.

77 LC to Lilette Ougier, 5 July 1965, FLC, doc. G3 07, 230.

78 Two-page document, signed by LC, 9 Oct. 1961, FLC, doc. U3 9, 102.

79 LC to Paul Delouvrier, 6 Oct. 1962, FLC, doc. E1 18, 193. LC wrote a note about himself in the third-person singular: "Mr. Malraux a précisé qu'il n'était pas nécessaire d'expliquer 'qui est le plus grand architecte du monde.'" See *Le Corbusier Sketchbooks*, vol. 4, S-70, sketch 1039.

80 See LC, *Oeuvre complète*, 7:220–29.

81 Ibid., 220.

82 Ibid., 220.

83 See LC to Jean Dubuisson, president of Le Cercle d'Etudes Architecturales, in which LC asks advice about hiring a lawyer (FLC, doc. 13 14, 50). A week later he wrote to his former financiers: "I was offered the chair Auguste Perret at the Institute, which I refused, for I know how to resist temptation," and followed by enumerating his most recent contracts, prizes, honorary degrees, and the fact that his book *Creation Is a Patient Search* had come out in six languages. See FLC, doc. 13 14, 60–61.

84 *Le Corbusier Sketchbooks*, vol. 4, S-70, note on sketch 1039 dated 21 Nov. 1963.

85 Telephone conversation, transcript, LC to Mr. Anthonioz, chargé de Mission pour la création artistique, 17 Apr. 1961, FLC, doc. E2 14, 286.

86 "Conception verticale—conception horizontale," 16 pp., 8 Nov. 1956, FLC, doc. A3 1, 308–23. As far back as 1930, LC wrote: "The biological unit: the cell of 14 square meters per occupant." This cell was dedicated to the CIAM Congress, and LC was absolutely persuaded that it "would lead to the expansion and flowering of man's lives in a machine age." LC, *The Radiant City* (New York: Orion Press, 1933), 144.

87 See Caroline Maniaque, "Lettres aux clients, lettres aux artisans: Le cas des Maisons Jaoul," in *Le Corbusier: Ecritures* (Paris: Fondation Le Corbusier, 1993), 55–65.

88 LC, *U.N. Headquarters,* 6.

89 Ibid.

90 LC to Robert Bordaz (not sent), 15 Nov. 1962, FLC, doc. E 1, 9–36.

91 This movie, to be directed by André Michelin, Chaumaine Productions, was never realized. The script by Michel Bataille is dated April 1961 (FLC, doc. B3 09, 10).

92 From "Le Corbusier in New York: A Memoir by Costantino Nivola," trans. Richard Ingersoll, in *Le Corbusier: A Marriage of Contours,* catalogue of the exhibition "Le Corbusier: Drawings from the Collection of Costantino Nivola," (New York: Princeton Architectural Press, 1990), 3.

93 LC, *Precisions,* trans. Edith Schreiber Aujame (Cambridge, Mass.: MIT Press, 1991), 23–34, esp. 33–34. In 1933, LC wrote a book dedicated to bringing down the academy: *Croisade, ou le crépuscule des académies* (Paris: Editions G. Crès et Cie, 1933). This dislike was reciprocated: around the time of the hotly contested l'Unité d'Habitation project (1951), La Société des Architectes Diplômés par le Gouvernement (SADG) —academically trained architects with government-granted degrees—issued a scandalous article on LC's project entitled "La Maison du Fada." The piece was so slanderous, in fact, that Bernard H. Zehrfuss, a colleague and holder of a Prix de Rome, whom LC considered his nemesis, came to the architect's defense and resigned from the SADG.

94 LC to Jean-Pierre de Montmollin, 15 Mar. 1965, FLC, doc. U3 9, 214.

95 LC to his parents, from Munich, 29 June 1910.

96 LC to his parents, from Berlin, 28 Oct. 1910.

97 LC to M. Lallement, du Cabinet Civil du Maréchal, Paris, 8 Jan. 1943, FLC, doc. A2 17, 248.

98 For more details, see the communication between the Vichy administration and the Académie des Beaux-Arts to the secretary of state for national education and youth, Beaux-Arts, 12 Feb. 1943, FLC, doc. A2 17, 249–50.

99 Confidential memorandum signed by LC, dated 4 Jan. 1956, FLC, doc. U3 07, 17–18.

100 See Témoignages: Iannis Xenakis, who worked in LC's atelier from 1947 to 1959, describing how he, Maisonnier, and Tobito were let go, in "Le Corbusier l'atelier 35 rue de Sèvres," 16–17.

101 "Le Corbusier parle . . . et écrit," *Spazio e società* (March 1985), 57.

102 "Presentation of the Royal Gold Medal to Le Corbusier (Charles Edouard Jeanneret)," *Journal of the Royal Institute of British Architects* (April 1953), 215–18.

103 *Le Corbusier Talks with Students from the Schools of Architecture,* trans. Pierre Chase (New York: Orion Press, 1961 [orig. publ., Paris: Editions Denoël, 1943]), 4.

104 Petit, *Le Corbusier lui-même,* 125.

105 LC was not the only one to raise questions about the Grand Palais's suitability as an exhibit hall. The journalist Jacques Michel wrote an extensive piece, "Vers un renouveau de l'équipement culturel," inquiring into the palace's outdated functions, in *Le Monde* (30 Sept. 1964). LC read this article, marked it, and made several annotations, among them "Parler avec Malraux, important." FLC, doc. 13 18, 148–49.

106 Exhibitions continued to be presented in the Grand Palais, up through the summer of 1993, when bolts started falling from frames holding the glass roof. Although nets were erected to catch the bolts, leakage, the rotting of the wood foundations, and the rusting of the palace's delicate metal dome continued apace. Experts were brought in to study the palace and rescue it. Thirty years after LC's death, the estimated 34 million francs required to renovate the palace vindicated his dire predictions.

107 For the text of the entire interview in French, see "Reponse téléphonique de M. Le Corbusier," 16 Nov. 1963, FLC, doc. 13 18, 185–87.

108 Miguel de Cervantes Saavedra, *The Adventures of Don Quixote,* trans. J. M. Cohen (New York: Penguin, 1977), part II, 937.

109 Eugène Claudius-Petit, "Le Corbusier: Dernier projet pour Paris," *L'Architecture d'aujourd'hui* 249 (February 1987), 1.

110 LC, *Le Poème de l'angle droit,* part A-3 (1955; rpt. Paris: Fondation Le Corbusier and Editions Connivences, 1989), 29.

111 LC to André Wogenscky, cited by Pierre Joffroy in *PARIS Match,* 11 Sept. 1965, 58, noted by Joffroy as being written "at the time of Wogenscky's mother's death." In a letter to the author, 22 Jan. 1985, Wogenscky corrected this to refer to the occasion of his *father's* death.

112 Petit, *Le Corbusier lui-même,* 140.

113 Petit, *Le Corbusier parle,* 20.

114 Dr. Jacques Hindermeyer, taped interview with author, Paris, 8 and 23 July 1994.

115 Petit, *Le Corbusier lui-même,* 120–21.

116 Ibid., 132.

117 Jean-Pierre de Montmollin of Neuchâtel to M. Besset and M. Pomey, 31 Mar. 1965, FLC, doc. E2 16, 203.

118 Robert Rebutato to Dr. Hindermeyer, 20 Aug. 1965, FLC, doc. E2 11, 181.

119 For a moving text of this Mediterrean "monastic retreat," copiously illustrated with photographs and drawings, see Bruno Chiambretto, *Le Corbusier à Cap-Martin* (Marseilles: Parenthèses, 1987).

120 LC to Professor Renato Gambier, Venice, 16 June 1965, FLC, doc. G3 07, 197.

121 Albert Jeanneret to LC, 23 July 1965, Bibliothèque de la Ville, La Chaux-de-Fonds, doc. X, 17.

122 LC, "Unités d'habitation de grandeur conforme," Paris, 1 Apr. 1957, FLC, doc. U3 07, 176.

123 As related by Sylvain Zegler, "Le Corbusier m'avait dit: 'Le Musée du XXᵉ siècle doit être aux Champs-Elysées,'" *Le Figaro littéraire,* 2–8 Sept. 1965.

124 Dr. Jacques Hindermeyer, taped interview with author, July 1994, and Hindermeyer's unpublished witness account, "Le Corbusier intime" (n.d.).

125 From author's interview with Henry Pessar, August 1995. Pessar wrote this recollection down (in English) after the interview; that brief text, included here, has been edited but not abridged.

126 "Vous savez, je suis un vieux cornichon, mais j'aurais encore dans la tête des plans pour au moins cent ans. A tout à l'heure, donc!" Stanislaus Von Moos, *Le Corbusier: L'architecte et son mythe* (Paris: Horizons de France, 1971), 302–3.

127 See Kenneth Frampton, "Opus Circulatorum," prefatory note to Richard A. Moore, "Alchemical and Mythical Themes in the Poem of the Right Angle, 1947–1965," in *Oppositions* 19/20 (Winter/Spring 1980), 109. The original text read "swimming *for* the sun," which has been adjusted here. When I asked Soltan to corroborate LC's statement to him, he answered: "No, it wasn't to me that he said it, but to André Maisonnier, who told me about it at Le Corbusier's wake." Conversation with author, Philadelphia, 11 Dec. 1995.

Mise au point

1 This introduction, though not signed, must be by Jean Petit, editor of Editions Forces Vives, which first published this booklet in French (Paris, 1966). A more recent edition, combining *Mise au point* and *L'Urbanisme est une clef,* and containing an expanded introduction by Petit, was published during the LC centennial (Geneva: Editions Archigraphie, 1987). This second edition contains an expanded introduction signed by Jean Petit.

2 The expressions "Nothing is transmissible but thought" and "The law of life: death" already appear in LC's *Quand les cathédrales étaient blanches* (When the cathedrals were white) (Paris: Plon, 1937), in the chapter "Cities of the World," 30–31; cited from English-language edition, translated by Francis E. Hyslop, Jr. (New York: McGraw-Hill, 1964).

3 "Il faut de nouveau creuser dans la vie afin de refaire de la chair." From Henry Miller, *Tropique du cancer* (Paris: Editions Denoël, 1945), 121; book in LC's private library and now at the Fondation Le Corbusier (hereafter cited as FLC). Curiously, LC did not mark or underline the passage quoted here, although his copy contains other markings. "The cancer of time is eating us away," Miller wrote on page 1. *Tropique du cancer* was published in Paris in 1934, became immediately famous, and was banned in English-speaking countries. It was first published in English by Grove Press in 1961; the English translation of this passage is cited from *Tropic of Cancer* (New York: Evergreen, 1980), 98.

4 It is not clear whether LC is referring to André Gide's *Les Nourritures terrestres* (The fruits of the earth, 1897) or to Gide's *Les Nouvelles Nourritures* (The new fruits, 1935), a copy of which was in LC's library and contains several markings that find their resonance in *Mise au point,* e.g., LC's marginalia Rabelais (17), death (87), and "la vie . . . sans pitié" (88). His marginalia on p. 116, "toute la peinture! la poésie, l'invention: mécanisme informulable" echo the ending sentiments of *Mise au point.*

5 In his dedication of the book *Le Corbusier: Les plans de Paris, 1956–1922,* LC wrote to Jacques Hindermeyer: "La vie est une longue patience . . . Non?" (Life is a long patience . . . No?) To which the doctor replied: "Et votre exemple est là pour me rappeler la persévérance" (And your example is there to remind me of perseverance), December 1958, FLC, doc. E2 11, 146.

6 This paragraph can be found almost verbatim in the statement LC made concerning *Le Corbusier, 1910–65,* ed. W. Boesiger and H. Girsberger (Zurich: Les Editions d'Architecture, 1967), 6 (FLC, doc. U 2, 18–24), as well as the letter to his elder brother, Albert Jeanneret, the day of his arrival at Cap-

Martin that final summer. Thus this passage is still alive in LC's memory; unfortunately, he does not seem to remember any larger context for it. The letter, dated 29 July 1965, is full of defiance. For the complete printed text, see Jean Petit, *Le Corbusier lui-même* (Geneva: Editions Rousseau, 1970), 139–40.

7 Gen. 32:22–32.

8 Both ideas expressed in this passage—truth and the moral about material versus spiritual pursuits—were themes LC expressed to a group of more than three thousand students at the Sorbonne in a lecture of 4 Feb. 1960. They reappear as the closing paragraph of *Creation Is a Patient Search* (New York: Praeger, 1960).

9 Maurice Jardot was a longtime friend of LC's; their correspondence dates from 1940. Jardot held several positions at several government agencies, including the Caisse Nationale des Monuments Historiques. He wrote the preface to *Le Corbusier, textes et planches* (Paris: Vincent Freál, 1960), a visual documentary of LC's work in several mediums, including architecture, urban planning, and art. Jardot also provided the introduction to *Creation Is a Patient Search,* entitled "Sketch for a Portrait." Their friendship seems to have preserved a happier and more relaxed tone than most and lasted until the end. See LC to Jardot from Rocquebrune, containing a joke and a caricature, 28 Dec. 1944, FLC, doc. E2 05, 193.

10 The reference is to the Royal Institute of British Architects (RIBA) Gold Medal, awarded 31 Mar. 1953.

11 Dr. Plichet, psychiatrist at the Hôpital Saint-Antoine and president of the Medical Association of the Seine-et-Oise. The polemics against LC's project at Marseilles were much broader than one individual. It included the Society of French Architects and even a group of concerned citizens, who brought a lawsuit amounting to twenty million francs; the Society for the Preservation of the General Aesthetics of France" claimed that LC and his associates

should pay damages because the building was unhygienic, dangerous, and brutal. The court at Marseilles ruled in LC's favor; for his part, LC claimed philosophically that "struggle was good for building character."

12 *Petits lits blancs* were glittering fund-raising balls given annually at the Paris Opéra. The well-to-do invitees paid a high entrance fee, and the proceeds were given to charity (children, home care, and hospitalization).

13 When speaking of himself, LC often switches to a more detached third-person singular. A poignant example of another switch from "I" to the second-person plural can be found in a letter LC wrote to André Bloc on 9 Mar. 1964, at the time of reprinting *The Radiant City* (New York: Grossman, 1967 [orig. publ., *La Ville radieuse,* Paris, 1933], 347. In *Le Modulor,* LC adopts, in addition to his typical distancing "il," another detached variant: "notre homme" (our man) or "notre architecte" (our architect). See *Le modulor* (Paris: Fondation Le Corbusier, 1983), e.g., 25, 26, 27, 29, 30.

14 The idea of time passing, "page qui tourne," recurs often in LC's mature texts, speeches, and proclamations. Note a second instance later in the paragraph. The phrase is the title of an essay written and signed "Paris, le 14 septembre 1961" (see FLC, doc. U3 9, 93–99), most of which appears in *Mise au point* (1966), 28–47. It is not clear for what occasion LC used this seven-page text, which found its way into *Mise au point* with only minor changes. See also the note 25, below, for a similar text, "'Le graphique irrécusable . . . ,'" of 17 Oct. 1961.

15 The tone in which LC describes New York City is dramatically more negative and condemnatory than is his hopeful, optimistic passage in *When the Cathedrals Were White:* "New York has such courage and enthusiasm that everything can be begun again, sent back to the building yard and made into something still greater, something mastered" (36). See note 2, above.

16 In English in original.

17 "Si haut que soit le trône, si moelleux que soit le
    siège, on n'est jamais assis que sur son cul." Mon-
    taigne, *Essais,* book III, ch. 13 ("De l'expérience").
    Here LC cites the sentence inexactly; he cites it cor-
    rectly as an epigraph to the chapter "Explications,"
    in part II of LC's book *Une Maison, un palais* (Paris:
    Editions G. Crès et Cie, 1928), 86.

    LC was much taken by this sentiment of Mon-
    taigne's. He also tried it out at a seminar at Prince-
    ton University while discussing plans for his villas.
    He writes proudly of it in his book on his American
    visit: "Expressing myself (modestly!) in the
    manner of Montaigne," he wrote, "'Gentlemen,
    you never have more than one bottom to sit down
    on!'" Corbusier expected that the chairman of the
    department, one Mr. Labatu, would translate it to
    the students; but "No, you will not translate such a
    remark in the beautiful, green, Gothic town of
    Princeton." See *When the Cathedrals Were White,* 142.

18 The Modulor is a proportional system based on the
    human body (a man with a raised arm, measuring
    seven feet, six inches), the first proportional system
    based on the human body since the Renaissance, to
    be applied in art, architecture, furniture, and manu-
    facture. LC's comment here appears to be a hidden
    quotation of the words of Frédéric-Louis Sauser,
    known under the nom de plume Blaise Cendrars,
    born at La Chaux-de-Fonds the same year as LC.
    Sauser wrote to LC thanking him for a signed copy
    of *Le Modulor* but added, "Ton Modulor je m'en
    fous" (I don't give a damn about your modulor).
    Cited in Jean Petit, letter of 22 Dec. 1949, in *Le Cor-
    busier parle* (Geneva: Editions Forces Vives, 1967),
    18. See also *Modulor I and II,* trans. Peter de Francia
    and Anna Bostock (Cambridge, Mass.: MIT Press,
    1973).

19 The travel sketchbooks D-14, D-15, D-16, and E-20,
    as published by MIT Press and the Architectural
    History Foundation in 1981 (*Le Corbusier Sketchbooks,*
    vol. 2: *1950–1954*), contains entries recorded in

    Bogota during 1950. LC had been invited to Colom-
    bia to study the master plan for Bogota. This was a
    precursor to Chandigarh, where the principle of
    dividing the land into urban sectors was first
    applied. Sketchbook D-17 contains a drawing (271)
    dated 19 May 1950, with the message: "'La pierre
    amie de l'homme . . .' Pour Jardot Dr. des Archives
    photogra. de France."

20 Giacomo Barozzi da Vignola, Italian architect
    (1507–73), known for his treatise of 1562 on the
    five architectural orders (Doric, Ionic, Corinthian,
    Tuscan, and Composite), which were standardized
    during the Renaissance and which for LC epito-
    mizes all that is wrong with the Beaux-Arts educa-
    tion. LC wrote in *When the Cathedrals Were White,*
    "American instruction is . . . timorously founded on
    'Vignolesque' traditions" (140), and in *Le Poème de
    l'angle droit,* "Et Vignole—enfin est foutu! Merci!
    Victoire!" (1955; rpt. Paris: Fondation Le Corbusier
    and Editions Connivences, 1989), 68.

21 The correct dates are 1907 and 1911. The young
    Jeanneret first visited this monastery at Galluzzo
    near Florence in 1907. But he returned to it and
    sketched it on the way back from his *Voyage d'Orient*
    in 1911. See his description in *Journey to the East,* ed.
    and trans. Ivan Žaknić (Cambridge, Mass.: MIT
    Press, 1987), 23, 247n5, and LC's drawings, 244–45,
    translator's note.

22 This sequence of identity markers was stable for LC
    in his last years. He expressed much the same senti-
    ment in a BBC broadcast on 15 Mar. 1959: "I am
    seventy-one years old. I built my first house at age
    seventeen and a half and, for more than fifty years,
    I have continued to be occupied with many adven-
    tures and difficulties, catastrophes, and from time
    to time, success. My research, like my feelings, have
    been directed toward what is the principle value in
    life: poetry. Poetry is at the heart of man and is the
    capacity to enter the richness of nature" (interview
    recorded in LC's apartment, 27 Jan. 1959).

23 LC is alluding here to his principle of *Les Trois Etab-*

lissements humains (The three human establishments), a book he wrote in 1945; see note 27, below.

24 Serge Alexandre Stavisky (1886–1934), a Russian-born French swindler, sold forty million francs' worth of fraudulent bonds to the French. In December 1933, when the deception was discovered, it brought down two ministries.

25 This text, "'Le graphique irrécusable, 'La ligne irrévocable,' ou 'La fin du potard,'" is an eleven-page manuscript dated 17 Oct. 1961, Paris (see FLC, doc. U3 2, 236–46); the text with the same subtitle was incorporated exactly as typed into the French original of *Mise au point,* 28–47.

Three weeks later, on 10 Nov. 1961, LC mailed another copy of this manuscript to Jean Petit, to whom LC's secretary wrote, "Monsieur, Veuillez trouver, ci-joint, l'article de L-C 'Le Graphique Irrécusable,' M. Le Corbusier m'a chargé de vous joindre également une copie de sa lettre du 12 octobre 1961 à M. Jean Jacques Duval concernant le 'Graphique Irrécusable.' Je vous prie d'agréer, Monsieur, mes salutations distinguées. La secrétaire."

The letter of 12 Oct. 1961 begins in the text with the words "I am sending you a first copy of my text 'Le Graphique Irrécusable'" and is reproduced in its entirety over the next two pages (27–28), except for the closing paragraph. Both this letter and the appended text were in Jean Petit's possession until the publication of *Mise au point* in 1966, whereupon he incorporated LC's cover letter to Duval, and the text LC sent to Duval, into the final text of *Mise au point.* For more on Duval, see note 33, below.

26 *Zazous* was a nickname given in the early 1940s to the eccentric youth of Paris. It derived from the English "swing"—more precisely, from a song by Johnny Hess, "Je suis swing," which employed American jazz rhythms. The refrain went like this: "Je suis swing / Dza zou, dza zou / C'est gentil comme tout!" Another song of Hess's from 1943, "Ils sont zazous," mimicked the dress habits of the new generation. See "La libération des zazous," in

"Le plaisir des mots par Claude Duneton," *Le Figaro littéraire,* 22 July 1994, 2.

27 This phrase echoes the title *Les Trois Etablissements humains* (Paris: Editions Denoël, 1945), which LC wrote for the Collection ASCORAL (Association des Constructeurs pour une Rénovation Architecturale, which he directed) in collaboration with N. Bezard, J. Commelin, Condouin, J. Dayre, H. Dubreuil, Leyritz, Hanning, Aujame, and De Looze, who participated with LC in 1942 at ASCORAL. Corbusier returns often to this theme (see especially *Creation Is a Patient Search,* 301), including several times in *Mise au point.* A compressed version of LC's twenty-year search for humane town planning in an industrial society, dealing with the Three Human Establishments, the Four Routes, and the Linear Industrial City, can be found in "Towards a Synthesis," in *Le Corbusier: Oeuvre complète, 1938–46* (Zurich: Editions d'Architecture Erlenbach, 1946), 69–75.

28 As early as 1937, in *When the Cathedrals Were White,* which LC wrote upon his return from the United States, he commented at length on the unfortunate influence of the Ecole des Beaux-Arts in Paris— which reached as far as American architectural education. He considered the teaching in many universities to be "dull, flat, dreary and academic," concluding: "The diploma was glorified by the words D.P.L.G., 'Diplomé par le Gouvernement (français).'" He further observed, "I thought that the function of government was to administer its own times and to lead people on the paths of an ever-changing life; not to set up obstacles" (119). At the end of 1940, the Vichy government created the Institute of Architects and, in a ministerial decision, authorized three individuals who lacked official degrees to build. They were Auguste Perret, Eugène Freyssinet, and LC, considered widely to be the three fathers of modern architecture in France. So much for gratitude on LC's part!

29 The French edition uses *maireries* here, not *mairies.* Because *maireries* does not exist in French and because LC placed it in quotation marks for empha-

sis, I have assumed that LC deliberately created a neologism from the word *mairies,* city or town halls, and that this was not simply a typographical error. In fact, he uses the same word in quotation marks in his manuscript "Page qui tourne," 2. See note 14.

30 "Think of the stupidity of a 'Grand Palais" of 1900, in which several Academicians had a chance to speak their message in enormous dimensions!!!" *When the Cathedrals Were White,* 6.

31 In English in original.

32 The Palais du CNIT (Centre National des Industries et des Techniques), located at La Défense, sometimes also referred to as Nanterre, built in 1958. At the time it held the world's record for surface covered by reinforced concrete (236,680 square feet, or 22,000 square meters); its triangular form measures 781 feet (238 meters) on each side. R. Camelot, J. de Mailly, and B. Zehrfuss, architects; N. Esquillan and J. Prouvé, engineers; P. L. Nervi, consulting engineer. LC is clearly referring (with some resentment) to the image that appeared in the journal *Construction moderne* 1 (January 1959), a copy of which was found in LC's library with the annotation "Paris Demain." The image shows the outline of the Palais du CNIT superimposed over the place de la Concorde, indeed covering the entire place in a single span. "Paris demain" was intended as a title for a film, but the project was never realized.

33 Collaboration between engineer and architect is a subject that preoccupied LC for years. The ASCORAL emblem appeared in *Creation Is a Patient Search,* 307, full page and in color; on the facing page LC wrote: "Under this symbolic composition I have placed two clasped hands, the fingers enlaced horizontally, demonstrating the friendly solidarity of both architect and engineer engaged, on the same level, in building the civilization of the machine age. This is the emblem of the 'constructors'" (from *Science et vie,* August 1960). LC corrects the misassumptions made by *Science et vie,* insisting that his emblem leads to peace, collaboration, and efficiency, not the dominance of one over the others.

On 6 Jan. 1964, LC wrote to his old friend the engineer Jean-Jacques Duval, commenting on Duval's book "Le Corbusier vivant," in manuscript since 1962, for which LC had written a one-page introduction. LC refers to this very image and asks Duval to turn it by a quarter-turn and feature it full page and in color, precisely to indicate this collaboration between engineer and architect. FLC, doc. E1, 20.

Jean-Jacques Duval (b. 1912, interviewed by the author in July 1992) met LC at L'école polytechnique at Zurich. They renewed their relationship in Paris in 1934, and after World War II, Duval was among those who attracted LC to a project for reconstructing the city of Saint Dié, which the Germans had leveled. Although the city plan was rejected, Duval commissioned LC to build his factory, Manufacture Claude et Duval, 1947–51, still operating today. Duval is still working on his book. In the latest version, entitled "Rencontres," in a chapter entitled "L'atelier 35 rue de Sèvres" Duval uses several versions of "clasped hands" (ms. p. 218).

34 See *Le Poème de l'angle droit,* section B.4, 67–68: "The clock and the sundial brought to architecture 'the sunbreaker' installed in front of the windows of modern buildings. An architectural symphony readies itself under the title: 'The House Daughter of the Sun' . . . and Vignola is finally done away with! Thank you! Victory!"

35 On completion of the United Nations Building in New York, LC wrote a letter to Senator Warren Austin (Vermont), president of the Commission of the Site Planning Committee. In this letter, LC explains and warns about the dangers of not taking his 1929 invention, the *brise-soleil* (sunbreaker), seriously. "My strong belief, Mr. Senator, is that it is senseless to build in New York, where the climate is terrible in the summer, large glass areas which are not equipped with a brise-soleil. I say this is dangerous, very seriously dangerous!" With ample diagrams and explanations, LC in this very long letter illustrates the use of the brise-soleil along with the

"neutralizing wall"—both, he insists, essential for assuring comfort. See the letter printed in the *Architectural Review* (July 1950), 69–71. More than ten years later, in a lecture delivered at the Faculty of Medicine in Paris on 3 July 1961, LC explained the success of his application of brise-soleil at Chandigarh, a savagely sunny climate.

36   As this passage indicates, a part of this book was indeed written in 1961; the entire book does not date from 1965, as stated in its Introduction. A small text entitled "Page qui tourne . . ." (see Introduction, note 17, and note 14, above; it is basically the same text as "'Le graphique irrécusable . . .'"), in the form of a typescript dated 14 Sept. 1961 is located at FLC (docs. U3 9, 93–99, and A3 1, 344–50). This text appears in *Mise au point* (1966), 28–47, with a slight variation toward the end of the passage.

37   LC was actually applying these ideas to his projects of the time—that is, to his Regional Plan for the City of Meaux: "Ville Radio-concentrique de 17,000 habitants située dans le cadre de la région à 44 km de Paris." In his preliminary design booklet for Meaux, LC clearly illustrates and color codes these routes: "route de terre, route de fer, route d'eau." See the Meaux portfolio "Grille CIAM," FLC, doc. B, 72.

38   [LC's footnote] An example: U.S.A., *When the Cathedrals Were White* (Paris: Plon, 1936 [1937]).

39   The expression "We must localize industry" meant, for LC, that we must accept the "Third Human Establishment," the Linear Industrial City—part of his proposal to resolve the problems of contemporary planning. The industrial city could not be radioconcentric but must be linear, LC insisted. (See, e.g., his conference talk in Brussels, 26 June 1958, FLC, doc. U3 04, 216–21.) The repeated references in *Mise au point* to the Three Human Establishments and the Linear Industrial City have resonances elsewhere in LC's mature work. See, e.g., his letter to Nehru of 14 Feb. 1962 concerning possible industry to be located in the proximity of Chandigarh: "Hindustan Machine Tools wants to install an industrial city. . . . It would be outrageous to destroy the immediate approach to Chandigarh by an industrial city, and especially at this very moment, when the theory of the 'Linear Industrial City' appears as the social, political, geographical and demographic solution," Corbusier wrote. "My dear Nehru, I am the government architectural adviser. My duty is to intervene." For the complete letter, see Petit, *Le Corbusier lui-même*, 127–28.

40   See *Les Trois Etablissements humains,* Collection ASCORAL (Paris: Editions Denoël, 1945). Also *Urbanisme des trois établissements humains,* ed. Jean Petit (Paris: Editions de Minuit, 1959), and *L'Urbanisme est une clef,* ed. Jean Petit (Paris: Editions Forces Vives, 1966), 53–60. Also LC's notes in *Mise au point* (1966), 43.

41   A thalweg or talweg is a geological term for the greatest degree of slope serving as watershed. LC explained "Le thalweg" as a technical term in a lecture on the Three Human Establishments (Brussels, 26 June 1958, FLC, doc. U3 04, 222); it has now been universally adopted to mean the "trail of the valley" that all three routes have a tendency to follow. In S-70, LC marks a full page of notes dealing with "Three Human Establishments": "The linear industrial city, the three routes, *les thalwegs,* etc.," documenting his preoccupation with this topic. These notes are mostly from 1964–65. See *Le Corbusier Sketchbooks,* vol. 4: *1957–1964* (Cambridge, Mass.: MIT Press, 1982), 1041.

42   In a letter of 12 Oct. 1961 to Jean-Jacques Duval, LC writes: "Je vous envoie une copie de la première frappe destinée à la plaquette dont je vous ai parlé: 'Le Graphique irrécusable.'" LC appended the early version of a sketch for the illustration that appears in *Mise au point* (1966), 42–43, and page 9 here. Under the sketch he wrote: "12 October 1961: sent on Nov. 7, 1961, enclosure to Duval "along with the text" (see also note 25, above). In the same letter LC mentioned that he was sending a copy of the

same letter, text, and sketch to Paul Ducret, who worked for LC as administrator until his death in October 1964.

43 [LC's footnote] Collection Urbanisme de CIAM-ASCORAL, sections 5a and 5b, "Une civilisation du travail": *Les Trois Etablissements Humains* (Denoël [1945]).

44 Several versions of the manuscript (16 pp.) and typescript (8 pp.) are extant: "Conception verticale—conception horizontale," written for BIT (Bureau International du Travail), Geneva, copyright by LC, Paris, 8 Nov. 1956. There LC writes: "This work had a poor reception by the authorities; however, the six thousand copies of this printing were quickly sold out. To my knowledge, no reference was made to this book, neither in the daily press nor in the professional journals. In the meantime, one day in 1946, at the Hotel Matignon (seat of the head of the French government in Paris), I heard the President of the Council, in the presence of André Gide, say: 'I read *The Three Human Establishments:* it is the most extraordinary book I have ever read in my life' (the head of the government was Léon Blum)." Cited as per pp. 5–6 of the above ms., FLC, docs. A3 1, 308–23, U3 07, 768–75, and U3 04, 216–31.

45 [LC's footnote] *L'urbanisme des trois établissements humains* (Cahiers "Forces Vives," aux Ed. de Minuit [1959]).

46 LC is remembering his visit to the United States in 1935 and an invitation to lunch by the president of Carbon Carbide Chemical Corporation, then the world's largest producer of chemical products. During LC's visit, the president showed LC a variety of plastic goods: toothbrushes, plastic cups, and so on. LC's response: "Introduce this plastic substance into the building industry!" See "Urbanisme, témoignage d'une société," ms. dated 13 May 1958, FLC, doc. U3 07, 375.

47 Here LC is alluding to the French health insurance system, Sécurité Sociale, enacted in 1945 and giving all salaried persons access to medical treatment (patients pay the doctor and are later reimbursed; depending on the nature of the treatment or hospitalization, reimbursement varies from 70 to 100 percent).

48 In English in LC's original.

49 In English in LC's original.

50 Here ends the text "'Le graphique irrécusable,' 'La ligne irrévocable,' ou 'La fin du potard,'" the eleven-page manuscript that LC sent to Jean-Jacques Duval on 12 Oct. 1961 (see note 25, above).

51 "Le logis est le temple de la famille" (The dwelling is the temple of the family), wrote LC to Mr. Vincendon, editor of *Science et vie,* on 15 Jan. 1963. In this essay LC comes back to his old idea of the need to manufacture machine-made dwellings. This idea had preoccupied him ever since the Pavillon de l'Esprit Nouveau, when he tried to find a universal solution to satisfy this universal need. LC perceived industry as the only hope to solve the problem by standardization and then by industrialization. See FLC, doc. U 39, 160.

52 LC, *Oeuvre complète, 1946–1952* (Zurich: Editions Girsberger, 1953). These illustrated early volumes of LC's complete works were published under his direct supervision to serve as a standardized reference around the world. LC would often tell his assistants: "Go check it in Girsberger."

53 In communist countries during the Stalinist era, *formalism* was a term of abuse applied to almost any deviation from the party line: an interest in abstraction or intellectualism, attention to aesthetic form at the expense of more traditional content that the "masses" could instantly grasp, apparent Western influence, and so on.

As a Pole working in the 1940s and 1950s, Jerzy Soltan was fully aware of these mislabelings and their potential political danger. In 1985, Soltan wrote: "as to the notion of Formalism, all possible vices were attributed in Poland in the early '50s to Le Corbusier. They were summed up with the word

'Formalism.' Depending on the subject matter, the notion of formalism was interpreted at the wish of the really not well informed critics. [As you suggested in your letter,] 'Formalism meant only non-party line.'" Letter to author, 22 Jan. 1985.

Soltan began working for LC on 1 Aug. 1945 and left four years later, on 1 July 1949. For an intimate and moving account of Soltan's experience in the atelier, see Jerzy Soltan, "Travailler avec Le Corbusier," in *Le Corbusier, Europe et modernité* (Budapest: L'Ecole d'Architecture de Strasbourg and Editions Corvina, 1991).

54 True indeed! Not only did Soltan think of Corbu when he worked, but he carried his admiration of his master much further, responding reverently to LC's personal insecurity in the face of history (so awkwardly manifest in LC's lengthy citation of this personal letter). See the letter Soltan wrote from Warsaw on 27 Apr. 1950, in which Soltan reassures LC that he thinks about him, remains grateful for all he learned at his side, and in a postscript adds: "Hanka (my wife) is most probably pregnant—if it is a boy, he will certainly be named Charles-Edouard!" FLC, doc. R3 04, 170.

Soltan and his wife did indeed have a son in 1950 and named him Charles-Edouard. LC declined to be formal godfather, although he kept his "godfatherly" attitude.

55 This one-page paragraph from *Mise au point* can be found verbatim in Jean Petit's *Le Corbusier lui-même* (Panorama Forces Vives, 1970), 133, a book that, according to Petit, was corrected and annotated with LC's help.

The idea of the Open Hand Monument first occurred to LC in 1948, "spontaneously, or more exactly, as a result of reflections and spiritual struggles arising from feelings of anguish and disharmony which separate mankind and so often create enemies. Little by little the open hand appeared as a possibility in great architectural compositions. The notion of setting up such a monument at Chandi-

garh is reported to have been Jane Drew's, for she felt that the symbol of Le Corbusier's philosophy should be made evident to the people of that city." *Le Corbusier,* ed. Willy Boesiger (New York: Praeger, 1972), 210. See also FLC drawing 5825, showing the elevation-section with the measurements and a Modulor Man standing by; also drawings 5838 and 5845.

Concerning the Open Hand Monument, Soltan wrote, "I had several conversations with Le Corbusier on the subject. Many allusions, associations, and metaphors popped up on these occasions: the contrast between the *unarmed hand* and the fist, potentially a weapon-holding one." Pers. comm. with author.

56 LC's correspondence of January–March 1965 reveals the sense of urgency that he attached to this monument, both its symbolism to him personally and its overall importance to modern architecture; see his letters to Jeet Malhotra (28 Jan. 1965) and to Pierre Jeanneret, chief architect and town planning adviser to the government of Punjab (15 Feb. 1965 and 17 Mar. 1965). As he writes to Pierre Jeanneret: "I think that you, and you particularly—helped by Prabhawalkar and Malhotra (all three authentic visual artists)—could be proud to do this for Corbu, who is over 77 years old and has created this 'Open Hand,' which is surely the expression of an intense moment of modern society. It is not politics: it is modern 'history.' This thing standing up against the sky of the Himalayas is worth doing and must be done. I count on you. Cordially yours, Le Corbusier." LC to Pierre Jeanneret, 17 Mar. 1965, FLC, doc. G3 07, 103.

The Open Hand Monument was not finished in LC's lifetime. It was completed twenty years later, in 1985.

57 A series of little five-by-five-inch booklets, was published by Editions Forces Vives under the editorship of Jean Petit and includes *Textes et dessins pour Ronchamp* (1965), *L'Urbanisme est une clef,* rpt. ed. (1966), *Le Corbusier parle* (1967), and this very text.

58 The first recording was made on 6 June 1961 by Hugues Desalle for Alliance Française: *Le Corbusier: Mes pensées à 73 ans*. The collection, entitled "Français de notre temps," was devoted to great names in major fields and targeted primarily at foreign audiences. In the recordings, each roughly twelve minutes long, the personalities talk about the highlights of their life and work.

Desalle's second recording took place on 25 May 1965 and, when edited, carried the date 27 Aug. 1965, the date of LC's death. This last 33-RPM record is entitled (side A) "Le Corbusier revit son enfance, sa jeunesse, son aventure" and (side B) "Le Corbusier vit ses combats, le monde, son architecture, sa poésie."

59 The greater part of this paragraph appears in Petit, *Le Corbusier lui-même*, 132, in quotation marks, and is dated 28 Mar. 1965. If this passage from Petit's volume, like the previous one on the Open Hand Monument, is indeed extracted from the manuscript of *Mise au point*, it not only indicates the time LC was working on this short essay but also hints at what has been conflated and rearranged in these texts and even, perhaps, the location of the *Mise au point* manuscript itself.

60 A *braguette* is a slit or fly (in trousers) or a codpiece. Sometimes Rabelais evoked the container to mean the contents. *Balletron* is an obscene word made up by Rabelais.

61 The above lines are the first tercet of Stéphane Mallarmé's "Le guignon" (The jinx), the first of his "Premiers poèmes" (1862, reworked 1870s). The initial version contained only five tercets instead of the twenty-one in the final versions from which LC quotes. In this poem, Mallarmé dwells on the sad fate of the poet in the world ("biting the golden lemon of a bitter ideal"), and its final line—about a disillusioned and impotent poet hanging himself—recalls the suicide of Gérard de Nerval in 1855. "Le Guignon" is believed to have been conceived as a counterpart to Théophile Gautier's *Ténèbres* (a work focusing on death and hell). English translation cited in text by Henry Weinfield, *Stéphane Mallarmé: Collected Poems* (Berkeley: University of California Press, 1994), 4.

62 LC finished proofreading *Le Voyage d'Orient* on 17 July 1965, and the book was published by Editions Forces Vives in 1966, the same year as *Mise au point*. For an English translation, see my translation, *Journey to the East*.

63 Augusto Tobito Acevedo, a Venezuelan, worked with LC's at 35 rue de Sèvres from 1953 to 1959. He left France to take a position at the School of Architecture in Caracas. In his comprehensive list of his collaborators, wishing to acknowledge a special contribution made by the trio who were let go in 1959, LC wrote: "Maisonnier, Xénakis, Tobito, who left the atelier in 1959, have asked to be designated as Project Architects." List of collaborators, FLC, doc. U3 14, 175–76. The list also appears at the end of *Creation Is a Patient Search*.

64 The Revelation of Saint John the Divine, 8:1: "And when he had opened the seventh seal, there was silence in heaven for about half an hour."

65 LC uses very similar words in dedicating *Le Voyage d'Orient* to his brother Albert at about this time (July 1965): "May our affection remain firm, constant, absolute—like that distant horizon, between Limnos and the Aegean." There was a time when LC reduced the meaning of life and death into this unbending Cartesian axis, vertical and horizontal, life and death, heaven and hell. In fact, he wrote to André Wogenscky: "La mort est l'horizontale de la verticale, complémentaire et naturelle." Wogenscky to author, 22 Jan.1985. Perhaps the most appropriate homage to this Cartesian world order is LC's *Le Poème de l'angle droit*, especially part A.3.

66 LC died while swimming one month later, at the end of his vacation, on 27 Aug. 1965.

The Final Year

1 Eugène Grasset, *Méthode de composition ornementale* (Paris, 1905).

2 The school was not Yale but Vassar, where LC lectured on 1 Nov. 1935 after he had lectured at Yale on 30 Oct. 1935. See "Schedule of Le Corbusier Lecture Tour," New York Museum of Modern Art Archives, doc. no. 11.1/71(7).

Index